11 HOURS ON THE LEDGE

11 HOURS ON THE LEDGE

Madness, Mob Mentality, and the Media

Jerry Jamison

BLOOMSBURY ACADEMIC
NEW YORK • LONDON • OXFORD • NEW DELHI • SYDNEY

BLOOMSBURY ACADEMIC
Bloomsbury Publishing Inc, 1359 Broadway, New York, NY 10018, USA
Bloomsbury Publishing Plc, 50 Bedford Square, London, WC1B 3DP, UK
Bloomsbury Publishing Ireland, 29 Earlsfort Terrace, Dublin 2, D02 AY28, Ireland

First published in the United States of America 2026

Cover Design: Corey Jamison
Cover Image: Nick Brama

A catalog record for this book is available from the Library of Congress.

ISBN: HB: 979-8-216-37182-3
ePDF: 979-8-216-37183-0
eBook: 979-8-216-37184-7

Typeset by Integra Software Services Pvt. Ltd.
Printed and bound in the United States of America

For product safety related questions contact productsafety@bloomsbury.com.

To find out more about our authors and books visit www.bloomsbury.com and sign up for our newsletters.

Disclaimer

Now that all of the principal players in this drama have passed away and faded into the pages of history and are long forgotten, I strove to bring all the people in John's world to life again with their unique personalities and agendas and, in some cases, unattractive purposes. To best accomplish this, I changed some names, combined characters, created portions of dialogue where it was not available, shifted some events, and expanded situations to make them more understandable and readable, all in what has been called a narrative nonfiction style.

However, combining acceptable creative license with solid and verifiable facts—all of this story comes directly from newspaper articles of the day—the result is that this is an absolutely true and accurate story.

CONTENTS

PREFACE

As the long-time owner of a national advertising agency, I am always on the hunt for inspiration. The sources for this are many and varied, and I learned long ago never to discount where the "next great idea" for a campaign might come from.

Thus, on one peaceful weekend morning, I found myself combing through some old and yellowed magazines, having come across a desire to educate myself on advertising in the 1940s. I was hoping to create a retro campaign in the style and presentation of the early "Mad Men"—the gin-and-tonic, chain-smoking advertising teams that proliferated during that era along New York's Madison Avenue.

During this particular foray—while I was perusing ads for formal gowns from Lord & Taylor that cost a whopping $10 or a night's stay at the tony Ritz Carlton for $21—I saw an article entitled, "The Man on the Ledge" by Joel Sayre. It was pages long in tiny print, with no photos, and wound its way through other features about a Dude Ranch in Colorado, J. Edgar Hoover's scotty-dog named "G-Boy," and the latest *objets d'art*.

It didn't immediately catch my attention, but eventually, I started skimming casually. To my great surprise, I instantly found myself fascinated by a story for which I was totally unprepared. At the top, it was captioned in large print: *This is not fiction. It is a true story!*

The editors no doubt felt that disclaimer was required because virtually no readers would believe it was based on fact. And for good reason. It strained the imagination.

The article—published on basically the tenth anniversary of the actual event—told the story of an otherwise unknown 26-year-old man who, on a bright and clear July morning, inexplicably climbed through an open window on the 17th-floor of the Hotel Gotham in midtown Manhattan and carefully made his way along a stone ledge.

As his lengthy eleven-hour standoff became the focus of all of New York and much of the nation, it soon dominated every radio stations.

A crowd—generally estimated at between 10,000 and 35,000, though many estimates went as high as 200,000—gathered below to ogle the action along with more than 800 (some said 1,000) police officers who were present to try and convince him to come back inside while controlling the growing mob.

Opera glasses were being sold to get a better view of the young man who was teetering between life and death.

Ice cream, popcorn, and candy vendors made their way through the crowds, hawking their goods.

Buttons commemorating the event were hastily made and sold on the streets.

Diners on neighboring balconies ordered room service and sipped wine as they were being entertained by the anonymous man on the ledge.

Reporters from highly competitive and voraciously hungry sensationalist newspapers and magazines gathered like swarming flies to the scene. They surrounded the building while scores used subterfuge and deception to make their way up to the 17th floor to get a bird's eye view of the developments and inject themselves into the action.

With newsreel cameramen feverishly setting up their tripods—even fledgling television networks were present—an equal number of photographers from the dailies and wire services took up positions in the apartments and offices across the street.

Down below on the street, nearly two dozen more lay flat on their backs on the sidewalk in front of the entrance to the Gotham in hopes of capturing the shot of their careers—a falling young man tumbling down in their direction.

Most of these were sporting "Big Berthas"—cameras with long-range lenses that were a relatively new development at the time and which, up until this point, had only been used to cover large sporting events.

Perhaps this would be the year's greatest sporting event, as play-by-play commentary for nearly a dozen hours was provided to stations nationwide through the Mutual Broadcasting Network, preempting other popular programming.

At the height of it all, one radio station offered the man $100 to set up one of their microphones on the ledge to capture conversations of the attempts to lure him to safety.

The man on the ledge, in fact, was John William Warde, who lived with his parents in the snooty, exclusive village of Southampton, New York. They were—what was called at the time—"a socially prominent family of some renown."

John lived a life of prestige, entitlement, and materialism with all the trappings of wealth and access.

The public's fascination with the events—aside from the lure of hopefully seeing someone plummet to their death—was that they couldn't grasp how a handsome, fastidious, wealthy, young fashionista somehow managed not to have a wife or girlfriend or a career.

The press dubbed him a "dashing playboy"—a somewhat glorified and enamored term of the day—and they despised his life of carefree excess during what came to be known as the Depression Era. But on this particular day, he was the loneliest young man in Manhattan.

"He always felt himself an outsider. Different than the other boys, you know," a fellow classmate once remarked. It might have been, as we well understand in this more enlightened era, a description of a different lifestyle choice.

In my previous books that have focused on true crimes committed by some of the most fascinating—and indecipherable—human beings ever to live, I tended to focus on the psychology—or, better said, pathology—of these individuals who look and act like everyone else but whose minds are deranged in some profound way.

I believe this exercise provides valuable and educated insights into their minds and helps—one would hope—give us a better picture of what signs to look for and how to help these tortured people. Psychological examinations of killers—often ordered by the courts or unearthed later by researchers—generally show how their brains function abnormally, physiologically, emotionally, and socially. Hence, the word psychopaths.

This story is different for a couple of reasons.

First, we know very little about what was happening inside the head of John William Warde on the day he decided to stand on a stone ledge hundreds of feet in the air over one of Manhattan's busiest intersections.

Although he had struggled with mental issues in the past, on this particular day, he chose to share little of his inner feelings. There is even some evidence that he never intended to do as he did but rather made a snap, irrational, in-the-moment decision.

There is—with one notable and quite significant exception that you will discover later in the pages of the story—a feeling that he termed "this thing inside me." That "thing" is threaded throughout this book's pages, but it just might hold the key to understanding the mind of John Warde when he was making the most important decision of his lifetime and is a direct reflection of the restrictive era in which he lived.

The second reason this project will not be a customary deep dive into the individual psychosis of the man is that I made a tactical decision to take a different approach to the entire event. Rather than focusing wholly on the man himself, I wanted to explore the impact of this most intimate and gut-wrenching of all personal choices—whether or not to consciously end one's life—in terms of how it affected the world around him.

John Warde's apparent split-second decision to step out on a ledge instantly altered the lives of everyone in his orbit, whether or not they were familiar with who he was. For most of the observers on that day, in fact, he was both nameless and faceless. Yet, their lives were profoundly affected by his simple act that required only five short steps.

Similarly, in writing a script for an eventual 1951 Twentieth Century Fox film, screenwriter John Paxton—who largely fictionalized the story—decided not to use flashbacks to explain why the lead character was up on the ledge.

Richard Basehart, who eventually starred in that movie, said, "Paxton treated his central character as a pebble thrown into a pool of water. Without losing sight of the pebble, he concentrated on the ripples it raised and wrote dramatic vignettes and one act plays around the people they washed over."

Well-stated, I believe.

That approach resonated with me as well because, it seemed, the most fascinating aspect of the entire ordeal was how the myriad of people surrounding one man's decision chose to respond to it. In the end, the story is more about them—and American culture—than anything about the sad man who was struggling with inner demons.

This perspective, then, is sociological rather than psychological. If the latter is the study of the individual mind, then the former is the science of understanding the "group mind"—how people think, respond, and react as a group or groups.

There can be no better example of this than Mr. Warde's unfortunate situation from long ago, where there was infinitely more activity whirling around the poor man on the ledge than he was experiencing alone on that shelf.

Using the sociological approach also allows me to finally make use of my sociology undergraduate degree, which, until now, seemed like a quite expensive but not entirely useful major. My parents, were they alive, would be proud of this fact.

I also need to take a moment to discuss the authenticity of this story since, in so many ways, it will undoubtedly seem unbelievable to some readers—and understandably so. Let me begin by saying that *11 Hours* is indeed based on real events and unfolded just as I have depicted here.

I was compelled to take some literary liberties in crafting this story in part because very little is known about John Warde or the events on this day in his life. To fill in the gaps, I created reasonably informed scenes based on what would make the most sense given the activities on either side.

There is no way to know exactly what happened during every minute of this ordeal—or, for that matter, before or after it—but I believe my depiction is a fair representation of how it all unfolded that day under the microscope of New York City and its media.

It was also helpful to me and quite fortuitous that in 1948, scriptwriter John Paxton—who was not far in time from the actual events—was able to access eyewitnesses, police files, reporters' notes, and memories from bystanders who were present on that day.

In the story he was crafting, he went even further into the full story than the information I was able to access in Sayre's column, which focused primarily on the hard facts and not the emotions of the day. Paxton's solid reporting helped inform my story.

This project also involved an immense amount of research—provided by my invaluable assistant Julie Estrada—which included locating thousands of newspaper articles from 1938 that covered the event in real time—some hour by hour. A pulsating account of the event that transfixed Manhattan emerged from these cracked and yellowed pages.

Finally, although we can gather facts, we seldom can recover the personal thoughts and conversations that take place in any historical event. Since some of these will forever remain missing—and impossible to retrieve—I sought to fill in those gaps to add some humanity and context to what otherwise might appear as little more than a two-dimensional character: *merely a man on a ledge.*

Now that all of the principal players in this drama have passed away and faded into the pages of history and are long forgotten, I strove to bring all the people in John's world to life again with their unique personalities and agendas and, in some cases, unattractive purposes while remaining firmly anchored to the known facts.

To accomplish this, I changed some names, combined characters, created dialogue, moved some events and expanded situations to make them more understandable and readable, all in what has been called a narrative nonfiction style.

However, combining this creative license with solid and verifiable facts—virtually all of the story comes directly from those newspaper articles of the day—and the actual names and backgrounds of the people involved, the result is that this is a true and accurate story with just a touch of added flavor and spice.

Hopefully, all of this adds up to the heart-pounding, soul-searching, tension-inducing experience that beckoned me to this true tale when I first read about it in an aging antique magazine that serendipitously came across my path one morning.

Such a story, however, does not come to be without some impact on the author.

In doing my research on the events of that day so long ago, I found myself cringing at the thoughtless and ill-conceived approaches to rescuing the man, as well as the total misunderstanding of mental illness and how to help an individual who suffers from a medical condition.

In so many ways, *11 Hours* is a cautionary tale on mental health and the treatments available for people who suffer so mightily from this disease, as well as a more evolved understanding of lifestyle choices. It is hard not to feel empathetic toward John Warde while at the same time abhor the reactions of the onlookers, reporters, and curiosity seekers who are desperately hoping to see a man leap to his death.

As a society, we are still far from having the necessary compassion and understanding to help those so terribly afflicted. However, in contrast to past generations, we are at least making strides in the right direction.

In any case, it is my sincere desire that we have moved far beyond that uninformed time. And hopefully, you will enjoy this journey of discovery and insight.

Jerry Jamison
Chula Vista, California
jerryjamison.com

1 The Early Hours

"Harder. Harder. Harder, Mr. Warde! You gotta work harder, harder, harder if you're gonna make it in the newspaper business. Hard isn't enough. Hard doesn't cut it anymore. Hard is for losers and pipsqueaks. Harder, I tell ya. *Harder. Harder. Harder!*"

Manelli had been the city desk editor for as long as anyone could remember. Some said as long as there was a city. That might have been an exaggeration, but no one would have said it to his face. That was because no one ever said anything to his face.

Manelli—nobody could remember his first name—was cut out of old cloth. A newspaperman since the turn of the century, he did it his way, and everyone else stayed out that way. Even the publisher, the esteemed N. Herbert Mayflower, steered clear of the old goat. And for good reason. There was no reason to spoil a perfectly good day by running into Manelli.

July 26, 1938, was a perfectly good day.

Manelli navigated the ninth floor of the Staniforth Building on Fifth in Upper Manhattan. Five of the top floors had been leased to the *New York Tribune* since the day of the ribbon cutting. That meant that before there was a building, there was a Manelli. "Older than dirt" had been said more than once.

Older and tougher.

He moved through the maze of desks like a shark thirsty for prey. Had it not been for the fact that he dragged one bum foot on the hardwood floor, he might have moved in complete stealth. His eyes were ever darting, his fingers constantly rolling an unlit cigar.

Manelli was eternally a man in a vacuum because wherever he went, people subtly and subconsciously moved out of his path, creating a void. Like Moses, the sea parted before him and then swallowed up the open space behind.

It was John Warde's singularly poor fortune to have found himself trapped between his desk and the mail cart when Manelli made his turn along the seventh floor's west wall. It was the old man's regular route on any given Tuesday, but John couldn't have known that. He was, what was called at the time, a cub reporter. *A newbie.*

After nearly a year of being unemployed—not an unusual circumstance for a young man during the Great Depression—it was his first day on the job. Nobody had bothered to tell the new kid to stay out of Manelli's path, and now he found himself in this unfortunate situation.

Besides, it was a bit of a rookie initiation. The staff was looking forward to it.

John glanced around and saw the chuckles and smothered smiles and knew he was the butt of the joke. After a while it felt like everyone in the room was pointing and laughing, mocking him. He hadn't been in his intern position for even an hour, and he was already a failure.

A failure again. A failure like always. A big, fat failure.

Shortly, the voices in his head started to whisper. Then they began to shout. Then they were screaming. This time, it was happening faster. The words in his cramping brain were tumbling in and upon themselves.

And the day had started out so well . . .

After returning from Chicago on a short but pleasing getaway with some friends, John was anxious for a fresh start in a new job. Well, it was not a job—just an internship, they were calling it. That was something different for him, but it was his father's idea, so enough said.

His father, after all, knew best. That was what he had told him all of his life.

John Warde Sr. was a powerful executive with the American Railway Express, a national package delivery service that arranged transport using the railroads—not unlike UPS or FedEx use roads and air transport today.

He was not just powerful but quite wealthy too.

It was that wealth which had provided John William Warde with a life of luxury and privilege as he grew up in the exclusive enclave of Southampton along the eastern coast of Long Island. The village, which during his youth had a population of four thousand, was best known as a summer resort for not just the wealthy but the *extremely* wealthy.

He and his sister, Katherine—named after their mother—who was four years his junior, had enjoyed a charmed life. With each other as their primary playmates, they were able to navigate the social expectations placed on them as they grew and matriculated through that world.

Of course, none of that sophistication or training in proper manners could have prepared him for this moment with a crude, brusque, cigar-chewing old goat who made it his hobby to berate and belittle those under him. With this cub reporter now in his sights—a punk he was forced to take on at the demand of the publisher, a friend of the kid's father—he was almost salivating.

Thus, Manelli—invigorated by serendipitously stumbling across an unwitting victim—pounced on the twenty-six-year-old rookie and leaned in close to John's face without saying a word at first. If he thought that might be intimidating, he was correct.

The cigar was now in the editor's mouth, still unlit, and was bobbing up and down as the huffing Manelli sought to catch his breath from his morning stroll. His eyes, less than a foot from his victim, were squinting, piercing, unforgiving. His breath was fetid, and his forehead was beaded with sweat. His chins—there were several—jiggled as he gasped for air.

"Harder. Harder. Harder, Mr. Warde. You gotta work harder, harder, harder if you're gonna make it in the newspaper business!"

There was no real reason for John Warde to be singled out or dressed down. He was a capable young man and a reasonably good writer that people seemed to like. He trusted he could make it in the newspaper business—heck, he was confident he could do anything he put his mind to. It was just that most things didn't interest him.

This new job—or whatever it was—was just the next thing in a long line of "ideas" his father had for him, primarily designed to not allow him to embarrass the family any more than he already had. He had a bit of a reputation as a playboy, fastidious to a fault and an unabashed flirt with all the girls.

John had to admit, which he willingly did, that he liked fine things and was quite exacting about how he looked and carried himself, and he always presented a polished image for all to see. He knew he was quite handsome and made sure he looked the part.

In fact, on this particular morning, he had spent hours picking out his outfit for the day, ensuring that it not only matched perfectly but featured the latest in fashion for sophisticated men. He wanted to make sure that he was the cat's meow of the newsroom, though that was less of a challenge than he had expected. On his way in, he stopped to have Sammy shine his shoes to perfection.

However, at this moment, it was just John's poor fortune to be caught in the path of Manelli's normal routine of tracking down someone on the floor and reminding them that they were a failure.

"Hard isn't enough. Hard doesn't cut it anymore. Hard is for losers and pipsqueaks. Harder, I tell ya. Harder. Harder. Harder!"

John was nodding as Manelli spoke—spit flying from his mouth and spattering the kid's glasses. Not that he heard much. Mostly, there were just grunts and barks coming out of his mouth, but occasionally he could pick up a sentence or two. The word "harder" came up often enough to make it memorable.

To the cultured sensibilities of John Warde, Manelli was little more than a gorilla in trousers and suspenders.

"Listen to me, ya little nobody, and listen good. I don't care if you are some hoity-toity rich kid. It don't mean a damn to me! Ya gotta get out there and dig, hear me? Dig, dig, dig. Stories don't just fly out of a monkey's ass and land on your desk. Ya gotta go dig 'em up. Make stories outta nuthin' if there ain't nuthin' there.

"And if you can't find a thing, then you make yourself the story . . . but whatever you do, don't bother comin' back here if you ain't got a story for me."

John's primary takeaway was that he had never once considered that a news story might fly out of a monkey's ass and land on his desk.

He was open to it, though.

After Manelli finished with his tirade, he left the kid pressed against the wall—where he stayed for nearly a minute. The old man then went out, like a heat-seeking missile, in search of a new victim. A vacuum instantly formed before and behind him.

After the dust had settled—and the screaming in his brain died down to a manageable roar—John felt like he needed to clear his head and decided to take a walk. Having never really been able to hold down a job for any length of time—other than a stint working for the Bank of Southampton some years after high school—it never occurred to him that people actually maintained set hours.

In fact, there were few parameters on John's privileged life. He enjoyed marching to the beat of his own drum and felt few restrictions or, for that matter, guidance. His father, who occasionally stayed at home, more or less lived a separate life from the rest of the family, especially his wife.

They both had their social responsibilities in town—which Mrs. Warde carefully tended to like a manicured garden—but for the most part John Sr. was involved in his work and then enjoyed evenings at the supper club sipping scotch and smoking cigars while telling ribald stories. He was the prototypical "man's man" of the era.

John Sr. was in fact a valued member of the esteemed Maidstone Men's Club, which was—and still is—considered to be the most elite, prestigious, and difficult to get into of all the clubs in the Hamptons. This, in turn, was the summer haven of New York City's most wealthy and socially connected families—even in the throes of the Great Depression.

Amid the familial maelstrom, John's life was mostly lost in the shuffle. Neighbors noted that during his preadolescent years, the boy exhibited an overwhelming conviction of inferiority. After high school, he dabbled in higher education, but with a generous allowance and little encouragement, he saw no need to continue.

John eventually took a job at the Long Island headquarters of the New York Telephone Company at 101 Willoughby Street—built only a few years earlier and as a monument to man's sense of world dominion during that heady era. Decorated in an Art Deco style, it towered over every other building in the borough and featured stylish designs of chevrons, diamonds, and starbursts.

Although John reportedly enjoyed dressing up professionally, he found his responsibilities boring and without challenge. Coworkers later said that he was clearly intelligent and well mannered, but his volatile personality made him seem strange to them, and they tended to shy away.

John, however, was little more than a tiny cog in a very big wheel at the telephone company and showed little interest in advancing. Bright and capable, he seemed to feel that the job was beneath him, and instead of being inspired by the new technologies, he found himself more interested in fashion, art, and recreation. It was actually the building's stylish architectural design that had initially attracted him to the position.

He left his post within a year and was welcomed back home by his mother, who saw it as an "unpolished career choice." There, he lazed around and flitted through social events intended to showcase him to eager and, hopefully, well-connected young women.

His father, who was priming his son for a management position at American Railway Express, was becoming frustrated with his son's obvious lack of ambition. Placing him in a bank owned by a fellow Maidstone member, he thought, would solve the problem.

On this day as John exited the *Tribune* building, he was already second-guessing his father's decision to take on this whole journalism thing—especially starting at the bottom. He envisioned himself more as management material. Already, this felt like little more than a school assignment that he had to endure but not enjoy.

What he did enjoy, however, was the new concierge charm school he had recently created advising young, soon-to-be debutantes on the proper etiquette for those emerging into the social scene of the Hamptons.

Here, John felt completely in his element, despite behind-his-back whispers from friends. While instructing young ladies on preparing for their introduction to 1930s proper New York society by refining them with approved etiquette, behaviors, and social decorum, he felt fulfilled and appreciated for contributing to someone's social success.

It was, in essence, his dream job.

John had recently begun setting up classes—without the benefit of any clients—on fashion and appropriate dress, rules of introduction, proper greetings, and how to open a conversation and carry it.

As soon as his father got word of it, however, John Sr. called it a sissy idea and promptly set up the *Tribune* job. That would turn out to set in play several events that would redirect his life forever, though any such thing was far from his mind.

Instead, he was walking out the heavy glass turnstile doors of the Staniforth Building with plans to think this whole damn thing out.

Less than fifteen minutes after leaving the newspaper offices, John Warde was walking along Sixth Avenue and turning on Thirty-Fifth Street in a hopeless search for "the story." At least that was what he was telling himself. There was little evidence that it was there among the teeming, faceless commuters that streamed down the thoroughfares of The City without a story among them.

But that isn't really true, John said to himself.

"Everyone has a story. Everyone has a story to tell. Packed down, hidden away, kept in the dark, locked up for good. Yeah, there must be a thousand stories—and a million secrets—right in front of me, and no one will ever know. The City doesn't allow it. The City chokes them out."

The City was indeed a cruel, jealous taskmaster. It demands all of you and gives nothing back in return.

To John Warde, The City was no different than his father. His father was no different than Manelli. They were all cruel, insensitive masters who didn't have a whit of understanding or culture. John knew he also had his own secrets, packed down and safely out of sight.

His mother wasn't much better in his eyes. She had spent much of her life explaining to John what a terrible person his father was. How inattentive he was. How he caroused with younger women. How he was an alcoholic who had learned the tricks to cover it up. How he never loved or cared for his son. If it were not for her, in fact, young John would have no life at all. He owed his very existence to her.

Katherine Warde needed him to be her "good little boy" and make mommy proud. The perfect young man, with the perfect manners and wearing his perfect summer outfits of white linen striped suits and straw hats. All he needed to be for her was a Hampton boy.

To Katherine Warde, that was an admirable career in itself.

John walked for some time, jostling through the crowds with their blank expressions and summer outfits on a beastly July morning. The temperature was already up to eighty-six and promised to rise from there. He had no destination. He had no ideas or feelings. Just one foot after another.

One foot after another, waiting for a story to fly out of the proverbial monkey's ass.

But, of course, there were things to think about. Things inside of him that he kept close to his heart—that he shared with no one, not even his dear sister, and that he dared never let see the light of day. Walking helped. He felt he could best sort out what he called "deep thoughts and strange feelings" when he was alone.

That was, alone with the other million people in New York City on this day.

The crowds' dull, sheeplike, monotonous thudding stood in sharp contrast to the colorful displays of the summer season contained in the show windows of Bonwit Teller on illustrious Fifth Avenue that were alongside him. Not that anyone noticed.

Not that they noticed the animated robotic characters of women pausing on a make-believe beach—a hand-painted brightly striped cabana in the background—"their children" playing with colorful balls and building sand castles.

There, forever happy both night and day, they continued in their awkward, stiff, endlessly repetitive mechanical motions. Lifting a pail, putting it down. Lifting a toy shovel, putting it down. Lifting a martini, putting it down.

Lift it up. Put it down. Lift it up. Put it down. Lift it up. Put it down.

For a brief second, John preferred the state of the automatons. *Harder, harder, harder.* They never needed to be that. Just the same, never changing. Plus, never being bothered by the thousands of people who passed by looking but not seeing. No expectations. Those mechanized robots never even cared, either. Life was nothing more than *lift it up* and *put it down.*

Mister and Miss Perfect also beckoned shoppers into Bloomingdale's with their fashionable swimsuits, stylish broad-brim hats, and ideal tan bodies. Her, with her virginal white but slightly daring bathing ensemble, him with bulging muscles covered with a horizontal striped top and belted body-hugging bottoms. "He's Mr. Perfect, all right," John thought to himself as he stopped to take in the scene.

Mannequins beamed their painted smiles out to passersby and displayed the pastels and bright colors of the season as if they had been flash-frozen in place at a lawn party and then arranged on tiers in a socially acceptable lineup. Their drinks never went empty, the air never grew chilly, and their trendy sunglasses and cigarettes with long filters provided the air of sophistication for which all New Yorkers strove.

Evening fashion—long, bejeweled, and appliqued gowns and black-tie tuxedos—was on display for the social set in Bergdorf Goodman's windows, with tunes from Count Basie and his orchestra broadcast out into the streets. There was a giant martini glass in their midst with a machine that sent bubbles bouncing merrily into the air of the display window and out into the street.

A few people had stopped to admire the window display. Clearly they were tourists from Iowa, Nebraska, or Kansas . . . or wherever they came from. John had nothing but disdain for these hayseeds.

Somewhere along Fifty-Fifth Street, John took stock of his location for the first time.

In front of him was the towering nineteen-floor Hotel Gotham, a fixture in the ritziest part of town from the moment it was erected in 1905. It was the only destination for the socially connected in town—and a permanent city residence for many of the nation's wealthiest—as well as celebrities who booked rooms whenever they visited Manhattan.

The Gotham—as it was affectionately called—was where all visiting Broadway stars were housed. Anything less would have been an embarrassment to the shows' producers.

Outside, the doorman, Walter Vickers, stood at attention—dressed impeccably in his long, blue, double-breasted coat with brass buttons and burgundy trim. His top hat was perfectly perched upon his head, and his entire carriage showed immaculate posture. *He may have been a commoner*, John thought, *but he certainly knows how to play the role.* He admired people who could "pull it off."

All of this, of course, went unappreciated by the hardworking doorman busily ushering guests in and out of the hotel while whistling for cabs.

It would be hard to tell how long John stood there, but it was some time. It would be nice to say he was pondering something deep. However, he wasn't at the moment. Mostly he was just thinking about how The City was little more than a sweltering, uncaring monolith that sucked the life out of everyone within its reach.

All of these stories floated around, and there was no one willing to tell them and no one interested enough to listen. It didn't go much deeper than that.

John was at his destination—what he had been aiming for all along—but there was still a decision to be made. Life had gotten under his skin. He was annoyed, bugged by everything, as he stood staring at the gray neoclassical limestone exterior that seemed from his vantage point to disappear into the heavens.

"The Tower of Babel . . . that's what it is. The Tower of Babel surrounded by canyons of steel." Warde was "in a mood," as they say.

"What's that, buddy? What'd you say? You coming or going?" Vickers, the doorman, was waving impatiently at him. "In or out. Make a decision."

John smiled. *Make a decision.*

Seconds later, he was entering the Gotham and standing in its vast lobby. He was scheduled to meet his sister, Katherine, and some family friends for lunch in their penthouse suites on the seventeenth floor.

He was bored before it even began.

Going up to give the hotel clerk his name so that his sister could be alerted, John was instead given a note saying that she was requesting he join her in Room 1714, where they would have room service prepare and deliver their lunch—an even more mundane option for this boring day.

That was the exact moment Mr. John William Warde had an idea.

"If you can't find a thing, then you make yourself the story." That was what Mr. Manelli had said. *You become the story.*

So that was what John decided to do.

2 Zero Hour

John Warde's arrival at Hotel Gotham—although it appeared to be a spontaneous decision—was far from it. He had predetermined that he would meet up with his sister, but, more importantly, he was reconnecting with Patrick and Isabella Katherine Valentine—who went by her middle name socially—a compassionate couple that had taken the troubled young man under their wing. He liked them.

The Valentines had stepped in and provided more stable footing for the likable but disturbed young man who had spent some time in a mental facility. Katherine had known him before his breakdown and lobbied hard for her husband to give him a job—anything really to keep him close to their home. And to her.

"Giving him the job didn't seem to help much," Patrick Valentine said much later. "He seemed to think he was a failure from the outset. We didn't really know what to do with the young man."

Katherine had a solution. She suggested that they take a short getaway to Chicago—the location of their primary residence—to allow John to clear his head and prepare him for his new position at the *Tribune* the following week.

"So, my wife and I took him to Chicago," Patrick explained. "Along with his sister, to cheer him up and get him back on his feet. We spent a few days there, mostly the weekend, and to tell you the truth he seemed all right to me."

John was especially looking forward to reuniting with his twenty-two-year-old and recently married sister. The foursome swam in Lake Michigan, went to Wrigley Field to see a Cubs game, and attended a band concert with a picnic in Grant Park. It was a fun-filled and busy weekend, and the Valentines were convinced that their guest had turned a corner and was ready to face the days ahead, hopefully succeeding in a new job.

Despite the best efforts of the Valentines and his sister, however, nothing seemed to cheer John up as they traveled by train back to New York. On the Monday following the weekend getaway, Patrick needed to return to his office, where he oversaw a large and quite successful travel agency.

Valentine handled both the Chicago and Manhattan offices of the Clara Laughlin Travel Service, established by a "midwestern maiden lady" whose guidebooks had become nearly standard equipment for the American tourist in the thirties.

His office was little more than two blocks away. After a couple of hours going over the paperwork that had stacked up over the weekend, he was to meet his wife back at the hotel for a bite to eat at lunchtime.

Isabella Valentine—whom John affectionately nicknamed Bella—and his married sister, Katherine Bull, settled into the Valentines' city townhouse in the Hotel Gotham with John. They planned to do some shopping that afternoon in the exclusive fashion district surrounding the hotel. They were concerned about the midtown heat, but little more than that was on their minds.

John, of course, had work the next day and began to grow despondent about having to give up the fine life to become a blue-collar worker, from his perspective, as well as miss out on more clothes shopping.

Away from him, the two women talked about his mental state and wondered if there was something they might do to help. Perhaps a call to the family doctor or one of the psychiatrists at the state hospital? Unfortunately, given the era and their role as women in society, few to no tools or insights were available to them on how they might help.

So, on Tuesday morning, as Patrick went off to work at the travel agency, Mrs. Valentine phoned back to her Valmay summer home in Southampton and inquired about the children. With all well, the ladies took off for Macy's to attend to their social responsibilities with every expectation that life would continue to move along the same lines they had previously.

When John left for his new job in the city that morning, his brain was like an ever-tightening mainspring threatening to explode at any moment and with the slightest provocation. Not that that appeared to be the case from the outside.

John was always affable when in a "manic phase," but he tended to be dull and silent when things in his mind seemed overwhelming and turned dark. Though he was not in a good frame of mind, few, if any, could have ever picked that up.

So, on Tuesday, July 26, 1938, all the voices in John's head seemed to be speaking at once and simply became too deafening.

Having been walking for more than an hour through Manhattan's most trendy streets, he was now in the elegant lobby of the Hotel Gotham to have lunch with his sister whom he loved dearly. Pausing only momentarily at the front desk, he prayed the voices would subside at least long enough for him to enjoy his meal.

They would not.

What took place over the next eleven hours would captivate the entire city of New York and the surrounding area and reverberate down throughout the nation in a nearly inconceivable manner. At the time, no one on earth knew the dark demons that were swirling around inside his handsome head or the secret he had held so closely within his soul that tortured him daily—the thing that was beginning to make his brain splinter and disintegrate.

* * * * *

"I trust, sir, that you will be comfortable here," the bellboy said. "If there is anything else I can do for you, sir, please don't hesitate to ask. Here at the Hotel Gotham, our goal is to provide superior service at all times. You may ring the desk at any moment, and one of our experienced staff members will be at your doorstep pronto. Have a nice afternoon, sir."

The bellboy—a man of about fifty and four feet, ten inches tall at best—was pleasant but well rehearsed. It was a message he had delivered at least a thousand times in his years—all for about fifty cents on average.

"Another casualty of The City," John said to himself, not bothering even to consider if perhaps the man enjoyed his job or was thankful for it.

John took a minute to check out his surroundings. He had entered Room 1714, which was one of two permanently leased by the Valentines, who used it intermittently throughout the year, mostly when they were in town to catch a Broadway show. They also had taken Suite 1716, which was connected by an adjoining door and where his sister and Mrs. Valentine were now resting.

Both rooms were massive by today's standards. They constituted a legitimate, multi-room living space for the socially connected family as well as a convenient place to entertain guests from the Manhattan social circuit.

"Story of the century," John said somewhat enigmatically, again speaking only to himself. He was in a fragile state, however, and he recognized it. With enough psychiatric therapy to spot the triggers that might set him off, he tried to settle his spirit and calm his nerves.

About that time, his sister came through the connecting door from the adjacent room and immediately gave him a big hug.

Katherine was wearing a modern, quite fashionable green and pink satin summer dress with white flowers that flared out at the bottom, featuring slightly padded shoulders and multiple layers of fabric. On her head, resting at an angle, was a broad-brimmed pink straw hat with a single green band that dropped down her back. Her hair featured soft waves just set at a Fifth Avenue salon.

"Hello, brother. I can't wait to hear about your morning. First, though, I want to show you a handbag I got at Barneys. It's delightful. I'll save it for the fall, though."

John had already lapsed into one of his darker moods. There was no particular reason for it, but it felt as if a heavy blanket were descending with a mind to suffocate him. His eyes were darting around the room. He noticed the large recessed window with long white draperies on either side and wanted to open it to get some fresh air into the stuffy room.

Moving over to the edge of the bed in the room, he sat on the bedspread, bouncing a bit on it to judge its firmness, and then fell backward onto it with his hands clasped behind his head. The material was a soft, cream-colored chenille. Very nice. Very plush.

"Do you want to see my new bag, John? Are you even interested? I thought you would like it."

Without acknowledging Katherine, he picked up the phone on the nightstand and—with his best-cultured voice—requested room service.

"Can I please have a French dip sandwich *au jus*, rare please, with mushrooms and onions. I'll have fried potatoes as well, please. Oh, and do you have white cake? A slice, if you don't mind. . . . No, make that two. A bottle of champagne—your finest—and a pot of coffee.

"Yes, charge it to the *New York Tribune*, please. Attention Mr. Manelli. Yes, that will be all. . . . How long? All right, thank you. See you shortly."

"John! What in the world are you doing! We've already ordered for all of us. Patrick will be coming up soon. You're crazy, brother. I should call a doctor and make an appointment for you." After a weekend with her moody older brother, Katherine had had it with him.

She could have no idea at the time how consequential those words would turn out to be for her, her brother, and for all of New York on that summer morning.

Fine . . . he can eat alone, she thought. *I'm tired of babysitting him*. With that, she walked through the connecting door to Room 1716—leaving it partially ajar—and started to explain to Mrs. Valentine that her brother was already in a mood and they should just let him be.

That sounded good to the very tired Katherine Valentine, and she lay down to rest while awaiting her husband's arrival for their lunchtime meal. She pulled out a copy of *Modern Screen* magazine with movie star Sylvia Sidney on the cover, wearing culottes and a halter top and playing tennis. The headline read: *Hundreds of Intimate Pictures!*

A moment later, her brother called to her from the adjoining room. "I'm going out." Unconcerned and still annoyed, she thought that maybe the fresh air would do him some good and that when he returned for his lunch, he'd be in a better mood. It was often like that with him.

Hearing her brother take off his coat, fold it carefully, and lay it over the back of an armchair, she called back to him playfully, "All right, all right, don't be such a fussbudget. Just keep your hair on." Then she returned to her magazine.

* * * * *

Exactly twenty-seven minutes later, Tommy Hardesty knocked on the door of Suite 1714. He knocked twice. He knocked another two times. "Hello, room service. . . .

Hello, sir?" It was not uncommon for someone not to answer—bathroom break or telephone call in most cases—so the bellboy pulled out his giant ring of keys and started sorting through them until he got to 1714. Inserting the key and opening the door only an inch or two, he again announced his presence.

No answer.

Opening the door fully and pushing in his linen-covered cart covered with silver domes, he moved it smoothly across the Oriental rug and positioned it next to a table set off a few feet from the window. "Enjoy yourself, sir. *Bon appetit!*" he said to no one. It was part of his normal routine, and so it just came out reflexively.

Waiting a second without a response from anyone in one of the other rooms in the suite, he began moving toward the door, wondering if he would still somehow receive a tip for his service. He lived off of them, after all. Unfortunately, some guests—even the wealthy ones—took to hiding when it was time to tip. *The greedy bastards.*

Backing out the door with head slightly bowed—another essential sign of respect that Hardesty had been taught when he was just a novice on the job thirty years ago—he noticed at the last second that the deeply recessed and ornately framed window was open, the curtains billowing in dramatically.

"He might want fresh air," the bellboy mumbled to himself. "But this is ridiculous. It's already ninety degrees out there, and he's letting in nothing but the heat. Gimme a hundred years, and I'll still never understand these rich folks. They've never taken care of a house, that's for darn sure."

In nine steps, Hardesty was attempting to push the starched white linen curtains back out of the window—in a hopeless battle with the stiff, sweltering breeze—while grabbing hold of the bottom sill of the raised window to force it down and into place. At that moment, one of the curtain panels decided to make one last escape attempt, and Hardesty leaped to pull it back in.

That was when Hardesty noticed a pair of Florsheims directly to his right.

Shoes, feet, legs, and then—moving his eyes slowly up the pant legs—he was looking directly into the eyes of Mr. John William Warde. The man on the ledge—seventeen floors high above the summer shoppers on Fifty-Fifth Street—tipped his hat and said, "G'day, sir."

Hardesty leaped back and almost stumbled to the ground at the sight, letting out an involuntary howl. In a flash, both Katherines came running in from the adjoining room.

"Where . . . where is he? Where's John?"

Hardesty could only point to the open window with the curtains blowing in on either side. He jabbed in the direction of the window a second time and then said, "He . . . he . . . I mean, he . . ." The bellboy couldn't get the words out and, fearing the worst, Katherine Bull clamped her hands over her mouth.

She was convinced her brother had leaped out the window to his death. Calling out to Mrs. Valentine to come over, the two women cautiously and fearfully looked out and down from the open window. They saw John casually taking a drag on a cigarette and watching the puffs of smoke dissipate into the air.

Katherine Bull screamed.

From down on the street, the first moments of Warde's precarious vigil on the ledge were dramatic. Passersby on West Fifty-Fifth Street heard a piercing scream. They looked up idly—and saw a young man sitting down on the ledge as comfortably as could be, dangling one foot over the edge, midway between Room 1714 and the next suite. He seemed neither frightened nor overly concerned—just a man on a ledge on a summer day out soaking up some sun.

After gathering her wits, John's sister turned to face John, who had elected not to look in her direction. Katherine was confused, angry, and tired of her brother's histrionics. As she stretched out as far as she could, he turned to look at her, and with one look, she suddenly could not speak.

The gravity of the situation and her brother's apparent disregard for his own safety instantly overwhelmed her. Fainting across the sill, she nearly fell out of the window, and might have had not two officers grabbed her legs. "He looked different somehow. I really can't explain it. I was truly frightened for him. My heart fell," she later explained.

Mrs. Valentine quickly took her place and stuck her head out the window. "If anyone in uniform comes to that window, I'll jump," Warde warned. "I promise you that." She withdrew quickly and collapsed in a chair, her head in her hands.

By this time, her husband, Patrick, who had already gone to his office and returned home for lunch, joined his wife and leaned out the window. "Ah, come in, John," he said coaxingly. "We'll have a nice lunch together, and if you come in now, we'll go to the ballgame this afternoon. You know how much you love baseball."

"Who's playing?" Warde asked.

"The Brooklyn Dodgers and the Cubs," Valentine said. "I know you like the Cubs."

Warde sniffed. "I'd rather jump than watch the Dodgers," he said as he took a long pull on his cigarette without looking at Patrick.

The conversation effectively ended with that. John, now sullen, lit one cigarette after another and then stood up and began pacing back and forth. *If you can't find a story, then make the story.* Manelli's words kept echoing in his ears. However, this had now gone well beyond that. This story was for real. Perhaps this was already out of hand.

"If anyone comes near me," John said hoarsely to Patrick who was still leaning out of the window but was silent, "I swear I'll jump. I know what I'm doing. I just need some time."

Mrs. Bull—revived with smelling salts by this time—returned to the window after a pause to gather herself. This time, she had a rope tied around her ankle that ran under the bed and out the door to where some men were holding it.

"Please, please come in, darling," she pleaded. "We love you. We all love you. Come in and let's have a drink. It's awfully warm out there and much more pleasant in here. When people love each other, they feel it. You know how much I love you, Johnny.

"Come in and let us love you. Nothing will happen to you. I swear it. Come in and have a drink. Darling John, you have so much to live for—candy, food, good times, and . . . and . . ."

Katherine fainted once more. Policemen carried her back into the adjoining room and placed her on the bed while Mrs. Valentine took over.

* * * * *

"Hey, hey, Marsha, get me Mr. Harris real quick. I got a *sit-chee-ation* up here in 1714. You gotta get me Harris and pronto!" Tommy Hardesty was trying to catch his breath while attempting to talk to the hotel operator. He was desperate to get a hold of the front desk manager—his boss—and inform him of what was developing on the seventeenth floor. In all his years as a bellboy, he'd never faced anything like this.

Little did Hardesty know, Harris was already in the middle of his own crisis.

Like a whirling dervish, the revolving front doors to the Gotham were spinning into a blur as attendees from the New York City 1938 Shriners National Convention came rolling into the hotel foyer. As if a crack in a dam or a hole in a dike had broken open, the lobby was soon flooded with people of all shapes, sizes, and temperaments.

Mr. Harris, the tightly wound desk clerk, braced himself for the onslaught with a grimace but not a flinch. He had weathered similar blitzkriegs and survived to tell about it. This group was only distinguished by their silly maroon fez hats emblazoned with nonsensical embroidered emblems and black tassels flying behind them.

As the tidal wave of conventioneers reached the registration desk, nearly every clerk behind the counter stepped back.

But not Mr. Harris. No. He was prepared for the full frontal attack. *I was born for this moment*, he said to himself. *Born for the battle.*

"Welcome to the Gotham. I hope your travels here were pleasant. How may I . . ."

He stopped. A cacophony of unrelated sounds rose from the front lines of the guest brigade that would rival the volume of a jet airplane taking off. With arms raised clutching reservation confirmations and luggage being tossed to and fro by bellhops, it was a sight to behold.

* * * * *

Out in the hallway leading to the double suite, the officers and reporters who were now gathered there, from time to time, could hear snatches of the dialogue between the two Valentines and Warde and were hesitant to interrupt.

"Come on in, John," Mrs. Valentine was begging him. "Forget all about everything that's happened. We can do that. We'll just let it go. We can start afresh as if nothing ever happened."

"First, tell me, where's my sister?" he demanded. "Where's Katherine?"

"Katherine's asking for you also, John. She wants to be with you in here, though, in the room," Mrs. Valentine pleaded. "Come on in, darling, please. Come along in and have a nice lunch and forget everything. It's getting quite warm out there."

"Not if there are policemen in the room," Warde retorted. At the moment he was trying to squeeze past the oversized architectural ornament jutting out above the ledge to reach the window in the next suite where Mrs. Valentine had been resting.

Fearful that he might not be able to get back to his original position and then feel trapped and panic, she said, "If you're frightened about crossing that barrier, John, we'll get someone to help you. I promise nothing will happen to you. Everyone in here is your friend. . . . We just want you safe, that's all."

"No, you're wrong," Warde shot back. "They'll only send me away again. I know you've got cops in there, and they're just waiting to haul me away to Bellevue. That's what Katherine was saying to me. She called me crazy. She said she was going to call a doctor for me. She wants to have me committed!"

For the first time, they had a clue about what had triggered this entire unhinged series of events that had caught them all so off guard. Later, Patrick Valentine would tell reporters, "A remark was passed by Mrs. Bull that was so trivial that no one could even remember it. Apparently, it was not trivial to John. He twisted it into an indictment."

Bella Valentine was desperately trying to correct John's false impression of his sister's comment. "No, no, John, she said nothing of the sort. Besides, if she called you crazy, you know it was all in jest—on a lark. She doesn't mean that, John. You know she doesn't think you are crazy one bit. She loves you dearly."

With more people gathering below by the minute, John fell silent on the ledge. *Manelli would be proud of me*, he thought. The people at the *Tribune* must have been buzzing with excitement. He would make them all proud. However, his sister was not proud, and she was the most important person in the whole world to him.

"She abandoned me. If she loved me so much, why did she leave me for Earl Bull? Why did she go and get married? She didn't need anyone other than me. But she chose to leave me. And now you've called the police to come lock me up."

"I swear to God I haven't!" Katherine Valentine insisted. "Only me and your sister and Patrick. We're the only ones in here. If you come over and peek in, you can see for yourself."

"They'll send me away—back to that asylum," he insisted. "We both know that."

"No," she answered. "We all love you, John. When people love each other, they protect each other. Don't you see?"

"No, I don't. I don't see that at all. No one can protect me from what I feel inside."

"John, you know what I promised you—and I mean it. I won't break my promise. We'll never send you away. You'll live with us, and all will be fine. You can see your sister as often as you want."

"My father won't allow that. He'll send me away. I'm just miserable, Mrs. Valentine. I've fallen short of everybody's expectations. Now I might just as well fall myself."

John laughed grimly at his joke. Katherine Valentine shuddered.

The conversation continued on, though John seemed to have calmed down some. She felt that progress was being made, as she could see his body relax and his demeanor lighten. Hope was rising.

"Think I could have a glass of water? It's getting awfully hot out here." John, wearing a tight-fitting white vest, casually unbuttoned it and handed it to Katherine Valentine. "Please fold this up or hang it in the closet. It's one of my favorites." That was another positive sign.

Mrs. Valentine handed him a glass of water out on the ledge, and he drained it quickly. She also handed him a cigarette. Then she perched herself halfway on the ledge and took one herself.

"I'd light it for you, but, you know . . ." John seemed to be in a more congenial mood as he spoke to his good friend.

"I understand," she replied with a pleasant smile and a wink. This was the Johnny she knew and loved—witty, urbane, self-confident, and quick-minded. He was on his way to being back in his right mind. The manic phase was slowly diminishing.

Katherine Valentine later said she refused to give him the full pack of cigarettes as he had requested, believing it might encourage him to linger too long on the ledge on a sunny summer morning. She felt assured that he would be coming in at any moment. She, too, allowed herself to relax.

Finally, his sister returned to the window and leaned out, this time—based on her penchant for fainting—with the rope tied securely around her waist.

"Brother, this has gone on long enough. Your lunch is getting cold, and we are all very tired. Please just come in and get all of this foolishness over with. Really, John, it's getting quite warm in here, and all of this isn't helping one iota."

"You'd better leave me alone to work this problem out all by myself," he snarled back at Katherine. "I'm sorry to disrupt your day, but I have something to work through. Something I've been dealing with for a while. It's a problem for me, you know."

"There are all kinds of problems, John," the sister said. "Everyone has a problem. We all have problems. You can work it out somewhere else than out here. We've always been so close. Just like brother and sister. Well, I mean . . . more like two brothers, don't you think? You know what I mean, Johnny. So close . . . like twins, we are. I couldn't live without you, John. I don't really think I could. Please don't do this to me, I beg you."

"I'm nothing but a rotten rotter," he said softly and brokenly. "Nothing but a rotter to you."

"No, no, Johnny . . . you're no rotter. Why, you're the best brother in the world," Katherine answered. "There is no one better than you. You're a man of character . . . you have more character than anyone I know. More character than me. I just want you to live. I love you, John, you know that!" She gazed at him with tear-moistened eyes and was desperately searching for the right words that would turn all of this madness around.

Looking back at her, John reached his hand toward his sister, but not close enough for her to touch him. His eyes began to overflow with tears, and he mumbled something unintelligible. She asked him to repeat it. "It's something you would never understand, sis, something I have to work out inside myself."

Tears rolled down his cheeks. "I'm tortured inside, Katy. . . . I can't figure out how to deal with it."

After she heard those words, Katherine Bull fainted for a third time and was not to be revived for hours.

3 Hour One

A soul-shattering scream from a balcony across from the Gotham caught Patrolman Robert Devine's attention.

The scream—without the benefit of any words—quickly had Devine scanning the windows of the upper floors of the Colonial Arms Apartment Building where the sounds seemed to have emanated from. Sure enough, in seconds he spotted her. The woman would turn out to be Mrs. Jeanne Lubic, who had been setting some milk outside in an icebox on the fire escape to keep it cold when she saw something amiss.

With one more massive yelp and nearly frozen in place with fear, Lubic pointed a single finger of her outstretched arm across the boulevard to a window in the Gotham. Looking over in that direction, Officer Devine followed her pointed path through the air and was soon staring at the same object that had so startled the woman.

It was a man on a ledge. To the left of the man was a woman who appeared to be reaching out to him with one arm—stretching as far as she could.

His back and head were pressed tightly against the hotel's granite block outer wall, his heels as well, leaving him less than six inches on the remaining portion of the ledge before it dropped nearly two hundred feet to the bustling street below. At the time, he was positioned just three floors below the building's 232-foot height and only seventy feet from the busy Fifth Avenue corner.

One of his arms was stretched out to provide some balance, and he appeared to be nestled against the edge of a stone oval architectural ornament of floral design with a large decorative bow carved into its top. It was about a yard wide and almost shoulder high and protruded significantly from the building's wall.

Facing westward toward Sixth Avenue, the wind was whipping at the man's hat that was threatening to go sailing into the Manhattan air at any moment. The man was relatively tall and slender—a good athletic build—and could boast a head of thick, curly, tousled black hair.

He was dressed well and had the look of a professional about him. With freshly pressed gray flannel trousers and black shoes with a high shine, he modeled a hand-painted blue silk tie—quite the fashion statement—which was tucked into his shirt.

Then he did something quite inexplicable.

Warde sat down on the edge of the ledge and crossed one leg over the other—casually dangling the one tauntingly. Then he took his hat and, with one mighty flip, sent it sailing high into the Manhattan midday air. He lit a cigarette and leaned back on his two arms, scanning the streets in every direction. It was, after all, the best view in town.

At least from the street below—the fellow seemed to be absolutely enjoying himself.

When Patrolman Bobby Devine realized what was happening, he put in a distress call to his partner Charles Glasco, who was just blocks away, working Thirty-Seventh Street on foot patrol. As soon as he did, Devine recalled that he immediately rushed across the street to the hotel and ran to the elevator, going straight up to the seventeenth floor, which was where the desk clerk thought the man might be.

When he arrived, Devine found a woman—later identified as Mrs. Patrick Valentine—standing in the open door of Room 1714, who quickly waved him in and immediately pointed to the window without saying a word. Going over there, the officer started to climb partway out when he saw Warde.

"He looked like a regular guy to me, smiling and laughing. He was only a few feet away from the window, so I made an awkward grab at him, but he said: 'Don't come near me, or I'll hop off'a here.' He said it real calm-like too, like it was nothing more than a day in the park for him. He just sat there smoking and smiling at me.

"It was a strange look, though . . . not quite right. There was something in his eyes that made me step away from the window at once and telephone headquarters and the fire department."

Within fifteen minutes, hook-and-ladder trucks, the NYPD Rescue Squad, ambulances, and about sixty policemen—headed by an inspector—had arrived.

Shortly after getting the distress call from Officer Devine, Glasco also snapped into action.

Officer Charley, as he was known in the neighborhood, was an old-fashioned cop who was a proud member of the First District Traffic Summons Squad.

Beginning his shift at 8:00 a.m. every day for the past fourteen years, Officer Charley's duty was to serve summons on persons guilty of parking violations on Thirty-Seventh Street between Fifth and Ninth Avenues.

An amiable, rather rotund, and pleasant-looking man of thirty-five and better than average height, with sharp brown eyes and black hair quite thinned out on top, Glasco was proud to have been a New York Police Department officer for well over a decade and was highly regarded by the other members of his unit, Traffic C, as a teller of Irish folktales.

Glasco, in fact, was supremely proud of his Irish heritage as well, though a bit sensitive because his surname was often thought to be Welsh—a fact that grated at him dearly. As a result, whenever this was mentioned, he would do a slow burn and then produce his membership card in the Ancient Order of Hibernians—the largest and oldest Irish Catholic organization in America—which he carried for just such an emergency.

Officer Charley had covered both sides of the same three-mile stretch for well over a decade, and never a day in his life had he thought of doing anything different. He was born a cop, just as were his father, his brothers and uncles, and Pops—the oldest in the clan of Glascos.

Glasco began to run—or some imitation of that—to reach the police phone on the corner of Fifth Avenue. As soon as he picked up the receiver, he was instantly connected to the Sixth Precinct.

"Midtown. Whatcha need?" The dispatcher was a little casual.

"Herbie . . . Herbie . . . we got a 10-56 in progress—a jumper. Over on Fifth and Fifty-Fifth at the Gotham. He's way up there, too. I dunno, guessin' fourteen, fifteen floors up. Maybe more. He ain't movin' a muscle. Send some cars. Better block off the streets for several blocks. We gotta move, gotta move fast Lots of shoppers on the streets right now!"

Glasco was breathless. He'd run the better part of a city block—clearly not something he had done in some time. The cop had a bad feeling that this wasn't just some gimmick. It was the summer season, after all, not a time really for showing off or some publicity stunt. "No, this time it's for real," he said to himself.

Making his way back to the scene, he came up alongside a squad car and could hear the call going out: "Calling all units. A 10-56 in progress at 700 Fifth Avenue. Backup needed. Proceed with caution. Crowds beginning to gather."

As Glasco neared the intersection, he saw a gawking crowd on the sidewalks, as six police radio cars screamed up and skidded to a halt. Already, two hook-and-ladder trucks, a rescue truck from Police Emergency Squad Number 4, and an ambulance were parked with men hustling to get into position.

The firemen were hastily unfolding a fire rescue net, its center marked by a blood-red circle, beneath the ledge where Warde was now sitting. Lifting their arms high in his direction—much as a golfer measures a putt—they were estimating where he might land. As they did, they knew for a fact that the net would hold only those who jumped from the sixth floor or lower. It was a useless—though visibly important—exercise.

Officer Glasco could easily see from the street a man with his white shirt and dark trousers highlighted against the dull gray limestone of the building. It was an image he would never forget throughout his lifetime, and it would continue to give him chills at the very thought of the sight of the man on the ledge. A frightening scene seared into his memory.

People had stopped in place, transfixed, staring up and pointing. Another person, then another and another, joined the first group. Within five minutes, there were several hundred more spectators. Within an hour, the street would be packed from curb to curb and shoulder to shoulder. The crowd had also begun to spread out for several blocks, and traffic detours were being set up.

Sergeant Sean Murphy was standing on the south steps of the Fifth Avenue Presbyterian Church, at the northwest corner, mopping his brow. "Take a look up there," he said, pointing at the Hotel Gotham, directly across Fifty-Fifth Street.

As Glasco watched, a woman leaned out the window to the right of where the man was standing—her right side resting on the sill—and beckoned vigorously to him with her left arm. The man whirled in her direction, then crouched, holding on to the stone ornament with one hand and raising his other arm in a wild gesture. They seemed to be arguing, or at least in an animated conversation. She appeared to be desperate in her pleas.

Glasco was informed by the sergeant that the woman was the man's sister. The biggest concern at that point, apparently, was that the event would tie up traffic at one of the city's busiest intersections. If this lasts much longer, they knew they would have a mess on their hands as rush hour approached.

"Well, if they don't jump the first hour, they never jump," Glasco noted with some confidence. At least that was the story that had circulated among the Emergency Division in the department for years. At the moment, they were toying with the idea of just grabbing him and yanking him through the open window in the room.

"Can't get at him," the sergeant replied, still staring at the building while squinting into the intense overhead sun. "He's just far enough away to grab but threatens to jump if a cop even comes near that window. Bobby Devine is up there now, but I'm not sure what's happening."

"I could get at him, I bet'cha," Glasco said. "I'd just stop being a cop for a while and pretend to be someone else who wanted to befriend him. That's the way I'd do it anyways. And I bet you a cup of coffee I'd get at him too."

"Well, maybe you would, at that," the sergeant responded. "You always was a pretty fair actor, and you got a smooth way of talking too. You're a real storyteller, everyone says. It's worth a try, anyhow. Go on up to Room 1714 and tell Devine I sent you. See if you can get that poor loopy-loo in off of the ledge. They tell me he's only a kid. Con him in off the ledge, and maybe we can have a little peace down here."

Indeed, crowds were beginning to build. By the time Glasco—who did indeed have a reputation for having an easy way about him with some down-home charm—had made his way to the base of the hotel, there were already hundreds of lookie-loos all staring into the sky and pointing, their hands sheltering their eyes from the unrelenting midday sun. Already-sauced Shriners were joining in the fun as well.

As the officer took his position at the entrance to the Gotham, he suddenly felt as if he was in the midst of a circus. There wasn't concern or fear on the face of those assembled. No, he noticed with some surprise. There was excitement, anticipation—dare he say, *joy*?

Officer Charles Vincent Glasco looked down at his wristwatch as the onlookers rushed past him desperately to get the best viewing spot. It was past noon now, and it was hot. It was also unbearably humid, and the officer stopped to wipe his forehead with his handkerchief while pulling his cap down closer to shade his eyes. He was sweating profusely, and it reminded him that his wife had been pushing him to drop a few pounds. Well, maybe more than a few.

"This might be a long one," he said to himself. "Best tell the wife to put dinner on hold."

Thirty miles away in Woodhaven, a friendly neighborhood in the southwestern corner of Queens, Margaret Glasco—Maggie to her husband—was shopping for the evening meal with the promise that her husband would be having liver and bacon—his favorite dish—for dinner. Her husband was scheduled to get off at 4:00 p.m. that day, and as was always the case, dinner would be ready for him when he walked through the door.

Charley had not been feeling too spry, with a troublesome sacroiliac that had been acting up lately. To ease the pain, Maggie would strap his back with adhesive tape each morning before his shift and say a quick prayer for him. She was concerned about his health. His weight didn't help any, and she did anything she could to ease his discomfort.

It was a good marriage. Maggie was a good woman, and they both looked forward to having dinner together and then relaxing with a cigarette and a beer on the porch. *Fibber McGee & Molly* and Bob Hope's *Pepsodent Show* were on the radio that evening—two of their favorites—and she had baked a chocolate cake as a special surprise for him and their little girl. Yes, it would be a nice night together.

Until she received the call.

* * * * *

Outside the hotel, another frenzy was underway and growing rapidly. The crowds had tripled as midday shoppers, commuters, and lunchers were now all converging throughout the street and enjoying a little unanticipated entertainment. The police had set up barriers and roadblocks to control the car traffic, but the bystanders only treated those as little more than suggestions.

In fact, the more the cops pushed the people back, the more they pressed in. Shortly, reporters on the scene were estimating the crowd to be several thousand. If anything, radio and newspaper reporters were feeding the fire as best they could. Submitting their reports every ten minutes, there was soon an insatiable demand for news on the event, and the temptation was to exaggerate slightly to get a scoop.

Both in business offices and in their homes scattered throughout the five boroughs, most New Yorkers were tuned in to a live radio broadcast featuring Walter Winchell on CBS, who was doing his dead-level best to inflame the entire situation.

Shouting regularly, "I think he's about to jump. I think he's gonna go any minute!" Winchell fortunately had the presence of mind to remind viewers—with a message from his sponsor—that "French-milled Lux Soap is as fine as any skin care cream you'll find in Paris!"

An experimental television set in the laboratories of the Radio Corporation of America—today RCA—in the building directly across the street picked up the heart-pulsing drama and flashed it on-screen where curious onlookers crowded around the set in the window of the offices to follow the action.

At 711 Fifth Avenue, less than a block from John's perch, the pioneer television station of the National Broadcasting Company was telecasting the activities on the ledge and providing play-by-play commentary to a small group of viewers.

Three weeks later—when the outcome turned out to be a distasteful one—the pioneering television division proudly and sanctimoniously reversed its course and inaccurately pointed out that it had elected to ignore John Warde's suicide watch at Hotel Gotham, arguing that "it was too terrible to report." This, although the *New York Times*, with its famously high standards, considered it "news fit to print" and made the story a front-page feature.

Despite the flurry of inaccurate reporting and the incessant jockeying for positions outside the hotel, the police were solely focused on the job at hand: finding out who this person was and then getting him off that ledge.

"What room is it? How far up? How far from the roof? Does he have a weapon? Is he making any demands? Do we know anything about the man at all?" Questions were flying in every direction from the temporary headquarters the NYPD had set up in a room off the Gotham's lobby.

Eventually, Captain Pat McDonald—a mountain of a man—took charge by slamming a three-inch-thick phone directory on a table in the room, bringing everything to a halt.

Patrick Joseph McDonald was a bit of a legend in the department, having gained tremendous fame by winning two shot-put events in the Stockholm Olympics and then returning eight years later—interrupted only by serving with distinction in the war—and capturing the gold once again in Antwerp, Belgium, in the fifty-six-pound weight throw event. During the in-between years, he was a national champion in several throwing events.

Born in Doonbeg, Ireland, McDonald was listed as being six foot three and weighing 295, but those who knew him said those statistics were a vast underestimate. Longtime friends said he was closer to six five and 340, the biggest they had ever known, and they firmly believed that there wasn't a man on earth who would mess with him. Featuring bright red Irish hair in a mass of curls and fair skin, even in his late fifties he was considered handsome.

Nicknamed the "Irish Whale," everyone agreed that they'd never want to go up against him.

Certainly no one in the makeshift "war room" off the lobby of the Hotel Gotham had any intentions of standing up to the Irish Whale or even making any suggestions. Everyone was relieved to find someone finally willing to take charge of this mess.

"Where's somebody from the hotel who knows what in blazes is going on here?"

"Captain, my name is Mr. Easton Harris. I'm the desk clerk. Mr. Clive Randolph, the hotel manager, will be here shortly. I suggest that I escort you to room 1714, where the man in question exited through a window, creating the predicament in which we now find ourselves."

"OK, Harris, let's go now." McDonald, if nothing else, was decisive and a leader of men.

With that, the entire contingent was rushing toward the lobby elevators. Pulling a few startled guests out of the way, the men filled two cars past capacity and shot up like a rocket to the seventeenth floor. When the doors opened simultaneously, it appeared as if the elevators were vomiting them out.

As the detectives, street cops, hotel executives, and assorted reporters tumbled out into the corridor and rolled forward like a tsunami in the direction of the suites at the end of the hall, everyone was yelling directions and offering solutions to this quite upsetting situation.

Up until that very moment, Room 1714 might have been the quietest, most peaceful room in the entire hotel. Officer Glasco had arrived well before any of them and had managed to wedge himself halfway out the window, though he didn't feel it necessary to say anything initially.

He figured that was up to the nameless man on the ledge. This was his show, after all.

Before Officer Charley attempted to connect with the man, however, he had stopped in the lobby to borrow the coat and cap of the huskiest bellboy on duty. It seemed like a prudent thing to do at the moment.

Outside of Room 1714, Glasco stopped to put them on—the jacket wasn't quite big enough to button across his stomach and was a bit tight under the arms. He removed his cap, shield, pistol holster, and cartridge belt and laid them on the bed.

He was worried about his trousers, which didn't match the bellboy's outfit, because he feared John might recognize them as part of the regulation police uniform. But he figured that probably never more than the top half of him would be visible to the kid on the ledge. Glasco then headed for the partially open window.

As John Warde stood on the ledge, acclimating himself to the height where he now was, he began to survey the scene, limited though it was. Time was moving slowly for the young, mysterious man clinging to an eighteen-inch stone shelf. There was much to think about, much to consider.

He had become convinced that his sister Katherine was hell-bent on committing him to an insane asylum—something that was altogether untrue. This fear only ratcheted up his paranoia all the more.

What had been intended to be the ultimate expression of a person's free will—the decision to live or not live—had suddenly and quite unexpectedly exploded into a community event. When John put his first foot on the window sill, he was only thinking about himself, but The City refused to let him be alone in the choice he was about to make.

The City. Damn The City.

The City which had emasculated him, made him faceless and nameless, had stripped him of personality and robbed him of promise. It had ignored his secret passions and stolen his soul. Now it was about to offer him up to the masses as a sacrifice to indifference.

Standing on that ledge in the glaring hot sun, John was the loneliest man on earth. In the distance, sirens were echoing through the man-made canyons of Manhattan. Below, it looked like ants were moving methodically around in patterns driven by an unseen force. Across the way, the balconies and rooftops were filling with fascinated bystanders.

What was to be John's most intimate of all decisions was now a shared experience, and it frightened the troubled young man even further.

At that moment, John realized something very, very important: no one was particularly concerned about him and his inner motivations. They only cared about how his actions impacted their lives.

One day later, a reporter who had viewed the entire spectacle from beginning to end wrote the following in a 1938 editorial in the *Honolulu Star-Advertiser* under the headline "A Roman Amphitheater."

> Schoolchildren read with fascinated horror of bloodthirsty crowds watching the ancient Romans chucking Christians to the lions. Just the day before yesterday, in the year of 1938 AD, a vast New York crowd showed the same

> characteristics as those ghoulish Romans when thousands waited for hours hoping to witness the sight of a man hurtling himself to death from a 17th-story window—the result of mingled mania and exhibitionism.
>
> Some even made themselves comfortable with chairs on nearby roofs and sipped cocktails to add to their enjoyment. Others piped music from their radios to add a festive touch to the circus they were viewing.
>
> It might have unfolded differently, in fact, if John Warde's befuddled mind had not been affected by the sight of the enthusiastic and cheering crowd he had attracted. And John Warde fulfilled the ravenous desires of this fascinated crowd who desperately sought out a morbid thrill, just as the ancients thrilled when the lions jumped on the Christians.

John was finding himself drifting toward a deep, dark hole. What had begun as a silly, rash decision now was feeling ponderous. Repeatedly, as though speaking from the depths of an overwhelming feeling of inferiority, Warde mumbled something about "hating to be a quitter."

He needed help—he knew that—but he had no idea where it might come from.

4 Hour Two

"Who are you?" The suspicion in John's eyes bored into Glasco dressed in his undersized hotel uniform. The thermometer read ninety-four degrees as the two met each other for the first of many conversations that would stretch on for the next ten hours. Glasco was dripping with sweat.

"The name's Charley. Nice to meet'cha. I'm a new bellhop here at the Gotham. Matter of fact, I just got the job this morning. Listen, John—they tell me that's your name anyways—I don't want to butt in on what's strictly your own business, but I'd like to explain my angle on this situation to you.

"You see, I got me a wife and three kids. Before the hotel took me on this morning, we'd all been on welfare relief since, well, I can't hardly remember when we wasn't. Completely busted for a long time, and then I lucked out and got this job.

"You ever been on relief, John?"

There was no answer, but the suspicion had gone out of John's eyes, and his face had softened. He had steeled himself to face the police, but this man was an empathetic character. Glasco continued.

"Well, it's really tough, John, and I wouldn't kid you. Times have been really tough for me and the missus and the kids. Oh, I suppose if a man was single, it wouldn't be so bad, and the welfare relief people mean well and do the best they can, but when you got a wife and three kids—boy, I'm telling you! Well, John, I'm just giving you my angle on this situation, so please give me a fair shake.

"Cross my heart, if you don't quit this, it'll cost me my job. I've got the kids, and it'll go bad with them, too, if I lose out here."

"Go away and leave me alone, can't you?" Warde replied. "I feel blue. I don't want to come in. I'm not sure I want to live. Besides, it's nice and peaceful out here."

"Gee, buddy, you can't stay out there forever," the policeman-turned-bellboy responded.

"Why not?" Warde bounced back. "I'm getting all the fresh air I need out here. This is the most peaceful time I've had in six months."

Behind the scenes, however, nothing was peaceful.

Room 1716, where the Valentines and John's sister were waiting anxiously, was beginning to fill with reporters—welcomed in by the police who wanted their own names in the papers—additional officers, and an odd collection of uninvited crackpots who had somehow managed to reach the seventeenth floor. They were rapidly tossing out suggestions—everything from casting spells and religious incantations to alchemic solutions and divining the stars.

Patrolman Glasco, posing as the bellhop, had moved to sit on the window sill a few feet from Warde, attempting to entice him from his perch by regaling him with his own sad-sack story.

John paced most of the time, but between those high-rise strolls, he firmly gripped the stone ornamental flourish behind him. When he sat down, he did so with great care, as if he was concerned about the crease in his trousers. Carefully pulling up each pant leg first, as soon as he sat, he smoothed out the material and ensured that everything was properly in place.

Glasco shifted to a more animated approach.

"Hey there . . . I mean, look at me, fella! Have I ever done anything to you? Then, why do you want to ruin me? I'm just a lowly bellboy in this hotel. I have a wife and three kids. If you jump, people will say it's my fault, and I'll lose my job. Then what'll happen to my children?

"Come on in, son, and let's talk it over. Please, do it for me. . . . I mean, you'd really be saving my bacon if you did. I might even get a bonus or something if you come in."

Warde seemed touched by what a reporter would later call "these honeyed words," and he responded.

"Well, sir, I'm not looking to harm anyone, 'specially you. It's just that I can't seem to get over something. I have to make up my mind about it."

Officer Glasco continued. "Okay, so you're out there on that ledge, and it's strictly your own business—I'm being honest with you here—but think, maybe, about the rest of us. Suppose something bad should happen to you? You know what it'd do? Well, it'd cast a bad reputation on the hotel. That's what it'd do.

"John, once a hotel gets besmirched, its business gets lousy. Business gets real lousy, and the hotel starts laying off people. And who do they lay off first? The ones they took on last. So, if anything should happen to you out there, John, it's back on relief for me and the wife and the kids, and I'm not so sure I could bear it.

"I can't tell you how much I need this job—how much five people rely on my paycheck and my tips. I mean, I'm scared to even think what might happen to us, but we'd be on the street for sure. I ain't blowin' smoke up your ass, neither."

There was a long pause as John lit up another cigarette. He cast a curious glance at the gathering mob below.

Officer Charles Glasco was now stealthily leaning further out the recessed window to the ledge on his elbows with each word. He knew he wasn't authorized for such duty—this was far above his pay grade—but there was something about the moment that seemed to be calling to him.

The others who would come later might not have been able to put a name to it, but it was compassion.

The cop changed the subject, hoping to earn some trust. "Looks like we're in for quite a boiler for the next few days, if you ask me," Glasco said to a somewhat startled Warde. "Yup, I think we might be in for some whopping humidity too—record breaking, the papers say," he said while wiping his brow.

John subconsciously unbuttoned the top of his shirt around his neck as he stared into the void, only briefly glancing over at the man who was now peering out from the window. For a few minutes, the two men—inexplicably pulled together by fate—didn't speak or look at each other. It was just two fellows hanging out on a summer afternoon.

That same day—before the events of the day had even concluded—a newspaper had already published an article on the ordeal with the headline "Hamlet on a High Ledge: To Jump or Not to Jump." The subhead read: "Man Says 'I'll Figure This Out Myself.'" It provided moment-by-moment details that kept readers enthralled at a time when they had no idea how things might be resolved.

The reporter—with the enthusiastic style and colorful descriptions of a play-by-play sports broadcaster—first described the fifteen-minute period from 1:00 to 1:15 p.m. Noting that Warde smoked almost an entire package of cigarettes in that short time, he said that the man was nervously lighting one after another at a feverish pace, adding that he would frequently rest his chin in one cupped hand and look down into the two-hundred-foot chasm below, "as if he were pondering both his, and the crowd's next step."

He continued to describe that from his high perch, Warde could no doubt see that he had created a spectacle that served as "a magnet for ice cream vendors as they pushed their carts through the great throng while shouting their wares." Another man brought candy and peanuts to sell. Vendors were setting up on the corners.

Writing that firemen and police in rooms above and on each side tried to keep up rapid-fire conversations with him, he noted that although the closest window was only five feet away, the would-be rescuers were unable to reach him because of projections and the cornices outside the windows.

> Warde has so far turned a deaf ear to all pleas, continuing to smoke and occasionally walking with short, mechanical, purposeful steps as if he were playing a child's game. At other times, he jumps and hops along the ledge.

> The crowd below, when he did such things, roared with approval and found it all funny . . . to which he seemed to respond even more.

At 1:30 p.m., the man first mopped his brow with a handkerchief—the reporter commented—then he reached down to the ledge on which he was standing and picked up a glass filled with water and drank deeply.

> The crowd in the street found something funny in what he did and laughed uproariously. They seemed to be primed for a comedy show, and his every action for a stretch elicited laughter and howls of glee.

Responding to this reaction from the crowd, for a moment Warde hovered the glass tumbler off the ledge and over the assembled crowd, apparently threatening to let it fall and shatter into pieces. This brought a second wave of cheers that clearly delighted him even more.

To either taunt them or reward them as his audience, from time to time, Warde began to put a foot over the side, peered down, and then drew it back teasingly. Looking at the masses beneath him, as he would finish each cigarette, "he would flick the butts out onto the street, where spectators would scramble for them as souvenirs."

Police had quickly thrown a cordon around the space immediately below Warde, clearing it of pedestrians in order to protect anyone from "being hurt by a falling body and doubling the danger of the day." That was followed by a police emergency truck, filled with rescue specialists, which pulled up alongside the hotel. Fire apparatus suddenly began appearing from several directions, including a hook-and-ladder truck.

"At about 1:35 o'clock, three firemen in an adjoining window, pleading with him not to jump, appeared to anger the man, and he shook his head violently." An argument ensued, "though the content of that conversation is not known." The reporter commented that, in his opinion, perhaps Warde was disturbed that his high-rise act had been interrupted. Then he did something inexplicable.

Posing on the narrow, eighteen-inch ledge, with his hands outstretched as if he were all set to dive and his toes clearly over the edge, he caused an loud cry from the crowd. "He's off!" they yelled almost in unison.

But he wasn't. Warde changed his mind again, apparently, and casually lit another cigarette after he pulled back his feet and regained firm footing on the ledge, smiling and chuckling at the furor he had caused below.

Firemen on the ground reported that they felt paralyzed by his actions, saying they were "afraid to rig a net under him, fearing he might jump the minute we started getting it ready." Emergency squad policemen, however, carried scaling ladders inside the hotel with the hopes of installing them there.

The reporter marveled that "from the street came concerted roars from the massed thousands peering upward. For long periods, when there was no action above, the crowd would be virtually silent except for scattered voices with such shouts as:

'Make up your mind!' 'Go back!' 'Jesus can save you!' 'Don't jump!' 'Prove you're a man and jump!' 'Got any guts, buddy?'"

The situation on the ground was growing more dire by the minute. No traffic was able to move for blocks on either side of Fifth Avenue, though some adventurous spectators managed to worm themselves through the throng. The crowds, held back to Fifty-Seventh Street on the north by ropes and scores of police, continued to follow the drama as it progressed.

The ongoing drama had hypnotized the city since 11:40 a.m. when casual passers-by heard the initial scream after Warde clambered out on the ledge. Hundreds of people were now gathering around immobilized cabs with their radios blaring, listening to minute-by-minute descriptions by local broadcasters. Early on, the crowd was already estimated at more than twenty thousand people—most of them jammed behind ropes as traffic slowed to a stop in several places.

As the second hour of the vigil drew to a close, John Warde still remained on his seventeen-story perch while the many thousands in the streets below waited patiently for the ultimate decision of this one-man sideshow.

Below the activity on the ledge, chaos was indeed developing on the streets. People were now streaming in from the alleys and side roads and angling to get a good view of the non-action on the seventeenth-floor ledge.

In the adjoining suite—Room 1716—the crowd was growing even larger as the word had filtered up the law enforcement chain of command before finally reaching the commissioner's office. He was receiving minute-by-minute updates. Everyone seemingly wanted a piece of the spotlight.

* * * * *

Lewis Joseph Valentine—no relationship to the Valentines in Room 1716—was the New York City police commissioner. At the time, he was in the middle of a crusade to clean up the department, eventually making it one of the most honest forces in the nation.

"Muss'em Up" Valentine joined the New York Police Department at age twenty-one. After paying his dues as a beat cop, he began his heralded career combating police corruption. He eventually attracted the attention of Mayor Fiorello La Guardia, who then subsequently appointed him as the city's police commissioner.

Valentine would ultimately serve a long and distinguished career in that position. However, at this moment—only three years into the job—he was still trying to earn his spurs, win over his detractors, and impress Mayor La Guardia.

The excitement in the Commissioner's Office, the confusion in the adjoining room, and the chaos on the streets surrounding the hotel, however, was matched only by the activity across Fifty-Fifth Street.

Directly facing the entrance to Hotel Gotham was the stately and venerable edifice of the Fifth Avenue Presbyterian Church. It was perfectly positioned to play a critical role in the rescue efforts if the heads of the church were willing to cooperate.

The church had been a religious and architectural cornerstone of New York since its founding around the same time America was getting on its feet as a nation and President Thomas Jefferson walked up its steps.

Fifth Avenue Presbyterian would go on to leave its mark on America over the years by founding such organizations as the American Bible Society and Princeton Theological Seminary, inventing the concept of "Sunday school," and establishing the first free public schools, which later evolved into the New York Public School System.

The church's edifice was a masterpiece of the time and attracted attention worldwide. On this particular day—a day unlike any other in Manhattan—the church served as a towering backdrop to what was now a carnival of sideshows and barkers.

Eighty years earlier, when the congregation purchased a large, open field at Fifth Avenue and Fifty-Fifth Street for $350,000—a stunning investment at the time—it began construction of a new sanctuary. Church leaders believed that the recently established Central Park would serve as a natural barrier against business and factory expansion and thus provide them with a secluded and serene location.

When completed two years later, the church's steeple rose 286 feet into the air, making it the tallest building in Manhattan when it was dedicated in 1875. It also featured several technological innovations, including wooden louvers installed beneath the pews. This allowed coal-heated warm air to rise into the sanctuary from steam pipes in the basement on cold winter days.

On warm days like this one, enormous blocks of ice were delivered to the basement, where fans blew cooling air upward, making it one of the first air-conditioned buildings in the nation and, no doubt, quite an evangelistic drawing card. In fact, the cooling system was so effective—despite blistering New York summers—that modern air-conditioning would not be installed for another 128 years.

The church's exterior—exquisite in both ornate design and expert construction—is still one of the great landmarks in one of the greatest cities in the world. Built of red sandstone mined in New Jersey, the dramatically pointed clock tower featured

Swiss clockworks. To this day, it is not electrified and must be wound once a week by hand, much like an antique pocket watch.

Fifth Avenue Presbyterian's ominous presence and stately countenance were matched only by the unwavering resolve of its pastor.

"You cannot—you will not—use the Lord's sanctuary nor any portion of His House for secular purposes. It was dedicated to God's glory and not as a tool in a police action. I understand your desire based on our location, but I respectfully decline your request."

The Reverend Dr. John Bonnell was at the beginning of a storied thirty-year career as senior pastor of the church when he first spoke to Commissioner Valentine. It wasn't the only time they would speak in their lifetimes, but it was safe to say that it was not one of the most amicable.

Bonnell was refusing to allow the police to use their rooftop to string a line across the boulevard with the hopes of sending someone on a pulley system in a rescue attempt. Maintaining that the church—including the roof—was hallowed ground and could not be commandeered by the NYPD prompted a debate of some measure that would continue throughout the day's events and keep the commissioner fuming for some time.

To his frustration, the church—in all its glory and grandeur—seemed to stand coolly detached amid the commotion while providing Mr. Warde, from his solitary ledge, with a view of an enduring symbol of God's grace for mankind.

Whether he saw it that way, or viewed it as pointing a finger of harsh condemnation at his actions, is impossible to know. Yet the Fifth Avenue Presbyterian Church held its ground as it was swept up in the man-made hysteria of the moment.

Its front steps, however, were overrun by bystanders who scrambled to secure such a prime position to view "Jumper Johnny," as he was now being called.

On either side of the church were massive apartment and office buildings that featured wrought-iron balconies. The elite St. Regis Hotel was also across the street, with windows thrown wide open and curious onlookers poking their heads out into the hot sunshine.

By this time, all of the balconies and windows in the area were filled with curiosity seekers. Some had set up lawn chairs and were now enjoying beers and iced teas on the sweltering sunny day.

Bing Crosby and Perry Como could be heard wafting through the afternoon air as local stations intermittently broadcast updates on the Warde situation while spinning the latest tunes. It was turning out to be a nice summer day to share with family and friends.

Except, of course, for John Warde, and now also Charles Glasco.

Finally, Charley spoke up. "You gonna jump, kid?"

"If those cops come near me, I swear I will."

"Gotcha, kid. I ain't here to say one way or another . . . just was curious, was all."

"Who are you, by the way? What are you doing in my room?" Warde countered.

"Well, like I said, kid, I was on the floor below you and heard all the commotion going up the stairwell, and I thought I'd come see for myself. Thought the excitement might be kind of fun, I guess." Glasco wasn't being completely truthful—or even at all, for that matter. Still, he figured Father Reardon would forgive the white lie if he ended up saving the poor schmoe.

He continued with his ruse.

"So, you ain't much for cops, huh? Sometimes, I feel the same way, but if you stay out there much longer, kid, the joint's gonna be crawlin' with 'em. I can tell you that for sure. Only maybe they're gonna be a little sore about this happenin' on the day of the big parade. You see, their shifts end at four o'clock as long as there's no real action . . . but I'm afraid you kinda qualify as some real action, if you know what I mean.

"Look, it's up to you if you wanna jump—it ain't none of my business—but listen, I could sneak you down the stairs into Room 1603, on account it's empty and all, before too many of the coppers shows up. We could order some lunch on the house, you know, and then . . ."

Unfortunately, before Glasco could finish, Mr. Harris, the desk clerk at the Gotham, burst through the open door of Room 1714 and rushed directly to the window, nearly pushing an unsuspecting Charley headlong out the opening and into the clear, blue skies.

Poking his own head out, Harris yelled at the top of his voice, "Hey you, get in here this minute! I have a hotel full of Shriner conventioneers checking in today, and I do not need this distraction. You are not allowed to stand on a ledge at this hotel. We have a policy, and it is strictly forbidden. . . . Do you hear me, young man? There's already reporters out there. I don't want any publicity over this!"

It would be hard to determine who was more frightened—Officer Glasco or poor John outside the window—when the full mass of people poured through the door and into Room 1714 in hot pursuit of the desk clerk. Both men almost jumped out of their socks, and the poor guy on the ledge nearly did a swan dive on the spot.

As quickly as the desk clerk had arrived at the window, however, two officers each leaped to grab one of his legs and gave them a swift yank. From John's perspective, all he saw was a middle-aged man's head pop through the curtains one moment, say a few words that were lost to the wind, and then that same bald head disappeared from view the next moment.

Mr. Harris, however, was unceremoniously tossed into the corridor, where he was permanently exiled from the proceedings. As more officers arrived, they stepped over the still-rolling man as if he wasn't there.

Charley Glasco went back to his conversation.

"You know, it's a pretty dangerous thing you're doing, kid. You might fall off and hurt somebody. You don't wanna hurt nobody on the ground, do ya, kid?"

John shook his head. "Uh, no, not really. I never wanted to hurt anybody in my whole life." He looked down at gathering crowds and barricades going up. "They need to keep people away from the sidewalk because, well, you know . . ."

"Yeah, kid, I get it. So, wanna take me up on my offer for lunch in 1603?"

"I don't think so, though it's mighty nice of you, mister. I gotta think some things through. I'll come down eventually, but there's a lot on my mind right now. You know how it is."

"I guess I know. I mean, I don't really know, but I do know life is hard. But maybe not hard enough to be contemplatin' this here. Jumpin', I mean. Nothin' could be that bad."

As Glasco spoke in his comforting tones, he could hear a commotion in the room behind him. Glancing back to see what was happening, John suddenly tightened up.

For a second, Glasco pulled his head out of the window. Once again, John suddenly felt very, very alone. He called out loudly, though it was unknown if anyone in the room heard him. "No cops. I ain't kidding. No cops, or I'll jump!"

Sticking his head back out the window, Glasco gave it one last effort. He knew what was probably coming next and that it wouldn't end up well for the kid. Also, for the first time, John looked like he might be ready to give up. This had already gone on too long, and it was unfolding unlike anything he had originally planned. So, with a single sidestep toward the window, he began to reach out his hand to Charley.

In the room, however, a different action was underway as Officer Glasco was suddenly and forcefully grabbed by his elbow and yanked sideways away from the window.

5 Hour Three

"Who're you, buddy?" Chief Inspector Alexander Anderson asked. Apparently the situation had already percolated up the ranks and was now in the hands of the big boys.

"I'm Officer Charles Vincent Glasco, Chief." He stood erect at attention. "But ever'one calls me Charley. I'm the one who put in the call."

"Why are you out of uniform, officer?" The chief was not happy with what he was seeing. "You look like a clown. Disrespecting the uniform is never funny, officer!"

"Well, I was just trying to make a connection with the guy, and I knew he'd be afraid of cops. So I was thinkin' . . ."

"Oh, you were thinkin', huh? What's your beat, Officer Glasco?"

"The Traffic Summons Squad, sir. Been on traffic and parking detail goin' on fifteen years, sir. Proud to serve, Chief."

"I bet you are, but you ain't trained for this. . . . You're just a traffic cop, and we got guys 'specially for times like these. Okay, Glasco, get away from the window. We got this. You done your best here today, officer. You can go now. Go back and help with crowd control. . . . We got quite a situation brewing out there."

Officer Glasco saluted and, after gathering his coat and hat, was out the door in seconds. He truly cared for the kid on the ledge, but he was a man who respected authority, and he wasn't about to buck it now. He did not doubt that there were people better than himself at handling such delicate situations.

"Hey, wait a minute," Chief Inspector Anderson said. "Yeah, you . . . Officer Glasco. Before you go, what did you find out about the guy? Anything we should know?"

"Well, he didn't really say nothin' yet, but I think I kinda connected with him, you know. When you came in, I think he was just about to call it quits. Three more seconds, and I think he woulda been moving back to the window. I really do.

"Maybe if we could find out more about who he is, you know, we'd find out what's eatin' him up inside. Maybe he was in the army and, well, had a mental breakdown or somethin' like that. Nerve gas, or mustard gas, maybe in some of those drills they was doing. Lots of the boys got pretty messed up, you know."

Anderson added his thoughts. "Maybe some gal that he is sweet on or a boss he worked for. The family ain't much help so far, but there's gotta be some secret to this puzzle that we ain't figured out yet. Maybe a wife? A classmate? Ask Murphy to check around and see if any of the guys have a bead on him or anything.

"But I guess for now, you just get back out there and keep an eye on the crowds. We gotta keep this thing under control. I hear they're overrun and need some help. Tell 'em to bring in some off-duty guys if they need to."

"Well, I'd just say one thing before I go, Inspector. He and this Mrs. Valentine in the other room got a real connection. An unusual one, I'd say. They're real close. I don't think it's a romantic thing or nuthin' like that, but I don't know for sure. But I think you'll see it if you talk to her. Real close, that's all I gotta say for now. But I'd get her talking to the kid if I were to say anything. She has a way with him, I'm thinkin'."

With Glasco's exit, Chief Anderson was now in charge, fully and completely.

"Alright, everyone, listen up!" His voice was booming.

Square-jawed with sharp, full features, Anderson was a cop's cop, and he looked and sounded exactly like one might expect. Gruff and no-nonsense in his demeanor, he was a man of great loyalty to the department and driven by his commitment to "play it by the book."

Dedicated to his family—with an appreciation of fine whiskey and Camel cigarettes—at the top of his list was the department and the men under him. That was closely followed by the Yankees, the church, and his wife and children.

He was also given the highest honor of the day when he was made a member of Mayor La Guardia's hand-selected NYPD baseball team, which represented the department in a popular charity game against their counterparts in the Fire Department. Only months earlier, they'd had their annual showdown, and Chief Inspector Anderson, batting cleanup and playing the outfield, had driven in the runs that put his team in the lead.

Anderson was equally loved and hated by his men, but they never had to question whether or not he had their backs. The chief was loyal to a fault. You would never want to be on his shit list. Then again, there's no one else you'd rather have in your corner. On this particular day, there was no doubt who was now in control.

"Listen up!" It did not need to be repeated, but Anderson said it for effect.

"We got a command post set up on the steps of Fifth Presbyterian, and I've strung a line to an army field telephone from there to next door in Room 1716. From his position on the church steps, Sergeant John Tormey of the Emergency

Squad will be regularly relaying to Lieutenant William Klotzbach on what is happening outside from his perspective.

"We also have a phone line set up from that room to another phone that we can hand him so that he can talk to people he trusts without them having to lean far out of that window and risk fallin' themselves. We almost already lost one lady, and we can't let that happen again.

"We're gonna start by getting Mrs. Katherine Valentine—a close friend of the kid—on the line with him and see if she can talk him in. Right now, I'm thinkin' that's our best shot. I understand they are very, very close, and maybe we can just end this thing real quick now."

Anderson gave one of the phones to Katherine Valentine and then had Sergeant William O'Brien reach out the window to hand the other end to Warde and instructed that the line be connected through the hotel switchboard. The woman took a big breath and wiped away some tears before saying a short, silent prayer for wisdom and strength. Everyone in the room held their breath.

* * * * *

Isabella Katherine Valentine and John William Warde did indeed have an unusual and quite intimate platonic relationship.

That relationship began quite inauspiciously one day when Katherine—she went by her middle name socially—met young John while performing his banking duties in Southampton, the location of the Valentines' summer seaside home. There the family escaped the searing heat of Chicago, their permanent home where they were raising their two children.

Katherine was impressed with John's polished demeanor and sharp intellect, and the two clicked early on as she was taken by his quick wit. Over time, the Wardes connected with the Valentines, and they became social companions and friends.

Things had not gone smoothly for John as he moved into his teenage years.

Young John, by all accounts, was a quiet, intelligent, slender, good-looking boy with thick, meticulously groomed hair. Everyone said he was strikingly handsome. He was reportedly fond of baseball, music, and poetry. In high school, however, he had a reputation for being moody. No one really recalled him dating much or having a "steady." In fact, he seemed to have little interest in girls, though he was popular with them.

After graduation, John bounced around a bit before landing a job as a telephone operator—one of the only men in the profession at the time—and then as a clerk in a local bank, where he was reported to be a good worker, though a bit peculiar at times. Mostly, he was considered a bit of an "odd duck," but with his family's wealth and status, he was still included in most activities.

He was once described as "quirky and queer" by a coworker. Early on, there were questions about his mental health, though with America in the midst of the Great Depression, there was little recognition for or help with this disorder.

Nevertheless, this medical field was gaining increasing exposure through the studies and theories put forth by Sigmund Freud, an Austrian neurologist working out of London, who founded psychoanalysis—a newly coined and still much-disputed term.

Despite constant criticisms and repeated refutations, Freud's "psychological man" eventually replaced such earlier notions as a political, religious, or economic man as the twentieth century's dominant self-image. It was also the beginning of a more evolved approach to homosexuality, women's rights, racial equity, and what was called, at the time, "deviant behaviors."

Unfortunately, the breakthroughs that were occurring in the realm of mental health would be of no use to John Warde as he tried to navigate the events of the past few weeks and the demons taunting him on this warm and muggy Tuesday afternoon. Things had been changing lately for him, and the earth suddenly felt like shifting sand under his feet.

The most significant change came after an unfortunate turn of events just six days earlier.

With his parents somewhat distancing themselves from the social embarrassment of their "balmy" son, John became the unofficial ward of Mr. and Mrs. Patrick A. Valentine Jr.—that warmhearted couple in their mid-thirties who regularly summered in the family's vacation estate in Suffolk County's Southampton beach area.

Cleverly named Valmay—a combination of Valentine and May, his mother—their estate was known as one of the most impressive manor homes in the region, with expansive grounds, immaculate landscaping, tennis courts, vast lawns, and swimming pools, all swarming with scores of servants.

It was one of two family estates, the other being Danforth Lodge. That retreat, like Valmay, was extravagant and a reflection of the ostentatious displays of wealth of that era when many people were standing in soup lines and unemployment was reaching 35 percent of the population.

Located in Oconomowoc, Wisconsin, Danforth Lodge featured fifty-two rooms and more than thirty servants, as well as the most highly acclaimed "sunken gardens" in the western side of the nation. It was built on a V-shaped island—henceforth called Valentine Island—and had its own series of locks and canals.

After John was fired from his teller position at the bank—his second consecutive career failure—the ultra-rich and sincerely compassionate Valentines hired him as a caretaker and tutor for their two small sons. He alternately worked as a chauffeur and handyman for them—really anything to keep his mind and hands busy. It seemed at first to be the perfect cure for the increasingly unstable young man.

Their real goal was to provide a strong guiding hand for the wayward son of their good friend, John's father. Everyone hoped that a job in pleasant surroundings would help him overcome his melancholia and recover his self-confidence.

Mr. Valentine's father, already quite rich at the time, came to this country from Scotland when he was a young man and went to work for Armour & Co.—the massive meat-packing firm in Chicago—where he ultimately became its financial director. He then married the widow of business scion Philip D. Armour Jr. and was adjoined to her substantial inheritance.

Valentine promptly and dramatically purchased a mansion on Fifth Avenue from a famous steel baron for half a million dollars (more than $30 million in today's money) and moved his family to New York.

The Valentine family, at the time, was one of the wealthiest in the entire world. In fact, when Patrick's father died, his son—who was only thirteen years old at the time—received an inheritance of $8 million, a quarter of a billion dollars in today's money. Out of that, he was to be paid $1 million immediately (more than $60 million today), with the remainder coming when he reached the age of twenty-five.

Then, somewhat awkwardly, the young man fell head over heels in love with his first cousin—their fathers were brothers. In Illinois, it was both illegal and immoral for them to marry.

Love conquered all, however, and soon the twenty-five-year-old Patrick Valentine, fresh from receiving his full inheritance, was marrying the apple of his eye—curiously with the same surname—Isabella Katherine Valentine, in a London wedding, followed by an extensive European honeymoon during which there was no need for the bride to change the monograms on her luggage.

When they returned, they set up large homes in both Chicago and New York.

There, they combined their inestimable wealth, added a summer home in the Hamptons, and began to raise two sons. It was also there, during an afternoon banking visit, that Isabella met young and quite handsome John Warde.

Isabella Katherine Valentine appeared completely enamored with the dashing and witty young man. Soon she became his close companion, platonic confidant, and—some said—his romantic admirer.

With her husband often traveling back to Chicago for business, they spent countless hours walking and talking, swimming and sunning, reading and reacting to each other, until one day John's father announced that the summer playtime had run its course and it was time for his son to get a real job.

That decision sent John reeling. Like a petulant child, he warned that he might do something desperate to send a message to his father that he was unhappy with the interference and anything that would take him away from the life of leisure and attention that he was currently enjoying at Valmay.

When John Sr. doubled down on his demands, John Jr. made good on his threats.

Six days before he arrived at the Hotel Gotham to meet his sister for lunch, John drove in his father's car to the Ponquogue Bridge, a one-thousand-foot-long wooden drawbridge built only a few years earlier that connected Hampton Bays to the eastern end of Westhampton Island.

Parking his car at the peak of the bridge, he climbed over the railing and stood for a few minutes on the small outer ledge. He gazed down at the water, his toes dangling over the edge.

Noticing the young man from his small watchman's perch, the bridge tender dispatched a police boat to immediately head for the center of the river to intercept the jumper if he decided to leap. Afterward, he himself went sprinting in the young man's direction.

Seeing the boat steaming in his direction, Warde jumped.

In short order, the authorities were fishing him out of the river while the bridgeman was recording his car's license number. When John refused to provide his identity, the police tracked down the automobile's owner, where they encountered an angry father and a humiliated mother. After a stern lecture, John was delivered back to the Valentines, where Katherine quickly took the shivering young man under her care and provided an empathetic ear.

The event would have been concerning enough on its own, but it was doubly so because it was not the first time John had tried to take his life.

A year earlier, he had tried unsuccessfully to kill himself with a knife and came perilously close to being successful at it.

It had been a summer morning much like this very day—July 11, 1937—when John awoke to discover a note on the dining room table that his beloved sister had eloped with Earl Bull, an oil salesman who had come into town. Though four years his junior, Katherine was John's emotional rock and only true friend. The loss of her was insurmountable for him at the time.

Going into the kitchen, John pulled out a large butcher knife, held it lingeringly pointed at himself for a moment, and then promptly pushed it deep into his gut.

As he knelt on the tiled floor, watching the blood run down to his knees, he feared the wound wasn't sufficient to end his life—worse yet, it might take too long. So, grabbing a straight razor from the counter and lifting it to his throat, he pulled it slowly across his neck and opened what should have been a fatal gash.

At that moment—fortunately—a maid entered the kitchen. She screamed, and in minutes an ambulance was scooping him up and rushing with sirens blaring to Nassau Hospital, where his life was rescued by a team of surgeons who worked for hours.

During the many weeks of recovering, John's parents were determining their next steps. When he had fully recovered from his wounds, he was committed to Manhattan State Hospital for the Insane at Central Islip for observation and treatment. When he found out, he went into a hysterical fit of rage and had to be medically subdued.

Treatment for the mentally ill was far from evolved in the 1930s, and the prevailing approach at the time was to house and keep patients busy with the idea that they would get better with time. Although the field of psychiatry, and especially Freudian psychology, was beginning to take hold, it was far from being fully accepted or universally practiced.

The institution at Central Islip was a "hospital farm" located in central Long Island which, within a decade, would house nearly ten thousand patients, making it the second-largest psychiatric hospital in the United States next to Pilgrim State Hospital—also in New York—which was the largest psychiatric institution ever to exist in the United States. The buildings eventually grew to be a mile-long interconnected series of buildings affectionately, but not accurately, called the "String of Pearls."

Still in the grips of the Great Depression, a vast number of Americans—having lost everything—found themselves in the throes of mental illness with little help or support. The solution was to relocate these unfortunate souls to specially created farms where they could "work out their problems in the open air."

Through this treatment, patients received "O & O" (occupation and oxygen) and "R & R" (rest and relaxation) at the working farm, where patients cleared the land, constructed buildings, made furniture and mattresses, sewed their own clothing, grew crops, and raised dairy cattle, pigs, and chickens.

To arrive at his destination in Central Islip, John Warde was tragically placed on a special hospital train on the Long Island Rail Road, with bars on the windows and where patients were herded tightly like cattle. Undoubtedly a trip of terror, it only exacerbated the mental states of those who were packed shoulder-to-shoulder on their way to forced imprisonment with other dangerously unhealthy people.

However, to the Wardes, an even worse reality was at hand.

By committing their son to a mental institution, the family suffered an inestimable social disgrace—in that era, "mental frailty" was an unforgivable sin. Still, the parents felt that his mental needs were well beyond them, and even the threat of losing social standing was not sufficient to have them tuck him away at home out of sight.

By all accounts, John did well under the care of the psychiatrists and doctors at the hospital and regained form after some time. At the institution he was popular with the other patients and orderlies. With his modern and sophisticated training and winsome personality, he often led social events at the hospital and was the center of attention in the recreation room.

He also seemed to thrive in the outdoor setting and, despite his refined upbringing and cultured manners, took to gardening and appeared to have a green thumb of sorts by overseeing large and productive flower fields.

But all was not sunshine and roses. At other times, John was morose, disconnected, and surly. Emotionally up one day, down the next, it was determined that he was simply "moody," and the workers learned to "manage" him.

Six months later, at the beginning of 1938, according to Joel Sayre in his article in the *New Yorker* in 1949, John was released with a notation on his discharge papers that read: "The patient's manic-depressive psychosis seems to have arrested itself. He seems to be in a position to enjoy a healthy and happy new year."

* * * * *

Captain O'Brien had been tapped to set up a phone connection between Warde and Bella Valentine, but he was apprehensive. It seemed to him to be a big moment in this ongoing ordeal. A patrolman reached out to hand the phone to Warde but was quickly instructed by him to place it on the ledge instead and step back away. Inching his way over—while keeping his eyes on the cop—John picked up the receiver.

"Hello there, John, my name is Bill O'Brien," the sergeant answered. "I'm with the Sixth Precinct of the New York Police Department, and I have someone here who wants to talk with you. Before I hand this over, however, I just want to ask one more time . . . why don't you come on in, son? It'll be better for you and for all of us. For your family, you know?"

"I'm not falling for that. No, I'd get into trouble," Warde answered.

"No, sir, no, you would not. I'm not lookin' to arrest anyone. That's not our purpose here. We just wanna get you some help, that's all. I swear."

Warde was looking down at the crowd.

"They'd be angry with me," he added. "They expect something of me now. They'd be disappointed if I didn't jump."

"You don't know them, John. They are the same people who stare at airplanes. People that look blankly without a thought in their brain. People who got nuthin' better to do with their time than watch other people's lives. They're nobodies. You can't tell me you recognize anybody down there. And nobody knows you from Adam. I doubt if they even know your name."

"Yeah, they do, O'Brien. The radio is blasting my name all over town. I can't come in. They'll all laugh at me. I'll be the laughingstock of the entire city. You don't know what that feels like. What it feels like to be outside the circle of everyone else."

"Well, that's not entirely true, John. No one in this room would laugh at you. Hell, everyone in here cares. And besides, that bellboy friend of yours certainly cares. He wants to meet up with you someday. He just told me that. But imagine, that poor guy will get fired if you don't come in. He's got a wife and three kids. Don't you think that would be a pretty sad state of affairs?"

"Yeah, that'd be bad," John responded with genuine concern. "Real bad. Hope that doesn't happen, and I mean it. Hey, officer, have you got a cigarette?"

In seconds, a single cigarette was tossed out onto the ledge. Warde bent over to pick it up—the crowd cheering his move—and then thanked O'Brien for it over the phone. John was feverishly chain-smoking at this point, and Mrs. Patrick Valentine—wife of the man who had leased the room in whose hotel window Warde was perched—picked up the receiver from O'Brien.

"Hello, Johnny . . ." She started to cry and couldn't go on.

"Who the hell is this, anyway?" John sniffed out a trick with an actress playing the role of his friend. He didn't put anything past the cops.

"Oh, John, this is Katherine."

"Bella?"—that was his pet name for her—"Why are you saying 'Katherine'? Something stinks. How do I know it's really you?"

"It's me, John. I can prove it to you . . . you know that poem that we both hold close?"

"Yeah, well, tell me how does it start?"

Bella Valentine spoke a few of the lines in French for him.

"Okay, Bella, it is you. Only you know my favorite poem . . . and only you can recite it so beautifully," Warde said with his eyes growing misty. "But I won't come in . . . I just can't. My life is too sad."

Mrs. Valentine handed the phone back to Captain O'Brien, too emotional to continue. The process was beginning to resemble a tag team, with each person giving their best effort to bring the man in. Before he spoke on the phone, however, the captain covered the receiver with the palm of his hand and asked what the poem was about.

"It's a poem entitled 'Triste, Triste,'" Mrs. Valentine responded. "It's about a sad man contemplating his life." She translated for him.

O'Brien swallowed hard. The already morose situation suddenly felt a bit darker. The poem felt like an ode for a man contemplating suicide, not a fresh start to a new day. He decided to take a different angle in case John feared being arrested for a foolish act.

"Listen to me, John, you haven't done anything to worry about," he said soothingly. "I mean, a fellow can go out for a breath of fresh air if he wants to. There's no crime in that. No harm. That's all you did, son. You haven't committed a disorderly act. You haven't committed any crimes. I couldn't book you for anything even if I wanted to."

Warde disconnected the phone without comment. O'Brien threw his arms up in frustration, and Bella Valentine buried her face in her hands. John's sister Katherine was still recovering from the shock of the entire day.

Chief Inspector Anderson, angry at the time this was taking place, once again stepped up to take charge. "Okay, men, everyone away from the window. I'll take care of this myself. Yeah, I'll have him off in a minute, no problem. No kid is going to mess up my evening. I got plans!

"Hell, he's just a kid. I'll have him off of there in . . ." Anderson stopped to look at the pocket watch he always carried in his front pocket. "Let's see, it's about 2:50. Mark my words, I'll have him in custody before the three o'clock bells at St. Malachy's chime."

Every cop in the room looked at their watches. A few dollars changed hands.

Down on the street, the situation had already evolved into a major city event.

Hot dog and pretzel vendors were setting up temporary stands across from the Gotham and were in a bit of a turf war with the roasted nuts and popcorn guys who had staked this spot out long ago. They were continually barking into the crowd while simultaneously shouting obscenities at their competition.

The church's steps continued to be the hottest spot in all of Manhattan at the moment, and more than one fight broke out over who should get that prime real estate.

The New York spirit was in full bloom.

6 Hour Four

A major event also marked this day in New York City—the Ringling Bros. and Barnum & Bailey Parade through downtown. It had been planned for months to promote an upcoming three-week run at Madison Square Garden and had been the talk of the town for some time.

The Ringling Bros. and Barnum & Bailey Circus, without a doubt, was the number-one attraction in America in 1938. Over the years, its lineup of performers and crew had grown to more than 1,100 people, all of whom traveled with a menagerie of 16 camels, 26 elephants, 735 horses, and almost 1,000 other animals on 98 double-length railroad cars. Billed as "The Greatest Show on Earth," it would have been impossible to dispute that claim.

Best of all, the announcement that the circus had arrived in town was always accompanied by an animal and performer parade through every city's main thoroughfare.

In 1938, the company was also introducing the grand arrival of "Gargantua the Great" in the show's lineup. It had employed an audacious advertising campaign to transform the 460-pound gorilla into arguably the most famous creature of the twentieth century.

Each year the parade became bigger and more grandiose, and this year was widely expected to be the best ever. Heralded under a first-time banner heralding "The Year of the Woman," the event was also to feature highbrow New York socialites on display in a string of new Series 90, V-16, pink Cadillacs.

There was more, however. Much more.

The circus organizers had promised parade-goers along the six-mile route a "Marathon of Mirth" in full-page newspaper advertisements, and spectators—who had been lining up since early morning and now stood ten to twelve people deep—were in no mood to be disappointed.

Clowns, cowboys, and sword-wielding knights were accompanied by a menagerie of animals, including bears, zebras, twenty trunk-to-tail elephants, camels, and monkeys.

These were being marched by their trainers in and around the society matrons, while eight marching bands provided the soundtrack. Bringing up the rear of the parade was a float bearing the guest of honor—Mrs. Marie Fisher La Guardia, wife of the mayor himself.

By around 3:30 p.m., the parade had arrived at its halfway point. It was curling around Fifty-Ninth Street—the bottom edge of Central Park—and onto Fifth Avenue on its way toward the front entrance of Hotel Gotham, where now more than fifteen thousand onlookers were being entertained by a completely different diversion: a man teetering on a ledge more than two hundred feet in the air.

Unfortunately, the police had become so consumed by the unfolding events on the ledge that day, they completely forgot that the parade was heading their way. Then, as floats, matrons, bands, Mrs. La Guardia, and zoo animals suddenly collided with suicide watchers unwilling to yield their positions, the Fifty-Fifth Street intersection erupted in pandemonium.

A parade spectacular that was guaranteed to offer "memories that would last a lifetime" certainly delivered on that promise.

In little time, the zoo animals—which apparently did not enjoy a six-mile journey in one-hundred-degree temperatures—began to emit roars and growls and sent spectators running in fear for their lives.

This chaos was quickly followed by the tigers choosing to attack a large helium-filled Felix the Cat character balloon. It deflated agonizingly slowly—and grotesquely—to the abject horror of thousands of traumatized children.

Along with that, a little-known fact was discovered at this moment—namely that when monkeys become agitated, they begin to throw their feces at anyone considered a threat. In this particular case, the objects of their attention would prove to be the honored socialites who promptly received an unexpected dousing of the foul stuff.

The police eventually threw up their hands and let the whole scene play itself out.

Ironically, it was John who had the best view of the entire scene from his unobstructed vantage point high over the city, and he watched with wonder, and some delight, as he saw the madness unfold beneath his eyes.

Warde was taking it all in—examining the events and emotions that had brought him to this point—when a giant runaway Betty Boop balloon slowly made its way to the seventeenth-floor ledge of the Gotham and then hovered there for a bit, nose to nose with John.

With her doe eyes and coquettish grin, she seemed the perfect companion for this odd moment being played out before thousands on a bizarre stage in the sky. Then, as quickly as she had come into his world, she disappeared forever into the heavens.

For the first time in quite a long while, John Warde smiled.

* * * * *

"You there . . . boy! Get my bags! I'm in a rush. Got a train to catch. I've been standing here for five minutes." Clearly the man in the long, gray, woolen overcoat was an executive who was not used to waiting. Or being ignored.

Desperately trying to wave down a bellboy in the lobby of Hotel Gotham, the man's frustration level was building exponentially. Soon, that irritation became contagious and spread throughout the crowd packed like sardines at the front desk.

"Me too! Yeah, what's the deal? What kind of service you got around here? Next time, I'm going to the Waldorf." That sentiment—in various forms and with increasing degrees of obscenities—was soon being repeated throughout the lobby. The madness was growing, and the hotel staff was hunkering down under the onslaught.

"I demand to see the manager right this minute, buddy. No ifs, ands, or buts!" There was no "buddy," of course, so everyone conveniently convinced themselves it meant someone else. Except the long-suffering Mr. Harris.

In his most proper and cultured voice, he responded: "I'm sorry . . . Mr. Randolph isn't available right at the moment. There's a situation on the seventeenth floor, you see, and . . ."

"And you're telling me that that thing—whatever it is—is more important than me? Why, I never! That's no excuse. This hotel clearly doesn't understand priorities."

However, if anyone for one moment thought the chaos was confined to the lobby of the Gotham, they would be sadly mistaken, for outside a swarm of "lookie-loos" had transformed into a crushing and voracious mob. Completely unprepared for the scene outside, one guest—a Mr. Hawthorne P. Ludlow—rushed through the revolving doors in a futile attempt to hail a cab and ran smack dab into a pretzel vendor, which promptly sent a gallon of Gulden's mustard flying in all directions.

As an inevitable screaming match ensued—littered with colorful invectives—two older women, out for afternoon tea, stared at the upper floors and pondered the situation, which had them thoroughly enthralled.

"So what's your guess . . . advertising agency?" Doris asked.

"Could be it, could be, I guess . . . or those investor firms. They're always jumping, you know," Dorothy replied.

"Perhaps, but you know those ad men with the deadlines and the martini lunches. It's a bad combination if you ask me."

"A bad combination, indeed! I do hope they get it straightened out before seven tonight. Milton Berle is on, and I'd hate to hear it was preempted for this silly matter."

"It would be a shame, Dot, a shame indeed," Doris concluded.

Within seconds, the two were back on their way, waddling arm-in-arm and discussing upcoming plans for the Autumn Society Ball sponsored by the Women's Cosmopolitan Club of Manhattan. As they did, a contingent of firefighters were pushing away the crowd to form a large open circle in the middle of the street. That would have been intriguing enough, but it was what they were carrying that sent the crowd into an as-yet-unrealized frenzy.

Reaching the center of the circle, they unfolded a large hoop with a lightweight canvas stretched across it tightly to create a "safety net" designed to catch a falling body. As they scrambled to get the net in place, one cop who was following the action closely turned to his partner and said emotionlessly, "From that height, the poor slob would go through this thing like a bullet." It was more of an analytical statement.

"Yeah, well," his partner responded equally dispassionately, "at least it'll giv'im something to shoot for anyways."

The crowd was a mishmash of feelings and emotions. Some were empathetic and genuinely concerned. Others were terrified. A large percentage viewed the entire event as little more than entertainment. At the same time, an equal number were annoyed and angry at the disturbance it meant in their day—especially on the warmest day of the year—while a fair number enjoyed being amateur analysts and thinking through the myriad of concerns that might bring a person to stand on a ledge seventeen floors above a sidewalk, contemplating ending his life.

Psychologists would have a field day—and would for some years to come—examining the minds of these people. A sociologist would build a case study for a scholarly journal based on the situation.

The local parish priest would remember it as the day he had never prayed harder. The summer shoppers and tourists would recall it as a day they had never been more fascinated by such an unexpected, but not unwelcome, sight. A street-cart hot dog vendor would call it the best day of his whole year. The Checker Cab taxicab drivers—stuck in the biggest traffic jam in anyone's memory—well, they would call it their worst.

Everyone gathered inside, outside, and around Hotel Gotham on this day saw the John Warde drama as something unique to them. Thus, the day would be memorable for a thousand different reasons.

Few related to the guy nervously smoking cigarettes on the ledge.

* * * * *

Inside the hotel suite, while John had been exchanging informal introductions with Miss Boop on the ledge, Chief Anderson was preparing to bring all of this silliness to a quick halt and put an end to a situation that had the potential to embarrass the department even more than the feces-flying incident from earlier.

He was giving instructions like a machine gunner in the trenches—orders and demands were flying a mile a minute. Soon all of the key players were equally agitated and shouting their own directives. Too quickly, the scene was descending into utter chaos.

And into this tumult stepped four individuals who would change the course of the entire situation and forever impact the life of one John Warde.

The four were the hotel manager, a local doctor, a police negotiator, and the New York City commissioner of police himself. They entered shoulder-to-shoulder like the Four Horsemen of the Apocalypse and commandeered the room from the second they stepped through the door.

Clearly the situation had escalated, and Chief Inspector Alexander Anderson—both physically and psychologically—took a giant step back. It was now the commissioner's show to run.

If Captain McDonald and Inspector Anderson were the ultimate cop's cops, then Police Commissioner Lewis Joseph Valentine—no relation to Warde's friends in the other room—was the iconic image of the position, as if he had been selected for the role by a Hollywood casting director.

The look was there—a firm jaw, close-cut hair, six foot one, and a muscled body that filled out his uniform nicely. His voice was also that impeccable Irish baritone with enough of a brogue to make him sound, well, thoroughly Irish. He strode confidently, spoke with authority, and was imposing with his very presence—the perfect package when needed.

For moments exactly like these.

The dynamics of Room 1714 were rapidly changing, though all of it was outside the knowledge of the unfortunate person who had put everything in motion.

Also, now outside the circle was Officer Glasco, who obediently was on his way to returning to his role as a traffic cop. As he boarded the elevator to make his way back to the street, he came face-to-face with the other person involved from the beginning—Tommy Hardesty, the man who had delivered Warde's room-service meal.

"Did he jump yet? Has he already taken the nosedive?"

The bellhop was gleeful. After decades of having little more excitement than dealing with a sputtering radiator coupled with the disappointment of lousy tips, this was proving to be one of the best days of his career.

Officer Charley was disgusted with the question and refused even to address it. He was the only one who had connected with John and, though he knew little about the young man, he had developed such compassion for him that it was difficult to see the spectacle that the poor guy now represented.

Warde had simultaneously become the most fascinating and most despised man in the city.

In fact, he was no longer just a person. He was the central figure in an event—midsummer entertainment during the dog days that made the day a little bit brighter and a Tuesday with just a bit more energy than normal. Something to talk about—laugh about—while slogging through a weekday at the office or a sweltering day at home in front of a hot ironing board and a chicken baking in the oven.

But others were also impacted on this day.

Those for whom the entire situation was a source of anger. Cabdrivers and their passengers stuck in a historic traffic jam, those who couldn't make it to the subway and would be late for appointments, the shopkeepers who were furious over the obstructions to their entrances and loss of customers, and—of course—the cops who were looking at having to work beyond their shifts and possibly even to log overtime hours.

Finally, there were the entranced, the curious, the ambulance chasers who were hoping with all of their hearts they'd be able to see—once in their lifetime—a man leap to his death. To be an eyewitness at the bloody scene and, for the rest of their lives, be able to tell the story of this one monumental day. Their fingers were crossed.

Within fifteen minutes of reaching the street, Glasco was further down Fifth Avenue and helping some of his buddies set up barricades along Fifty-Fourth Street. The crowds seemed to be growing exponentially by the moment.

His mind and heart were with John, though, and it took some effort to concentrate on the job at hand. From time to time, in the background, he could hear the roar of a wild animal still on the loose from the parade—generally followed by a woman's scream—and the occasional cackle of a hyena, man or beast.

It was a bizarre day, to say the least.

Going about his job with the professionalism that made him so respected among his peers, Glasco was thinking about what must have happened to have brought this poor young man to the breaking point. In the short time they had talked, he didn't seem mentally sick or distressed or angry about something that had happened—some real or imagined slight that had pushed him over the edge.

No, nothing like that. Just a nicely dressed, nicely spoken, well-mannered young man who had—for some unknown reason—decided on this day to step through an open hotel window and stand on a ledge in the middle of a New York summer on an eighteen-inch ledge two hundred feet above one of the busiest districts in town.

Why? It was eating at the otherwise jovial thirty-eight-year-old traffic cop who couldn't seem to shake the tragedy of it all. As he pondered the eventual fate of John Warde, a man pushed him out of the way, shouting, "Get'cher 'Jumper Johnny' buttons here, folks. Real souvenirs of the most famous event of the year. Show 'em to your friends to prove you was here today!"

Officer Charley reached out. With one foot, he deftly tripped the man before twirling in the opposite direction and picking up a sawhorse road barrier.

In Room 1714, things were heating up as well. The commissioner had elected to put the situation on his own shoulders to ensure that it ended correctly with minimal humiliation to the police department. Once again, the orders were coming fast and furious.

"Where's the hotel manager? I saw him just a minute ago. Now, someone go get me . . ."

"That would be me, Commissioner Valentine. Pleased to make your acquaintance. . . . Sorry that it has to be under these most unusual circumstances. My name is Mr. Randolph." The manager reached out his hand to shake his guest's, but the top cop had already moved on.

"And someone find me the brain specialist! Get him over here pronto!" Several cops scattered with that command.

"Okay, Mr. Randolph, whadda you got for me? What can you tell me about our boy here? What can you tell about the kid in 1714?"

"Well, first of all, Commissioner, I need to explain that here at Gotham Hotel, we value the privacy of our clients. They are generally quite sophisticated and have come to expect a certain degree of . . ."

Commissioner Valentine—who fancied himself a bit of a handwriting analyst—leaned in close to the hotel manager as his eyes flared. "I don't give one goddamned red cent for your policies, see? I want to see the kid's name in writing to see if I can pick up anything, or I'll put you out on the ledge with him. . . . Hear me?"

Without saying a word, a man behind Randolph pushed the oversized hotel registry into the top cop's chest and pointed to a line on the ledger sheet.

Valentine put on his readers and traced the line with his finger until he came to John William Warde. Raising his eyeglasses to the top of his head, he spoke, his booming voice suddenly filling the room. "Get me everything there is on this idiot!" More cops dashed out of the room.

As they did, a distinguished but diminutive and round older gentleman stood in the doorway surveying the scene. His hair was thinning awkwardly, with only wisps and clumps remaining, though those were treasured and preserved. He wore a three-piece brown suit, which was quite ill-fitting and a poor choice for a hot and humid summer afternoon.

"And who the hell are you!" The commissioner didn't phrase it as a question, more like an extended expletive.

Unfazed by the brusque crudeness of the statement, the man responded, "I am, sir, Dr. Jacques Presner. My presence was requested by your department, Commissioner."

Dr. Presner was, in fact, the house physician at the nearby Hotel Dorset and had been summoned by the hotel manager, Randolph, because the Gotham's physician was out of town. He was also on the city payroll as a staff doctor on call for just such situations and was highly regarded by those in authority at the upper levels of city government.

The doctor was a French Canadian by birth—a small, dark, neat man with tortoise-shell spectacles—and a graduate of Montreal's McGill University. He was a general practitioner by trade.

Unlike other hotel doctors, however, he had developed a keen interest in the human mind's inner workings and some of its unique aspects.

Taking some advanced courses in the exciting new field of psychiatry, he was more advanced than the average physician. He had often spoken at seminars on the topics of manic depression, schizophrenia, and paranoia. None of this meant much to the hard-boiled commissioner, but, nevertheless, he was the beneficiary of such unexpected expertise.

"Oh, you're the brain specialist, aren't you? You here to figure this nut job out? How long do you think this is gonna take? I got a dinner planned for seven. You worked with these types before? Can you talk him down before it gets dark? Once the sun sets, we got one helluva new situation to deal with."

As Dr. Presner was launching into a lengthy explanation of the complexities of the brain as well as the evolving advances in the field of psychology, Commissioner Valentine was greeting the next wave of the suicide rescue team.

Although the good doctor was deep into his exposition of perceived needs concerning personal stigma, the fingerprint technicians captured Valentine's attention as they came rushing in with a report that there were no recoverable prints in the room. Apparently the jumper hadn't touched anything significant.

"Put 'em on the roof, and let's get this thing done with, then!" The commissioner was upset with the pace of the proceedings and was fraying around the edges a bit. "Get Klotzbach on the roof right now! He knows how to settle these things. He'll end this fiasco once and for all."

Dr. Presner had no idea what a "Klotzbach" was, but he knew his input was no longer needed and thus retreated to the adjoining Room 1716, where the bulk of the rest of the rescue team and reporters had been relocated.

Lieutenant William Klotzbach was indeed a legend in the New York Police Department in his day. A native of Oklahoma, he was rumored to have Cheyenne and Cherokee blood—though his last name argued a bit against that. Still, he wouldn't have received an argument over it from anyone.

Tall and lanky with high cheekbones and jet-black stringy hair, he resembled the beloved American humorist Will Rogers—a fellow Sooner—who had died only a few years earlier. Klotzbach spoke significantly less than Rogers, though. For the most part, he let his skills speak for him.

Klotzbach, in fact, was a lariat-and-rope expert for the Emergency Division of the NYPD, which meant he was the go-to man for situations such as this. The police and fire departments had several techniques for saving a person who was threatening suicide, and most of them involved getting their hands on the culprit before he realized his rescuers were coming.

None had proven more effective than Klotzbach at resolving such situations.

His approach was a simple one: make a rope lasso and hogtie the man before he ever knew what hit him. After years on the rodeo circuit, it was safe to say he never missed.

Without saying a word, Klotzbach made his way up to the corresponding window on the eighteenth floor. He readied himself to make the toss that would end this entire charade and get everyone home in time for their dinners. But just as he was testing his lasso in the hotel room, he noticed that the cornice of the hotel's facade extended out so far that he couldn't get the right angle to toss the rope.

Swearing in a language that resembled neither English nor Cherokee, Klotzbach tossed out more words in two minutes than he had in two weeks as he packed up his gear and headed for the exit to the stairwell.

Valentine's first and best shot had failed. This was unnerving to the man who was not used to failing at any level.

The commander of the city's chief rescue team had also arrived on the roof with the idea of dropping a large net over "the target"—their generic name for the man on the ledge. Several department negotiators were huddled in a corner, discussing strategies. They were preparing to catch him from above by trapping him against the building with the net and a team of men who would lower themselves in "bosun's chairs"—canvas seats much like those on a child's play yard swing.

That was when Captain William O'Brien of the West Forty-Seventh Street Station stepped in to offer a suggestion. This required no small amount of courage because, at the moment, Commissioner Valentine resembled a bull from a Looney Tunes cartoon, pacing and pawing and, with his chain-smoking, snorting smoke out of every orifice in his head.

"I got another idea, boss. I think we could get a fishing net and snatch 'im. Stretch it out below him without knowing, and then let 'im just jump whenever he wants, and we'll hav'im. Land 'im like a marlin, sir."

"What the hell kind of a harebrained idea is that, O'Brien?"

Bill O'Brien didn't think it was such a harebrained idea, but he was cognizant of who he was talking to. Valentine was the big boss.

"What're you suggesting? We stretch a net all the way across Fifth Avenue in New York City? We're cops, for God's sake, O'Brien, not circus performers. Wanna have some trapeze artists and tightrope walkers up there too, for heaven's sake? Geez Louise, Captain, I don't know why I put up with stuff like this."

"Well, beggin' your pardon, sir, but what I meant was we put together a net at the bottom of the hotel and hook it to some ropes on the roof and just ever so slowly pull it up out of his view—on account of the ledge an' all—and then if he jumps, he'll have no idea we got a net below 'im. When he goes, he'll only fall one story or two, and then we got 'im. Fish in a net, sir, like I said."

Valentine took a long pull on his Chesterfield. He blew the smoke out in a way that made it obvious to all that he was contemplating this idea. It was a big win for O'Brien just to get this far.

In the meantime, one of his assistants interrupted him. "We can't find no info on this Warde kid, boss. It's like he's a ghost or somethin'. No rap sheet on him at all. His name is John William. Mr. Harris checked the directories from all the boroughs, and there's no listing for him anywhere. We don't know who he is. The kid doesn't exist."

"Where's the hotel manager? . . . What'd you find, Randolph?"

"Nothing more, Commissioner. Looks like he just arrived earlier today to meet a friend with not a piece of luggage or anything. All we have is the name in the register to work with. He charged everything to the *Tribune*."

"Damn it! Damn it all! This is one cagey bastard, this kid. He's playing us for fools, and he knows it. Twistin' the whole NYPD on the day of the circus parade just for the hell of it. Son of a bitch. Any other day!"

The commissioner had expected the parade to be a major publicity coup for the department and for him personally. It never hurt to shine in the eyes of the mayor. His was a political position, after all. But now . . . now it was all going sideways. It made no sense. How could a kid—an unknown, snot-nosed punk—be outwitting the brightest minds of the city?

Thus, as a net was stealthily being lowered from the hotel's rooftop, the doctor explained the stages of development for a young male while the negotiators were still developing strategies. The commissioner was fuming and randomly shouting orders, sending his minions scurrying haphazardly.

The one thing everyone had forgotten about was John Warde, the young man sweltering outside on an eighteen-inch ledge on a July afternoon. In fact, it would appear that the only real concern—from anyone caught in the maelstrom that was now encircling poor John—was how his decision had negatively impacted their life.

And so, while the fury raged on inside the luxury suites, John was contemplating the one phrase that had managed to make it out to him from the inside. "The kid doesn't exist."

7 Hour Five

The adjoining suite, Room 1716, by this time was crowded with would-be rescuers. Two psychiatrists from Bellevue Mental Hospital had been called, and after conferring with Dr. Presner, the fifty-two-year-old Dr. Paul Shilder had moved over to the window and began to talk soothingly to Warde with a plan to befriend the man.

Leaning out of the window, Shilder said in a friendly, folksy tone, "Hey, buddy, this is a pretty tough day for you, isn't it?"

There was no response, so the doctor continued. "You're not the only one, believe me. We all got things we're trying to work through. Everybody does. If you could come in here, I'd make sure we're alone, and the two of us could just talk. Anything you want to talk about."

Warde flipped a cigarette at his face and laughed.

"You don't think I know what you're doing? I sat across from doctors like you at Manhattan State Hospital over in Central Islip for six months, and I can read you like a book. You don't have anything to offer me. Send in the next guy if you think he can do a better job."

Angry and humiliated, Dr. Shilder retreated and passed the baton to his colleague, a child psychologist by the name of Dr. Alexander Thomas, saying, "Let him jump for all I care!" Less than ten minutes later, Thomas had thrown up his hands as well. Warde was definitely a bright individual and always seemed one step ahead.

A priest from St. Patrick's Cathedral was next to take a stab at talking John off the ledge. He had just arrived as the two psychiatrists were exiting, and they wished him good luck. "I'll take a different approach, I think," he told the doctors. "I'll put the fear of God in him."

Taking his turn at the open window, he asked Warde, "Are you a Catholic?"

"No," Warde said indifferently. "No, I'm an Episcopalian, I guess. I'm not very religious, though."

Father James McCarthy wasn't dissuaded by his comments and entered into a lengthy presentation on why suicide was a mortal sin.

"The Church teaches that committing suicide is a sin—an act of blasphemy against God and therefore is unforgivable. It prevents you from entering heaven and achieving eternal life. Son, is that what you want your fate to be?"

Warde was noncommittal, and the priest continued with his sermon.

"The Church holds that one's life is the property of God, and to destroy that life is to wrongly assert dominion over God's creation. In the Catholic Church, you would not be allowed to have a funeral service if you killed yourself, and you could not be buried in a Catholic cemetery. It is a grave offense against the Creator."

"Again, Father, I'm not a Catholic . . . but you've given me a good reason not to become one."

After twenty minutes, Father McCarthy gave up and suggested they call one of the police chaplains to take over the spiritual duties.

Rev. William Ivie, a twenty-year veteran with the force, arrived shortly after and took a quite different approach to rescuing the troubled young man.

"John, the Scriptures have words for just such a moment as this. God's words are meant to bring comfort and hope. Can I read some to you?"

Warde, as before, was indifferent, neither objecting nor encouraging the pastor.

"John, the Psalmist says in Chapter 55, 'Cast your cares on the Lord, and he will sustain you. He will never let you be shaken.' Isaiah the prophet adds this too: 'Do not fear, for I am with you. Do not be dismayed, for I will strengthen you and help you. I will hold you up with my right hand.' John—even on this ledge—God promises to hold you up and strengthen you. Do you need strength, son?"

"I need a cigarette is what I need, Reverend. But yeah, I could use his strength. His forgiveness too, I guess." Something was eating away at the young man, and the intuitive pastor could sense it.

"Then, John, listen to the words of St. Paul: 'There is no condemnation for those who are in Christ Jesus because through him there is life. He has set you free from sin and death.'"

That verse struck a chord with Warde, who snapped back angrily.

"You don't know me, Reverend. You don't know my dark thoughts. You don't know the feelings I have inside me. No one knows. No one could ever understand. There are things that I know about myself that I could never share. Things God could never forgive."

"That's not true. That's not true at all, son." Rev. Ivie was sincere in his desire to bring hope to this troubled soul. "God forgives anything, everything, if we truly repent of our sins."

"I guess that's the problem, sir. I don't want to repent. I *like* my sin. I like who I am. It's everyone else around me who doesn't understand, who thinks I'm 'different.' I'm not afraid to meet my Maker. He created me, so I guess he understands."

Rev. Ivie could sense that there was little else he could do for John, but he refused to give up trying.

"Son, I only know this. The Lord loves you, and he is a forgiving God. Let me leave you with this: 'I am convinced that neither death nor life, neither angels nor demons, neither the present nor the future, nor any powers—not height, nor depth—nor anything else in all creation, will be able to separate us from the love of God that is in Christ Jesus our Lord.'"

John turned and, for the first time, faced the pastor who had been desperately trying to reach him.

"If you knew my secret—if I told you—then you'd say I could never be forgiven. God's love isn't powerful enough to understand me."

Ivie left heartbroken over the interchange and tragically would die mere months later, sharing that this conversation was one of the saddest in his long tenure as chaplain of the New York Police Department.

Minutes later, the compassionate minister was replaced by a woman dressed in a costume of long, draping silks of green and purple. Her name was Madame Damara. She said she hailed from Romania but was later tracked to the Queens neighborhood of Astoria, where she was known as Sharon Kafka.

Her red hair was tucked up into a turban—not an unusual fashion choice for the day—that was fastened in the front with a piece of jewelry that appeared to be a sliver of a moon embedded with colored stones. On her fingers were gaudy and garish rings, and layers of draping necklaces of varying lengths were around her neck.

Shuffling to the window, she pronounced that she could tell John Warde his future simply by doing his astrological chart. The police, obviously, were skeptical, but she had been invited into the fray because she had a reputation for resolving other similar situations—though there was no evidence of that. The cops felt that, at this point, nothing could hurt.

The self-proclaimed medium—who also promised that she could talk to the dead—quickly worked up a chart for John based on his birth date and assorted other information gleaned from his sister, who was in the throes of desperation.

Madame Damara—who later published her astrological reading for a twenty-dollar fee—was met with sheer silence by the young man on the ledge. He most likely hadn't heard a word she said because John's thoughts were neither on heaven above nor hell below nor the stars in between.

He had resumed his pacing, stopping occasionally to lean over the edge and peer at the growing crowd below. They pointed and groaned with each of his stops. From time to time, he would wave to them or dismiss them with a flicked lit cigarette, which instantly became a souvenir.

"Don't do it!" spectators shouted over from across the way in the luxury apartments and hotel rooms that fronted the Gotham.

"Go for it!" men shouted up from below. One of them had come across a bullhorn and was calling for John to take the leap, to his buddies' great delight and cheers.

When an appeal to the spiritual nature of the man on the ledge proved to be a complete failure, the brain trust of the police took a sharp right turn to embrace a radically different approach.

Six months earlier, Diane Gregal, of the Forest Hills neighborhood of Queens, had successfully coaxed a sixty-five-year-old man by the name of Maurice Nast off a ledge of Hotel Pennsylvania, less than a mile away from where John Warde now stood.

She, however, had used a less righteous angle to get the job done.

Described as a statuesque and voluptuous, peroxide blonde whose obvious physical features could not go without notice, Miss Gregal had lured Mr. Nash off his perch during the previous December by offering to "date" him.

With that in mind, a group of NYPD officers summoned her to the Gotham with what she later termed "an anonymous phone call." Once she arrived, she was ushered directly up to the adjoining Room 1716 and then brought over to the window. There, she leaned out and, putting her significant assets on display, began to talk to John.

"I went to the room, poked myself out the window, and said to him, 'Hello there, Johnny, remember me?'" she later explained with obvious pride. "We had never actually met, but I was pretty certain I could get his attention with that line.

"He asked me, 'Who are you?' and I said, 'I am Diane Gregal. Nice to meet you, Johnny.' Then he asked, 'Where are you from?' and I answered, 'Baltimore, remember me? Remember when we got together that night? Or maybe you were too tight to remember.' He said, 'No. I've never been with you.'

"So then I kind of gave up the whole charade and just was straight with him. 'Look, buddy, aren't you lonesome out there?' He didn't answer me. Then I said, 'Well, I'm lonesome. I'm really lonesome, Johnny. I could use a friend. Could you use a friend right now? Why don't you come in here, and then you and me could go get some drinks. Go on a date, fella, if you know what I mean.'

"He kind of just stared at me, and I tried to use some of my feminine charms that I've been blessed with, you know, so I was thinking we were getting somewhere. Then he just looked at me real blank like and said, 'I don't want love like that. I'm different from other guys.'

"And then, right at that moment, his sister Katherine yanked me back and wouldn't let me say no more. It was upsetting. I thought I was getting the job done, but if you ask me, I think the sister was jealous of me. Those two have a strange relationship, I think. Both of them women in there. It's real odd, I'm telling you."

Warde was once again alone and restless. The previous conversations had seemed to unsettle him, and the pacing continued. Lighting up cigarette after cigarette, he would puff hard and furious on each one as if it was helping him plan out his next steps.

He was also drinking glass after glass of water—one man counted thirty-three before the situation was resolved. At 4:30 p.m., John asked for a cup of coffee. When it was given to him, his brow furrowed, and a wry smile crawled across his face. "What, no cream? Who do you think I am, a street cleaner?"

Even in the face of crisis, Warde had managed to maintain his standards.

The coffee issue was quickly resolved, but when he received the cup, he sent it back once again for another sugar cube. Warde then sipped the beverage with all of the aplomb of a lawn-party guest. Lifting the cup with sophisticated etiquette—his little finger noticeably and delicately extended—he then handed back the cup as if he were delivering it to a white-coated server.

At intervals, Warde would purposefully send a wave of anticipatory horror through the mesmerized crowd, which could see him plainly from below and for many blocks. Often going to the very edge and then bending down low—taunting spectators with the thought that he might lose his balance—he would wildly wave his arms as if he were about to tumble, clearly delighted with the roar this elicited.

Striding up and down the long ledge with apparently no concern in the world, only the large decorative ornamental piece kept him from moving from the left window of Room 1716 to the right window of Room 1714. The ledge, however, clearly was his domain, and he was the man in charge.

For the two hours before five o'clock, John had largely constrained himself to a standing position to the left of the west window. It was open, and police sat near it, urging him to come in. From time to time, they would entertain him—with the hope of making some connection—with stories about baseball, the latest gossip on movie stars, and stories related to New Yorkers.

At times he appeared interested. However, at other moments, he seemed completely disconnected.

But for all of the tension felt in the sky, not everyone on the ground was as interested. In sharp contrast to the screaming crowds and pleading police negotiators, throughout the afternoon a group of nonchalant workmen continued their labors on the street as part of a renovation project for the hotel's ground floor.

Not one of them ever bothered to look up at Warde. Not one ever asked what all the commotion was about. Not one could give a damn. In many ways, they represented the real world of New York that, day in and day out, plodded along to keep the city moving forward. Scenes like this came and went, the workmen undoubtedly felt, but cement still needed to be poured, and the trash had to be hauled away.

In an attempt to better understand John Warde's mind, Katherine Bull—who had finally recovered from her series of fainting spells—sat down with the top cops in the room and tried to explain the young man's history. She told them that for as long as she could remember, her brother had been subject to periods of depression.

Sometimes seriously and frighteningly deep depression. Katherine implied that he seemed to hold some troublesome inner demon that had haunted him since he was a teenager. She suggested that they call her mother, who was ill back at her home in Southampton.

When they finally got Mrs. Warde on the line, her input was simple and to the point: "My son has mental issues. I have no idea what can be done to persuade him to come in off that ledge. He is troubled. Quite troubled. I do believe the source of his mental instability is his unrequited love for a woman that he had no hope of winning.

"He announced to me that her name is Miss Camilla. I believe she must have been of a different social status than he could aspire to, given his career history and unrealistic goals.

"He said she was his fiancée, but there seemed to be some lost connection between them. Camilla is quite a lovely girl, he assures me—and a talented singer—but I saw him express little romantic interest toward her, however, and never met her personally. I credit that to the difference in their social positions.

"John told me repeatedly that he had a passionate fondness for the woman, but he felt he could never hope to marry her. He just didn't see it ever happening.

"Other than that, I don't care to elaborate any further. I will have nothing more to say that could help you other than to say you all will be in our prayers."

Apparently Katherine, his sister, and Katherine, his mother, and Katherine, his friend, all had significantly misunderstood the seriousness of John Warde's mental health.

With little to no help from the family—and neither Patrick Valentine nor John's father much involved—the commissioner was turning to a new plan.

Without giving Captain O'Brien any credit for the idea, he had ordered some of his men to head over to the piers on the East River and locate a large net from some of the fisherman and dockworkers that might be a good size to catch a falling man.

After a great deal of explanation—and a round of laughter over the cops becoming "fishers of men"—the officers took off for the wharves but were unable to locate anything large enough to work.

Later, columnist George Tucker (1938) described how the cops procured a cargo net that was forty feet by twenty-five and built of sturdy woven rope, sufficient to catch any falling man from any height and not fray in the process.

> On the night of the John Warde tragedy, I was having an early supper with Commander John Baylis of the Coast Guard in the dining room at the Hotel

> Lombardy on East 56th Street. All through dinner, reports on the attempted rescue were communicated to the Commander by telephone.
>
> At this time, the melancholy young man had been crouching on a hotel ledge for more than four hours, threatening to jump.
>
> It was reported to him that, at the moment, 75,000 people in the street were milling underneath the boy. The police were desperately trying to devise some means of frustrating his suicide attempt and had yet to come up with a solution.
>
> Suddenly, Commander Baylis leaped up, "They ought to get a cargo net," he said. "He couldn't get away from a cargo net . . . it would be impossible!" He hurried to the telephone and instructed his men where such a net was to be found.
>
> Then, he came back, and we talked about Warde and about a hundred other things, I guess, from rescue work in the Arctic to tropical cruises.
>
> At about 10:15 I said good night and walked out into the street. All day, people had been saying, "Let's go down and have a look at that fellow on the ledge." But I hadn't gone. I didn't think he would jump anyway, not after waiting that long. It really hadn't captured my attention.
>
> But before I knew it, some force was dragging my steps toward the hotel. I took out my press card and stuck it into the band of my hat so the police would let me through the lines.
>
> And there he was, a tiny object on a far ledge, 17 stories above the sidewalk, illuminated by a powerful searchlight. He was smoking a cigarette. Suddenly, his cigarette descended in a full arc as it does when it is flipped in the dark.
>
> Meanwhile, from windows above the ledge hung long sailors' ropes well beyond either side of the man and out of his sight, to which was attached a great empty net positioned underneath, probably three or four floors away from the ledge.
>
> I smiled at the sight of it. It was the cargo net, the one recommended by Commander Baylis.

Indeed, as the flatbed truck that carried the net was arriving, city workers were standing by and ready to attach it to long ropes lowered from the far-above windows of the eighteenth floor, one up from the ledge where John stood. They were hoping he wouldn't notice.

Once the harness was in place, the net was slowly and surreptitiously pulled up from the ground so as not to draw attention to it from above. Folded and drawn up by its four corners, the net rose slowly and unevenly past jutting ledges on the eighth and twelfth floors.

As it reached the sixteenth floor, however, some of the ropes became tangled, and the net suddenly flattened against the wall and twisted and snarled there. Firemen in the street hastily pulled on additional ropes attached to its outer edges, but the net would not untangle.

Writer Joel Sayre, in the April 16, 1949, issue of the *New Yorker* magazine, wrote:

> The Coast Guard cargo net had been rising slowly in steady jerks for some time, passing the ledges on the eighth and twelfth floors, and there was a swelling hope among the onlookers that a true solution might finally have been reached.
>
> But, then, just as it reached the sixteenth floor, some of the ropes with which it was being raised fouled, and the net noticeably sagged against the hotel like a giant, empty woman's handbag.
>
> Firemen on the ground desperately tried to spread it back out by using the ropes attached to its lower end, but they could not manage. Then, riggers with pikes, who had been stationed at sixteenth-floor windows to keep a belly in the net when it was in position, began using their pikes in an effort to extend it.
>
> It was appearing to be a futile effort, though it captivated the crowd and most certainly, the men working the net never flagged in their desire and work to fix the monster handbag.

Despite this taking place beneath John's perch, he was unaware of the activity because his ledge was blocking his view. Soon men were crawling out of the windows on the sixteenth floor and into the net, where they extended out long poles in yet another attempt to try and poke the thing into shape again and loosen the knots.

The firemen were getting nowhere, however, and there was a sense that the clock was ticking on their efforts.

In the meantime, photographers on rooftops and in the upper windows of office buildings as far as three hundred feet away were madly snapping away to capture this dramatic development in the John Warde saga.

At 711 Fifth Avenue, a half block north from John's position, Dave Driscoll of the special-features section of Station WOR began putting John on the air—or, rather, a breathless description of his plight—with a play-by-play commentary worthy of the most exciting of Yankees–Red Sox games.

Opportunistic hawkers were now peddling cheap opera glasses to people on the streets, calling out: "He-yah! Get your binoculars, he-yah!"

Passengers craned and goggled at John from the buses now crawling along Fifth Avenue. Tour guides soon filled double-decker buses with ticket-purchasing customers who were promised a "bird's-eye view of 'Jumper Johnny' with moment-by-moment narration." Ironically, photos from that day show that the African American customers were literally seated "in the back of the bus."

As if it were the afternoon of the crucial game of a World Series, people all over New York gathered around the radios of parked taxis, the sound of which merged with news reports from the open windows all along Fifty-Fifth Street and Fifth Avenue. The switchboards of the West Forty-Seventh Street and East Fifty-First Street Precinct station houses were flooded with calls, mostly from givers of advice.

Another unexpected turn came when a crime wave erupted among the spectators as pickpockets roamed through the crowds taking advantage of the mesmerized watchers, causing more than one person to comment that Manhattanites were paying dearly that day for their curiosity.

Out on Fifth Avenue, animated conversations were in full bloom as onlookers offered up their opinions as to why this young and unknown man was making such a spectacle of himself. There was still quite a mixed opinion on whether he intended to take the plunge or if it was all for show.

"I heard it's a guy who's trying to settle a family scrap. He got all dramatic when he didn't get his way."

"I heard he's an accountant wanted for absconding. Embezzled his company of thousands of dollars, and they just discovered it. Soon as they did, he stepped right out that window right there where you see him now."

"Yeah. Someone told me that his wife's threatening to leave him, and he said he'd kill himself if she did."

"A fellow told me it's an investment broker who lost all his clients' money and can't face the consequences. Doesn't want to go to jail. Would rather die, I guess, than get locked up."

"Oh, you can bet your bottom dollar it's nothing more than an advertising stunt—a publicity gag or something. Pretty soon, I expect to see some big banner out there talking about a new picture show or something like that."

Bystanders seemed especially enthralled with the whole situation. Two women were talking to each other:

"My God, Louise! The way he's got his head turned now, he's a dead ringer for Tyrone Power. Wouldn't mind meetin' that fella for sure . . . if he don't jump, that is."

"You don't say! Gimme those binoculars, Brenda . . . and quick!"

With the ponderously slow process of rigging the net and lowering the ropes connected to it, Anderson knew he both needed to keep John occupied while still holding out hope that someone would be able to break through and talk the kid off the ledge.

So it came as a pleasant and timely surprise when John yelled loudly through the open window into Room 1714: "I wanna talk to the bellboy!"

8 Hour Six

"Glasco! Get Glasco—the traffic cop—get 'im up here pronto!"

Sergeant Sean Murphy, yet another proud Irish officer in a department full of them, took the call from Chief Inspector Anderson and was immediately scanning the increasingly unruly mob for the portly officer with the thinning hair.

The crowd had grown dramatically since Murphy had last surveyed the scene, and it caused his heart to drop somewhat. The entire situation was escalating far more rapidly than anyone could have anticipated. For a second, he wondered if there might be more danger on the street than on the ledge high above it.

Over the last hour it was also becoming harder to spot any of the policemen as the crowd continued to push and shove past the barriers to get a closer look at the action—or lack of it—on the corner of Fifty-Fifth and Fifth. The cops were virtually disappearing into the throngs and no longer had any control.

Despite the challenge, Murphy pushed into the mob and began a desperate search for Officer Glasco. He was well aware that time was of the essence. Finally finding him confronting a group of souvenir hawkers, Murphy signaled Glasco over and gave him the word from the brass.

"You're wanted back up there. The chief inspector just sent down the word and wants you on the seventeenth floor in a flash. Get moving, Charley!"

Glasco responded with a quick and curt salute and was on his way. He didn't have a clue what was happening with this new development, and he was hesitant to leave his traffic buddies because, in the streets, it was now an all-hands-on-deck situation. They had called in reinforcements, but everyone knew it was a losing battle.

The sergeant was calling in men from home—not a popular move with officers who had already settled in with their families for dinner—as it seemed they were increasingly overwhelmed with hundreds, if not thousands, joining the fracas every few minutes.

Patrolman Glasco began to realize that John's fate might rest in his hands. As a precaution, before heading up to report to the lieutenant in Room 1714, he stopped in the lobby to once again borrow the coat and hat of the bellboy on duty. He assumed he would have to employ his previous disguise.

Minutes later, he was stepping off the elevator and was immediately shocked to see the number of cops and reporters crammed into the relatively small space in the foyer, even overflowing down the corridors that branched off from there.

The men were shoulder-to-shoulder and barely able to turn. Now sounding like a roaring beehive, everyone was talking at once—no doubt promoting their theories on how to resolve the situation.

After being waved into the suite by an officer at the door, Glasco entered a nearly empty room—a stark contrast from the pandemonium in the corridor. There, he was met by the chief inspector, who was flanked by Dr. Presner, Chaplain Ivie, and Dr. Shilder, who had been invited back into the inner circle after the commissioner made his exit.

"He won't talk to anybody but you, Glasco. Don't ask me why, but you need to figure out something that'll work, or we're just going to make a play to snatch him. We're all growin' tired of this folderol. It's stretched into dinnertime, for God's sake.

"I'm tired of one man tying up the entire New York Police Department just to get some attention. I got half a mind to put a sharpshooter over on the roof of the St. Regis and take him out with a single bullet."

Glasco hoped that was just his frustration talking, but he couldn't be sure. An angry supervisor was not one to be questioned or fooled with.

One of the men then grabbed Charley by the elbow and gave a sideways head bob toward the open window. "He only wants to talk with you. That's what he's saying, anyways. You're the only one he wants. I guess he trusts you or somethin'."

Taking one more look at his bellboy uniform to make sure he hadn't overlooked anything, the officer took a big breath and started toward the open window. Before sticking his head out, he said a little prayer and crossed himself. He'd need all the divine help he could get this time around. There was a sense that time might be running out, that this might be the last opportunity to rescue the poor guy.

With this in mind, Glasco pushed aside the curtains and leaned out the window. "Hello, John," he said in a neighborly tone. John turned and smiled briefly. Then he lit a new cigarette and pulled in a lungful of smoke.

As Officer Charley spoke, he saw an iron-nerved Warde standing and carelessly dangling one of his legs over his precarious ledge. He appeared to be trying to excite the nervous mobs below as if toying with them for both their and his own amusement as a way to pass the time. Glasco thought at the time that John's mental condition might be deteriorating.

John didn't respond for a moment or two as he stared at the pavement and the neck-craning crowds below who were thoroughly enjoying every minute of this fine day. When he tired of that, he turned to Charley—the bellboy—and spoke.

"Gosh, Charley. I've been thinking about your situation, and I sure wouldn't want you to have to go back on relief. I'd be real sore with myself if that was the case, you know. It's making me feel real bad right now. Geez, I wouldn't want to do anything to hurt your family—they seem like real nice folks from what you tell me."

It's a good beginning, Glasco thought.

"You think I could please have another drink of water? I'm pretty thirsty. It's hot as Hades out here. Make it ice water, though. . . . I don't care for faucet water. Have the room-service people add some ice to it."

"Oh yeah, for sure, kid. Lemme get that for you," Glasco said, picking up the empty glass on the ledge. Ducking back inside the room, he put the glass down and ripped off the bellboy's coat. The heat in the room was almost unbearable at this point.

"He's thirsty. Wants ice, too," he told the lieutenant who was closest to him. "Rope me up. This time, I'll spread out on the sill and get as close to him as I can. When he takes the glass, I'll grab him by the wrist, and then you can reel me in."

Glasco rolled up the right leg of his trousers. The lieutenant put a slip noose around Glasco's leg, carefully concealing the rope with his pant leg. Through the room and then out into the hallway, eight burly policemen from the Emergency Division took hold of the other end of the rope.

Although Glasco's life undoubtedly depended on it, the men were confident that they could hold him because the NYPD Emergency Division always won the tug-of-war at the annual Police Sports Association games. It was a point of pride.

When the door to the hallway was first opened, Glasco was shocked to see that it had become a busy nest for reporters, cops, and guests who had made their way over to the scene. Typewriters were clattering, phones were ringing, and people were shouting.

In the nearest room, excited vacationers from Germany were loudly discussing the developing situation. Glasco, who knew some German, could pick up the gist of their conversation. It fell along the lines of: *This is absolutely fantastic, unbelievable, but completely crazy!*

Meanwhile, the hotel's flawlessly dressed manager, Mr. Randolph, was nervously striding up and down, up and down the corridor, doing his best to cooperate, while wringing his hands incessantly.

Glasco's thoughts were soon interrupted, however, by the lieutenant, who said, "Now listen to me, Charley, and listen good. If Warde falls or jumps after you get ahold of him, just keep hanging on tight. You won't drop more than a floor or two before you're in the net, so don't worry. We can haul you both up from there. But for God's sake . . . don't let go of him!"

Charley gave him a questioning look—a two-story fall while holding a 165-pound man was not that appealing. Still, he took a big breath and began to steady himself for the task ahead. First filling a glass from a pitcher of ice water, Glasco checked his leg and drew back the curtains. He sat down sidesaddle on the window sill with his left leg crooked under him and his right leg inside the room and invisible to John.

The patrolman was now facing east toward John. John eased away from Glasco and stood again on the edge of the ledge, "taut as a cat arching its back," as Joel Sayre described him in his 1949 article.

"Easy, now, take it easy," Glasco said, keeping his eyes on John's and thrusting the glass tumbler toward him. "Here it is, and it's good and cold, too. You're gonna enjoy this."

At first John inched farther away. His eyes once again filled with suspicion—and he seemed to be questioning if the man had some trick up his sleeve. To Glasco, he no longer had the look of the empathetic boy from just minutes ago. "No, I won't drink it unless you have a drink of it first," he said.

Glasco grinned back. "What? What'd you say, John? You want me to sip it first, is that it?

"Surely, John, you don't think I'd slip you a Mickey, do you?" To prove it, Officer Charley took several swallows from the glass. "See, John? It's just plain water, like you asked for. Here." He again thrust the glass toward John, but not very far, hoping that John would lean over close enough to be grabbed.

John stood his ground. "Give it to me with your left hand," he said, "so you can't make a play for me."

Thwarted in his plan, Glasco could do nothing but comply.

Slowly and cautiously, John reached for the glass with his right hand and took it by the rim between his index and middle fingers. Glasco noticed that his nails had been bitten to the quick. There was tension in his life. His heart went out to the poor soul. He wished he could bring him in for his own good.

While John drank, his eyes never left Glasco. He was squinting, and his gaze suddenly felt piercing, nothing like the young man who had been concerned about causing distress to Charley's family only a short time earlier. The cop was also on edge now.

As it turned out, he had a reason to be nervous as he watched John drink the ice water.

Dr. Presner, the doctor who had been summoned by the hotel management and was leading a team of three psychological specialists on location, had developed a plan that he felt might bring the entire event to a happy conclusion.

Their first thoughts were to introduce some medications into the liquids he was consuming with the idea that they might "heighten his mood." Although one New York newspaper called them "hypnotic tablets"—while a weekly magazine later spoke of "drinks that were liberally doped"—the reality was that the doses they gave him initially were, in the words of the reporter, "not enough to brighten the outlook of a bebop drummer."

Presner next concocted a strategy using Benzedrine—at the time, a heavy narcotic used for treating manic depressives—which he had scientifically formulated to deaden John's emotions and impair his physical strength without making him too weak to stand. By his calculations, after John drank one or two glasses, he would grow weak enough to be captured without a struggle.

Dropping several Benzedrine tablets into the water, which was being prepared to be handed to Warde, the psychiatrist watched the medication dissolve as he stirred it with a spoon and hoped that this would be the secret weapon to turn the tide.

John—who was often described as having a cunning born of mania—had circumvented this plan somewhat by guessing that someone might try to drug him. Thus, he made Officer Glasco his guinea pig.

The cop, to his credit, went along with the request—not knowing what impact it might have on his own body—and calmly took two big gulps of the medicated water. He felt it was worth the risk because, most assuredly, after Warde saw that there was no issue with the first glass, he wouldn't require a test from that point on.

That would prove not to be the case.

John Warde, who would go on to drink nearly forty glasses of liquid that fateful afternoon—water, coffee, tea, juice, and soda pop—would not take a single sip until someone had tasted it first. Yet, despite the vast quantities of liquid he consumed, not once did he show the slightest sign of being affected by the narcotics.

At one point, when Dr. Presner elected to double the dosage, the water became visibly cloudy and caught Warde's attention immediately. Calling one of the psychiatrists over, he demanded that the doctor drink the entire glass in front of him.

The man did as he was told, fearing a backlash if John felt he was being duped. The result was that that particular doctor was incapacitated for much of the remainder of his time on-scene.

The officers who rotated as testers found themselves becoming drowsy as well, often unable to stand and incapable of staying awake after a few doses. Eventually, every single officer, including the highest-ranking ones, had to take part in their share of the testing assignments.

Over time, traffic patrolmen were called up from their crowd-control duties to take turns sipping liquids and then recovering from them.

Perhaps more amazing was the fact that Warde never once indicated that he needed to use the restroom—something nearly all of the police brain trust were expecting to be the case. It had, in fact, been a central part of their overall rescue strategy—no doubt a unique one in the annals of the NYPD's storied history. The man proved to have the bladder of an elephant.

Later in the evening, however, as nightfall came over Manhattan, Glasco began to feel that John appeared a little woozy and was beginning to use the architectural ornamental element as support more often.

Then the tables turned, and within the operations team, there was a greater fear that Warde might die involuntarily by falling off the ledge unless a prompt rescue attempt could be made. The concern was that the narcotic might be building up in his system and suddenly overwhelm him, and he would pass out and fall.

Warde, however, seemed to become more cheerful, without any signs of ending his standoff. In one instance, as police shoved another glass of water in his direction and he stooped to pick it up, a gasp went through the crowd below, thinking he was beginning to fall. The mob below instantly broke through the police line to the sidewalk at the base of the Gotham.

Warde saw the activity. When he had finished drinking, he bent down and slid the tumbler back toward the window. As he did, there were more screams from below—women began covering their faces—and people began to point and shout, "He's gonna jump! Look, he's gonna jump!"

For a moment, John stood erect on the edge of the ledge, teasing them. Then he slowly teetered forward on the balls of his feet. Leaning precariously over the ledge, he stared at the crowd while waving his arms in a windmill fashion. The screaming became a roar.

Glasco felt sick to his stomach and bit his lip to keep from shouting back at the mob below.

"Look at those morons," John said cynically. "Look at them down there. They are hanging on my every move." Then he slowly leaned back against the wall, his eyes fluttering with weariness. Glasco began breathing again.

"You know, Charley, I'm ashamed to be doing this before all those people. It's humiliating. . . . It's beneath me," John said. "They're anticipating something from me. They're all waiting on me . . . all of them. They're the fools, not me. Everyone thinks I'm the crazy one, but it's really them. The mob down there. They could be home with their families, but they are just standing there for hours staring at me. Now that's crazy, if you ask me."

That gave Glasco an idea.

"You know what, buddy? Let's frustrate their intentions, then. Let's show 'em that they're the fools . . . just standin' out there in the sweltering heat and sweatin' up a storm all day long for nuthin'! We'll frustrate 'em to pieces! Yeah . . . that's the trick!"

John looked at him and smiled, one of the few during the day. "I've made up my mind. I think I know what to do."

"That's the way to talk, Johnny Boy! Sure, we'll frustrate the hell out of them and then you'll get the last laugh. Show 'em they are the damn fools on this day! That's what the papers will write too, I bet'cha. 'Crowd Is Crazy' . . . or somethin' like that."

But John had already turned. Now angry and resentful, John crushed his cigarette under his heel and twisted it hard. Then he picked it up and threw it down toward the street in a purposeful display.

John was pausing and thinking, rubbing his chin and squinting a bit.

"Like some more water, John?" With the mood change, Charley instinctively knew he needed to get him talking again.

"No, thank you. Not now."

"Care for a smoke?" Glasco shook a pack of cigarettes until one stuck up.

"Yeah, thank you, I would. Will you hold them in your left hand, please?" Every move by Warde was calculated. He was thinking far ahead of those trying to trap him, and the cat-and-mouse game was obvious. He was matching wits and winning at every turn.

That is, if teetering on suicide could be construed as winning.

John cautiously extracted the cigarette from the pack, lit it and smoked anxiously. "I see you're a Lucky smoker," he said. "I smoke Philip Morris myself. I've got some in my coat pocket in the room. No reason I should be smoking your cigarettes—not at seventeen cents a pack these days, anyway. That's not fair. I want to be fair with you."

"Think nothing of it." Glasco had no idea where this was heading. "Happy to help. . . . That's what friends do."

There was a prolonged silence. Both men just stared out into the vastness of Manhattan and smoked. Next, John shifted away from the earlier conversation.

"Why should you be kind to me, Charley? You never set eyes on me before. Who am I to you? I must be just another face in the crowd as far as you're concerned."

Glasco paused before he answered. This was a very real moment in an otherwise unreal situation.

"It's like I already told you, John, we're both tied up in this thing together. The way I got it figured, as long as you're in trouble out there, so are my wife and kids. In a way, their lives are dependent on you, if you catch my drift. Besides—and maybe this'll sound fresh coming from a bellboy—but you look like a regular Joe to me. You look like the type of fella I'd like to have for a friend. Do you think we could be friends, John?"

"Of course we could," John said. "I can see it."

Glasco leaned out the window and stretched his right arm forward to shake hands. John suddenly grew apprehensive. An expression of distrust returned to his eyes, and—somewhat dramatically—he extended only his right little finger until he barely touched Glasco's palm for just a second.

Glasco laughed. "You don't trust me much, do you, John? Well, listen, I trust you, and that not only goes for me but for the wife and kids too. We're trusting you not to let anything bad happen to you or to us. We believe in you, John. It's like you are part of the family in a way. The wife even sent me a note to say she was praying for you. Doing a rosary just for you."

Another silence settled between the two men who were proceeding cautiously, but genuinely with each other. Warde appeared to be deep in thought and ruminating on some troublesome topic.

"Here's the deal, though. I just can't get past it. Past this thing. I've got a momentous decision to make. This thing has got to be thought out. I have to . . . have to deal with it, you know, Charley?"

"Sure, I appreciate that, John. But maybe I can help you. I want to help you. I want to do anything I can. What's this 'thing' you are referring to? Maybe if you get it out in the open, we can talk through it together."

"I can't tell you, but thanks. I just have to work it out alone. It's not something I can say out loud."

The rope around Glasco's leg was suddenly jerked. He tried to ignore it, but the next yank was even stronger. It was annoying in this important moment.

"Well, whatever you work out, John, I want you to promise me that you won't do anything foolish. We're buddies now, so you gotta give me your word. Swear on a Bible kinda thing, you know?"

"I promise you I'll be working it out. I have to deal with it. I'm going to deal with it tonight. I can't go on like this."

"That's great, John. Tell you what, I'll be back in ten minutes. Gotta hit the can. Just don't forget that we're all in here rooting for you. My whole family too."

If others had become content to stand on the sidelines and enjoy the show, one man most definitely was not. Charley was convinced he could save this fella.

PHOTO 1 "The water is perfectly all right, no tricks" says Officer Charles Glasco to John Warde as he hands him a glass. As proof, Glasco drinks some of it himself. The water was laced with benzedrine but did not significantly impact either man. *(Getty Images)*

PHOTO 2 Sgt. John Tormey of the New York Police Emergency Squad directs the operation via phone by reporting "the antics of the maniac John Warde to others who are trying to rescue him." *(Getty Images)*

PHOTO 3 John Warde, on a ledge on the seventeenth floor of the Hotel Gotham, is coaxed and implored by his sister Katherine Bull—a rope tied around her waist to keep her from falling—to get him to come back in. *(Getty Images)*

PHOTO 4 John Warde (circled) "carries on his terrifying one-man show" high on the seventeenth-story ledge of the Hotel Gotham. *(Getty Images)*

PHOTO 5 Unmindful of the pleas of a chaplain and his sister from the window of an adjoining room, John Warde gazes above as if contemplating a climb to the eighteenth floor. *(Getty Images)*

PHOTO 6 Spectators of one of the greatest real-time thrillers in New York history crowd into the streets of downtown Manhattan at mid-afternoon to see the John Warde drama being played out. *(Getty Images)*

PHOTO 7 At its peak, up to 100,000 people were estimated to have jammed behind ropes at 55th and 54th Streets and beyond waiting for Warde to jump. *(Getty Images)*

PHOTO 8 A spectator uses binoculars to get a closeup view of John Warde perched on a seventeenth-floor hotel ledge. Vendors sold roasted peanuts and souvenirs *(Getty Images)*

PHOTO 9 John Warde (circled) stands on the seventeenth-floor ledge of the Hotel Gotham, towering far above the massive crowd that had gathered at its base. *(Getty Images)*

PHOTO 10 High above 55th Street and Fifth Avenue, John Warde accepts a cup of coffee with cream but requests an extra sugar cube after tasting it. *(Getty Images)*

PHOTO 11 Passengers on a passing Fifth Avenue bus, alert to the drama of life and death above them, gaze skyward to the seventeenth floor of the Hotel Gotham for a view of John Warde on his precarious perch. *(Getty Images)*

PHOTO 12 Once more from an adjoining window, John Warde's sister Katherine pleads frantically with him to desist from his mad campaign. John Warde answered with only a laugh before sitting down on the ledge. *(Getty Images)*

PHOTO 13 Photographers are on their backs on the sidewalk beneath the towering exterior of the Hotel Gotham capturing images of the ongoing ordeal over their heads. *(Getty Images)*

PHOTO 14 John Warde smiles in welcome appreciation as Officer Charles Glasco offers a snack to break up the monotony of the 11-hour vigil. *(Author's Collection)*

PHOTO 15 A few of the thousands who gathered to look up seventeen stories at John Warde, a tiny figure walking on an 18-inch narrow ledge, as people lean. *(Getty Images)*

PHOTO 16 Patrolman Charles Glasco hands a telephone to John Warde as the emotionally disturbed twenty-six-year-old man remains on the ledge outside Room 1714 of the Hotel Gotham. *(Getty Images)*

PHOTO 17 As rescuers close in from above, the sides and below, a cargo net is slowly raised from a lower floor with the hopes of trapping John Warde against the outer wall "like a butterfly in a net." *(Getty Images)*

PHOTO 18 Thousands of people gather to watch the high-rise thriller featuring John Warde. Hundreds of police were summoned to hold the throng in check as areas are roped off and traffic halted. *(Getty Images)*

PHOTO 19 Firemen rush to position a net under the seventeenth floor of the Hotel Gotham amidst construction workers hoping to catch a falling Warde. *(Getty Images)*

PHOTO 20 John Warde falls helplessly backward at the midway point of his seventeen-floor leap as he plunges toward the street below. *(Author's Collection)*

PHOTO 21 John Warde careens off of an outcropping near the sixth floor of the Hotel Gotham flipping his body in mid-flight shortly before striking the marquee of the hotel entrance. *(Author's Collection)*

PHOTO 22 John Warde tumbles lifelessly off the hotel marquee after landing on it at the end of his seventeen-floor fall. *(Getty Images)*

PHOTO 23 John Warde's battered body lies in the street gutter after just missing a police officer. One shoe was ripped off as he bounced from a sixth-floor ledge. *(Getty Images)*

PHOTO 24 Police place Warde's body on a stretcher to remove it from the street after he leaped. In the background, the phosphorescent flares of newsreel cameramen illuminate the area. *(Getty Images)*

PHOTO 25 A friend places flowers on the grave of John William Warde after he was buried at Evergreen Cemetery in Brooklyn. *(Getty Images)*

PHOTOS 26, 27 and 28 From left to right: New York Police Commissioner Lewis Valentine, Mayor Fiorello La Guardia, and Rev. John Bonnell, pastor of 5th Avenue Presbyterian Church. *(Getty Images)*

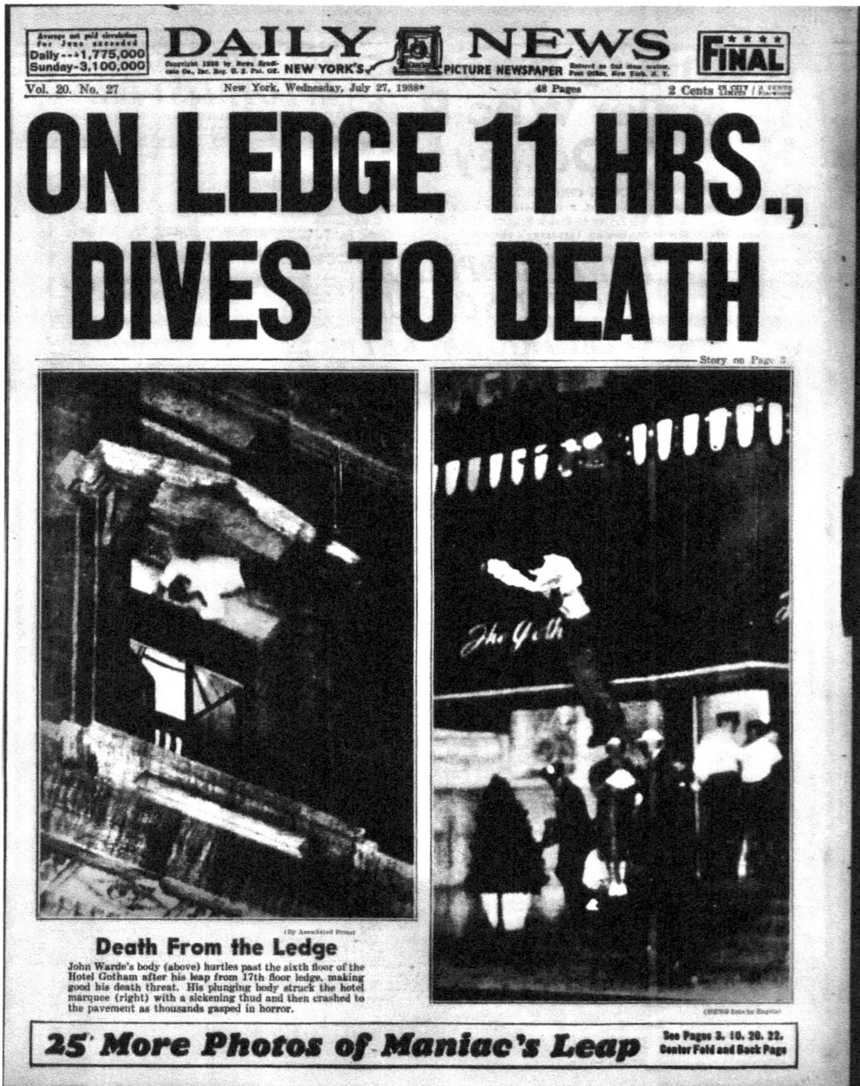

Daily---1,775,000
Sunday-3,100,000

DAILY NEWS

NEW YORK'S PICTURE NEWSPAPER

FINAL

Vol. 20. No. 27 New York, Wednesday, July 27, 1938* 48 Pages 2 Cents

ON LEDGE 11 HRS., DIVES TO DEATH

Story on Page 3

(By Associated Press)

Death From the Ledge

John Warde's body (above) hurtles past the sixth floor of the Hotel Gotham after his leap from 17th floor ledge, making good his death threat. His plunging body struck the hotel marquee (right) with a sickening thud and then crashed to the pavement as thousands gasped in horror.

25 More Photos of Maniac's Leap See Pages 3, 10, 20, 22, Center Fold and Back Page

PHOTO 29 The front page of the July 27, 1938, "Extra" edition of the *Daily News* promotes Warde's death in large bold type to its more than three-million subscribers. The special section included over twenty-five photos of the "Maniac's Leap." *(Author's Collection)*

9 Hour Seven

"What the Hell! Why was you guys yankin' on the rope? . . . You almost gave me a heart attack. I had something going with the kid, and you almost messed it up. Jeepers . . . you gotta be more careful!"

"Sorry, Charley," the men in the corridor responded sheepishly. "It wasn't our fault." A bunch of reporters had rushed in off the elevator and trampled the rope.

Glasco walked away, shaking his head. The entire situation appeared to spin out of control, and it was frustrating him mightily.

After stretching his tired muscles and a brief rub of his lower back, he returned to the room from the hallway. He huddled up with Dr. Presner, who had been present throughout the ordeal and began to discuss random other approaches that were being presented.

There was a certain desperation in the air—a growing fear that Warde might get too comfortable in his position on the ledge.

Meanwhile, John stood alone on that stone lip overlooking Fifty-Fifth Street in Manhattan during the dying hours of a warm summer afternoon. His head was aching with thoughts—thoughts about "the thing" that had been haunting him for years. He had, after all, promised he would deal with it by the end of the day.

"That kid out there is plenty smart—very foxy," Glasco said to Dr. Presner. "The way things are now, you can't get near enough to him to grab a belt or a sleeve or a trouser cuff, not to speak of an arm or a leg or a hand. I tried a couple of fast ones on him, but he saw through them in a flash. He's smarter than all of us, I'm afraid.

"He does go for that story, though, about me being a bellhop with a wife and three kids. I can tell it has him worried. I got confidence I can eventually talk him in, all right, only it'll take some time, I'm thinking. I'm not ready to give up."

The desperation among the others, however, was fully manifest when one of the officers in the room said, "Maybe if we could get one of those things they use in grocery stores to take cans and stuff down off the high shelves. Snap that on his ankle, give it a big yank, and bingo, you got him!"

"Or how about you catch hold of him with a pair of ice tongs?" another cop suggested. "You whip them into something fleshy like a leg or somewhere, and right away, his mind gets off whatever's bothering him upstairs and goes right down to where the pain is. Be a cinch to snatch him up after that, wouldn't it, Doc?"

"Those don't make a bit of sense," Anderson said, sparing the physician from having to express his horror at these suggestions.

The chief inspector continued. "If Charley went out there carrying ice tongs or a grocery grabber, that boy might take the leap after one look at him. You're forgetting that all he's got to do is make the least little twitch, and he's off the ledge. No, sir! This thing is strictly a kid-glove proposition. It can't be licked by anything but patience. We got to tire him out. It's our only chance.

"Glasco, get as much of that ice water in him as you can—pretty soon, he'll have to go to the bathroom. Anybody would. Keep on being nice to him. Get him talking about himself. You started out fine with him, so stay with it. You go take a look at him now, Doc, while Glasco catches his breath."

Glasco gladly slipped the noose off his leg and entered the crowded hall. The cops left as well.

For a brief moment, Room 1714 descended into an eerie silence. Not that there were ever many people or much talking in there—Room 1716 was the headquarters for most discussions. Still, the emptiness was strange. The silence hung in the air in a way that felt heavy and ominous.

Then, inexplicably, a boy of about sixteen dressed in a valet's uniform surreptitiously slipped into the empty room on tiptoe—his eyes glancing around in anticipation of being caught—and made his way to "the window."

Poking his head outside from between the flowing curtains, he looked out and up and was suddenly peering directly into the face of John Warde. He quickly removed his cap as if that was the appropriate sign of respect. John, after all, was a celebrity of sorts.

"Uh, well, hello there, mister." The kid's voice was trembling a bit. John offered no response other than to squint and blow some smoke in his direction.

"Well, mister, you see, someone paid me a whole dollar to bring this here note up'ta you, and I . . ." The kid had run out of words and just stabbed a folded piece of paper in Warde's direction while holding his cap over his chest.

"Left hand. Give it to me with your left hand, kid." John wasn't sure this might not be a trick and resorted to his proven procedure of requiring everything to come from a left hand, which would make it too awkward to grab him. Twice before, cops had tried that ploy while handing him cigarettes or water.

In one of those cases, when a patrolman made a violent grab for his arm, Warde nimbly stepped back out of range with one smooth move, and the man fell face-first on the granite ledge to both the horror and delight of the crowd. John towered over him, smiled, and kindly asked, "Need any help, officer?"

However, at this moment, John was looking at the note the valet had just handed him, reading it while a cigarette dangled from his lips. The slip of paper was direct and to the point: The Mutual Broadcasting Network was willing to pay the sum of one hundred dollars in cash if Warde would permit a live broadcast of the events on the wall outside Hotel Gotham. They would set up a WOR microphone on the ledge to pick up all conversations as well as anything Warde might like to share with their listening audience.

Looking back at the kid, he said, "Please tell the individual that sent you here that he can go to hell in a handbasket as far as I'm concerned." The boy disappeared from the window in a flash as John dramatically tore up the note and let the pieces flutter in the wind before disappearing into the crowd below as they cheered him on.

While all of this was occurring unbeknownst to anyone, out in the corridor, Glasco smoked a couple of cigarettes and thought about what the rope boys had told him earlier. It was something he had never thought about before. For the first time, Glasco worried that the "thing" John couldn't get past might indeed be impassable.

He later related that when he opened the door in the room leading to the corridor, the crush of people reminded him of the lobby of Madison Square Garden on the night of a big fight. From other rooms on the floor, he could hear the sounds of telephones ringing and reporters talking. Catching the eyes of one of the eight anchor men who had been holding the other end of the rope, one of them asked how things were going with Warde's sister.

He remarked that she wasn't in very good shape and that they were concerned for her. She was lying down and had taken a tranquilizer.

The man then asked Charley for a favor—to help him get home in time because he had a date that night. Glasco responded with a smile, indicating that he too had a date that evening—*with liver and bacon*. The man then followed with an unusual question, asking if Warde liked "dames."

Confused by the question, Glasco asked what he was referring to. Instead of providing details, the rescue worker simply winked, indicating that Charley knew what was meant by it.

Charley went back to the room, shut the door, went over to the bed, and sat down on the edge, holding his head in his hands. His head was aching something terrible. His eyes were smarting from the polluted air, and all the time on his feet had his sacroiliac screaming at him.

At that moment, a sergeant stuck his head out of Room 1714 and called to Officer Charley. Dr. Presner had returned from the window just seconds before Glasco entered the room. "He's asking for you again," the doctor told Glasco.

"'Where's that bellboy? Where's that bellboy?' was the last thing he said to me. We had a nice talk. I tried to impress upon him that everybody in here is his friend. He wasn't hostile at all. But he definitely has some affection for you.

"I think he'd like to come in, but he's afraid of the humiliation and possible punishment he'd have to face after causing all this hullabaloo. But to be honest with you, it strikes me that he's getting quite a kick out of causing it—of being, for once, the monarch of all he surveys, you might say. I get a feeling of a power drive there. Did he teeter on the edge and look down below while you were talking to him?"

"My God, yes!" Glasco said. "And it scared the hell out of me. I thought he was going to go. He looked like a diver ready to take the leap."

"Yes, I've seen the same thing. He actually has remarkable control of his equilibrium," Dr. Presner added. "And here's another thing. I've studied quite a lot about the subconscious mind, but this is the first time I've ever had a definite sense of watching it in operation. I'm seeing some things play out in front of my eyes.

"You see it whenever you put something up to him, and he starts thinking it over. It's in the way his face and hands and his limbs behave when the thinking is going on. You can almost hear one part of his mind tell him: 'You're a brave man, John, you're wonderful. All these people admire you for standing up for yourself and putting New York on its ear. That man who just talked to you is your admirer and friend.'

"And while this is going on, he begins to subconsciously nod. His head's nodding just slightly, and he seems to be telling you, 'Yes, yes, I trust what you're saying. Give me time. I'm thinking over what you just said.'

"But then the nodding will stop, and his body will tighten when the other part of his mind seems to say, 'Watch out! Don't do anything rash. There may be danger ahead. Don't trust this man!'

"This part of his mind will eventually dominate, and suddenly he'll shake his head and say out loud, 'Nope, I can't do it. Sorry. I just can't trust you.' But I'd say his willpower is by no means weak at this time, and he definitely has control over his faculties."

"Any ideas about what we can do, Doc?" Glasco asked.

"I think that our plan of attack ought to be to guide his thinking toward trusting us to help him make that difficult decision that he seems to be struggling with so mightily. Glasco, you're absolutely our best bet. You talk with him as long as you can, and whenever you get tired, I'll spell you. Hopefully the net will be in place by that time."

"Let's do it," Glasco eagerly responded as he slipped the rope around his leg again and returned to the window.

* * * * *

"You're late, Charley!" John announced angrily. He had on a wristwatch, and he looked at it. "You said you'd be back in ten minutes, and it's more than fifteen. Nearly sixteen. I'm disappointed." Warde was clearly perturbed by the lack of respect he was being shown. "Punctuality is an important part of trust, Charley." Warde was clearly upset.

"Gee, did I do or say something to make you sore? John, if I did, I'm sorry, and I apologize. Is there anything you want, John? Anything I can do for you? Just name it, and you can have it."

There was silence, and then John said matter-of-factly, "I want to talk to my sister."

"John, your sister's in bed with a terrible-sick headache. She's taken this thing very hard, you know, and she's in pretty bad shape. We better not bother her right now. She's taken a sedative. She's kinda out of it."

"I said I want to talk to Katherine," John said adamantly and with a flare of anger. Try as he might, Glasco could not dissuade him from his wish.

The police had installed a field telephone system to speed communication between the key players stationed in various parts of the hotel and to relieve the Hotel Gotham's swamped switchboard.

One line of the network extended across Fifty-Fifth Street to a sergeant standing on the church's steps. His job was to keep his superiors inside the hotel informed of John's movements as he followed them from the outside. A small cordon of cops even had to be set up around the sergeant, according to a reporter, "to protect him from zealots who squirmed through the police lines to press advice upon him on how to best save the boy."

There was, of course, an installation in room 1714 and also one in 1716. Glasco brought a telephone to the window for John, rang Katherine on her bed in the next room, got her on the line, and then started to pass the telephone to John.

John shook his head vigorously.

Understanding what he meant, Glasco switched the instrument from his right to his left hand—making a grab more difficult—and gave the phone receiver to him. "John then started talking, but he was kind of muttering," the cop later said. "I tried to listen, but John talked in such a low voice that I could not hear what he said.

"Then John lowered the telephone from his face and held it at his side. He was frowning and upset. I could tell when he did that, the conversation hadn't been satisfactory to either participant."

In Room 1716, Katherine put the telephone down and began to weep loudly and hysterically. She was screaming and crying to the extent that she had to be subdued again. Bella Valentine, who had been looking after her, picked up the phone and continued the conversation. She spoke gently, motherly, empathetically.

At first, Warde—perched high above the crowded streets in the early evening air—chatted as calmly as if he were sitting at his desk at home. Sitting on the ledge and chain-smoking cigarettes as they chatted on the telephone, as he finished each smoke, he would extinguish the stubs against the wall and place them on the ledge in a neat pile—now rather large—or toss them playfully into the crowd below his feet.

Bella then began to steer the conversation toward a more emotional vein.

"The children need you, darling. Both of the boys are asking for you. They are crying because they want you to be with them. We all need you, John, so why don't you come in? Tell you what, we'll play ping-pong. We'll go swimming together. Come on, darling, take one little step here, one little step there, show them you can do it. We want you, Johnny, we need you."

There was a long pause while Bella listened to his reply, and then she said, "Oh, Johnny . . . no! Please don't say that. Don't ever say that, please! Why can't you come in? I don't understand. I promise if you'll just come in, nothing will happen to you. They have all given us assurances."

Out on the ledge, Glasco could hear John saying, "But, Bella, I'd be so ashamed now. All those people down there are expecting something to happen." He lowered the telephone from his face and, for the second time, looked as if he might cry.

Glasco could tell the conversation was over, regardless of who had chosen to end the call. He pushed the phone cradle along the ledge toward him, thinking that when John bent down to put the receiver on it, he might be able to grab him.

However, once more, John was too cunning. He tossed the phone to Glasco and said, "You do it." Glasco put the phone on its cradle.

"Tell you what, Charley, I promise I'll come in if I get a document signed by the police commissioner promising that nothing will happen to me. It has to be from the commissioner himself, though."

It was an opening, a start, and an encouraged Glasco quickly withdrew from the window to set the telephone down and search out Captain O'Brien, who was in the next room.

"Warde says he'll come in if he gets a document signed by the police commissioner promising that nothing will happen to him." They discussed it briefly, and O'Brien was confident he could get approval for that. A quick call to the department's headquarters confirmed it, and it suddenly looked like the ordeal might finally be over.

Officially representing the New York Police Department, Captain William O'Brien of the West Forty-Seventh Street Station went to the window and formally told John Warde that the document of immunity he had demanded from the police commissioner was being prepared.

"But you don't really need it," the Captain added. "You can go to your buddies in Scarsdale or anywhere you want, without hindrance, if you'll only come in. You believe me, don't you? Don't I look honest to you?"

"No, you don't," John said. "You don't look honest to me at all."

A frustrated and annoyed O'Brien—who was not used to being treated like that by anyone—then yielded to Bella once more, who also felt like they were getting close now. As she approached the window, she heard a woman call from a nearby roof, "Don't do it, Johnny. We all love you. Go on back in like a good boy now. You just need to be a good boy, hear?"

"John, listen to me. Patrick and I will do the same. We'll make the same promise in writing. We'll write up a document and sign it as proof."

"What good is your name on a piece of paper?" Warde asked peevishly. "Aw, to hell with it all."

Bella continued to cajole Warde back into the room—first asking O'Brien to clear it of all policemen—but nothing she could say appeared to solace him in the slightest. "It's a long way down," she added as she watched her dear friend peer over the edge. "You don't want to do that. Please just come in, John."

John's tone had now oddly become caustic and dismissive. He callously laughed at the sincere pleas of his sister as well, who changed her previous tack, warning him that police were coming out to get him at any minute—a ruse intended to lure him in.

Then, at about 6:50 p.m., he abruptly stated, "If you let me talk to Mother, I might come in."

That was easier said than done. Throughout the long ordeal, law enforcement had been trying desperately to get Mrs. Warde to talk to her son by phone, but to no avail. Whenever they tried to contact her at her home in Southampton, they were told that she could not come to the phone, was not feeling well, or did not wish to speak to anyone. Knocks on the door by local police were not answered, and friends of the family refused to get involved.

Apparently, she had no desire to speak with John, who had greatly disappointed her and besmirched the Warde family's otherwise fine reputation.

However, this time the situation was different. It might be the difference between life and death for her son, and the NYPD twisted some arms to finally get her to agree to speak to her son. A long-distance direct connection to their Long Island estate was hastily set up.

Warde's mother, from her home in Southampton, finally came on the line.

The telephone was passed over to her son.

John put the receiver to his ear, heard his mother's voice, and, without a word, hung up on her.

Standing and crossing his arms across his chest, John Warde lit another cigarette. Charley Glasco eventually picked up the telephone and returned it to the room.

No one spoke a word.

10 Hour Eight

"Look, fella. I been feelin' real guilty since we last talked, and so I'm gonna level with you. I'm gonna come clean. I'm actually a cop, but I ain't the kind that shoots or arrests anybody, so don't be spooked by that. I'm on traffic detail, okay? I write parking tickets and deliver summons, you know what I mean?"

Charley had indeed begun to feel bad about deceiving John. The kid had already had a hard enough time with family, and he instinctively knew that Warde needed a friend more than anything in the world. So he decided to come clean on who he was.

"I was tagging cars downstairs, you know, when I first heard you was up here. I don't know from nothin' about what you think you're doin' or why . . . but you look like a nice kid to me. I hate to see you make a bad mistake. You ought to come in and think it over. I really think you should.

"The longer you stay out here, the harder it's gonna be. Nightfall is coming soon, and that'll be terrible for you. And these guys are only gonna make it rougher on you. I'm tellin' you, they're none too happy about havin' to work overtime hours about when the shift was to go home. And believe me, you don't want to deal with angry and hungry cops.

"Your room here is gonna be knee-deep with more big brass in another five minutes, so this is the time to skedaddle. You know you're gonna come in sometime, kid, so I'm askin' you to do it now, buddy. We'll go down to the station, do some paperwork, and you'll be home for supper. Me too. I got a wife and kid, you know."

John looked into the dusk-filled night air of midtown Manhattan and noticed that the lights were beginning to come on throughout the city. The City. It was The City that had brought all this on. The City that had wrapped him in social expectations since he could first remember.

The pressure had begun to build when he was a teenager. His father wasn't around, his mother was caught up in her affairs, and then, later, his sister abandoned him. He didn't fit in at school, he couldn't hold a job, he couldn't find that "thing" that could fill the empty hole inside. Now, here he was on an eighteen-inch ledge with the sun going down and his legs feeling weak.

"So, what's your real name?"

"Well, buddy, I was bein' straight with you there. It's Charley. Charles Glasco. I'm a patrolman. I mostly work over on Thirty-Seventh Street, between Fifth and Ninth, looking for parking violations. Been with the force a long time. Came from a family of cops, you know. It was in my blood." Glasco was trying desperately to reestablish trust. "And like I said, kid, I'm real, real sorry about not being upright with you. I feel real bad about that."

"It's okay, Charley. I know you were just trying to help. You've been the nicest of anyone, you know. You've talked to me like a friend. You've treated me like a person. Nobody does that. They think I'm an odd duck. Guess I am. I'm not like other guys."

Until then, Glasco had not seen what Dr. Presner called "the head nod," but now he saw it and knew he was getting somewhere. It was an exciting development, and he was confident that a breakthrough was just around the corner.

He felt like John wanted to tell him something but couldn't bring himself to take that step—just "couldn't get past it," as he had mentioned several times. But they were getting closer.

John and Officer Charley talked effortlessly for nearly an hour, and with surprising enthusiasm considering the situation. Glasco would later relate that they discussed a wide range of topics and that it was "a really enjoyable time."

"We talked about picnics, for one thing—whether a day picnic or a night picnic was better. John thought that night picnics were more romantic, but I pointed out that by day, the bugs weren't so bad, poison ivy was easier to dodge, children did not sit on food as frequently, and there were things like fat men's races and ball games between the marrieds and the singles that were always a kick.

"Then we talked about baseball for a stretch. He was a big fan of the Yankees. John said that he didn't think the Brooklyn club would finish in the first division. I offered to take him to a game if I could get off work—just the two of us having a beer and some peanuts on a nice summer day—but he refused my invitation, saying he hated the Dodgers.

"Then the talk turned to what sports John went into for himself. He mentioned ping-pong. I seen people playing that, but I ain't never played myself. I said I also enjoyed badminton—which we play a lot on holidays at home—but he had never heard of that and at first confused it with backgammon."

"Swimming is my favorite sport," John explained to the officer. "I love to take a long swim and then lie on the beach all covered with suntan oil. I like the feeling when someone rubs me all over with suntan oil. It's a good feeling, you know. I have a friend up in Southampton who likes that too. We both like sunning and tanning."

"Gee, that must be a great life, John. It shows in that streamlined build of yours. Even through your clothes, I can see you have a fit body. Do you also exercise regularly?"

"Oh, sure, and I work with dumbbells too. Listen, when I finally come in, I'll take you out to my house and show you the swellest set of dumbbells you ever saw. I got a real setup there. It has mirrors on the wall and everything. You'll like it . . . I know you will."

Glasco had just heard the words he had been waiting for for nearly seven hours and tried to keep the elation out of his voice. "Well, let's get going, then," he said casually. "Sounds good to me."

"What do you mean?" John answered, a bit puzzled.

"Well, I mean, let's go see those dumbbells of yours. Matter of fact, for a long time now, I've been wanting to get rid of some of this lard I'm carrying around, and probably working with dumbbells is exactly what I need.

"If I like yours, I'll get me a pair of 'em, and you can coach me what to do to develop a decent build. I'd really like that, and I bet the missus would too. Probably add some years to my life to get rid of this here belly. Come on, John, you got me all hopped up. Let's grab a train before it gets dark and go check them out tonight."

Then Glasco saw the other thing Dr. Presner had mentioned. The head bobbing had stopped, and John's body visibly tightened. The tone of their friendly conversation had abruptly changed.

"Not for a while yet," John said after a long pause. "I'm not ready yet."

"Well, when, then?" Glasco didn't want this moment to slip away. But it had.

"I'll let you know," John replied, barely above a whisper.

The man who tried for nearly eight hours to persuade John Warde—perched on a narrow ledge high above East Fifty-Fifth Street—to go on living later reported that John had made him "about seven distinct promises not to jump" by this time.

"Warde kept saying, 'Give me time. I have to work it out,'" Patrolman Glasco said.

"So I said to him, 'Well, will twenty minutes be enough?'

"He said, 'That depends . . . what time is it now?' He kept checking the time with me. He was very conscious of the time. But then he would let me down. He didn't stand up to his word. Whenever I would come too close, he would back away. He seemed to feel caught in a bind between something that was inside him and all those people out there that he felt he owed something to for waiting so long."

It was an odd dilemma for Glasco, who was trying to both rescue the young man—with the growing pressure of the entire NYPD on his shoulders—and be sensitive to his obvious mental instability. The officer was beginning to understand Warde better—he clearly had insight into his condition that no one else knew—and he truly had developed some affection and empathy for him.

"I could see him struggle with whatever it was. He was balanced on the balls of his feet all the time. I never knew if he was going to go over, and when I thought this might be the time, he'd back off, lean against that big wall ornament, and light up another cigarette. His moods would go up and down, just change in an instant.

"He didn't like the people on the street. They were bothering him, even though he would play to them at times. But he was mocking them to me. He'd say, 'Look at those idiots down there. Small people. Small in size, small in their minds.'"

Still, Glasco was not discouraged. He was convinced that the dam had finally begun to crack. During the long conversation, John had drunk quite a few glasses of water, each of which Glasco had sipped from first and then delivered with his left hand exactly as instructed by Warde. It was a bit of a routine now, and everyone seemed content to play by the rules.

The officer once again told John that he needed to take a bathroom break—explaining that he had a bit of a prostate infection and hoping that the subliminal message would get through to him. Before he left, however, with a lighthearted tone he said, "Gee, buddy, you know you can't stay out there all night."

"Why not?" John asked. "I've got everything I need out here."

In Charley's absence, John lit another cigarette—he was on his fourth or fifth pack by now. Sitting down on the ledge to rest his legs and tease the crowd a bit, he was pleased when they responded as expected with a roar that billowed up from below.

"Morons," he repeated to himself with a chuckle.

Dr. Presner replaced Glasco at the window, though they spoke little. After about five minutes, John turned to the doctor with fierce eyes and said, "I want Charley. . . . Tell Charley I miss him." As the physician was leaning further out the window to explain that Glasco needed a bit of a break, he heard a shrill, ear-piercing scream come up from below.

It just so happened that while Dr. Presner sat on the window sill trying to burn time until Charley Glasco could return, the doctor's wife and his sister, who was visiting from Montreal, were on a stroll up Fifth Avenue to do some light shopping—completely unaware of the activities going on in that area.

Then, like everyone else on that day, they were brought to an abrupt halt by the crowd at the Fifty-Fifth Street intersection, and they stared up in the direction where everybody else was looking. The sister suddenly uttered a terrified scream. "Isn't that Jacques up there hanging out of that window?" she said. Someone answered and said, "Yeah, the man up there is threatening to jump!"

Mrs. Presner, trying to stifle her terror, confirmed that it was her husband.

No one they asked could explain what was happening, so they struggled through the crowd to the hotel. There, they were refused permission to enter. Assuming that the man might be referring to her husband as the jumper, she rushed home in complete fear. It wouldn't be until later, at the home of a friend, that they found out what was happening from a radio account and were able to finally relax.

By this time, in fact, millions of people had heard radio broadcasts—featuring minute-by-minute commentaries—throughout the entire Western Hemisphere.

Ironically, sitting on the sill, the doctor could hear, booming through the hotel's open windows, the voices of announcers describing John's actions and his own. He complained about this, and the police made the thoughtless guests close their windows—on the hottest day of the year—or shut off their radios.

In the suburbs, women who had been listening to the broadcasts all afternoon phoned husbands and children working in the midtown section to stop on their way home and see the spectacle on Fifty-Fifth Street. Many firms whose offices afforded good views of the Gotham could not get their employees to leave at quitting time. Most were bunched around the windows until there was no more remaining space.

One person who tuned in late was Mrs. Charles Glasco, who had been busy all day with her housework at their Woodhaven home on Eighty-Seventh Street. At a quarter of eight, her telephone rang. It was Augie Schmidt, the neighborhood butcher and a family friend.

"Well, Maggie, with your old man out on that ledge, I guess you'll be keeping that liver and bacon on the back of the stove for a while," he said.

"Oh dear," Mrs. Glasco said resignedly. "What's he up to now?"

"You didn't hear yet? Ho, ho! Turn your radio on."

* * * * *

As the day wore on and the crowds continued to swell, Chief Inspector Alexander Anderson, who was once again running the show, kept sending for more men. At this point, there were more than four hundred police on the scene—as if numbers could swing the tide in this frustrating standoff.

The crowd had swelled to an estimated forty thousand spectators who were mobbing the streets, with newsreel crews positioned on rooftops and radio announcers broadcasting the midtown drama live to the world. The evening Broadway theater crowd was also now intermingling with casual spectators, and the crowd seemed to be growing exponentially, or at least becoming denser.

The mob had overflowed far away over to Sixth Avenue, between Fifty-Sixth and Fifty-Seventh, and the curious milled and jostled for positions on a small patch of sidewalk where someone had discovered that from that spot—through a space between two buildings—John's figure, lit up by the searchlights, could be easily seen.

A local newspaperman recalled spotting a young family where the father had his three-year-old daughter on his shoulders while the mother was shouting instructions:

"Hold Fernie a little higher, Daddy. Now, look up there, honey, way up high. See the funny man in the white shirt sitting way, way up there on the side of the building? Do you see him, dear? Oh, honey, you aren't even looking at the right building. Look. Where Mamma's pointing, looky. There . . . over there!"

An angry, sweaty policeman tried in vain to keep this stretch of the street clear. "Go on home and look after your own children," he kept shouting at the women. They laughed back at him in reply. "This is better entertainment than anything we can get at home!"

Meanwhile, John Warde kept smoking and pacing.

Deputy Mayor Henry H. Curran—the personal emissary of five-foot, one-inch bulldog Mayor Fiorello La Guardia—had also joined the ensemble in Room 1714 to encourage Anderson to get this thing wrapped up, something that was not received as a welcome comment. Curran came with Supreme Court Justice John E. McGeehan, who had been a former New York district attorney. Both were offering to take over the negotiations.

However, the most significant activity was taking place in the lobby of Hotel Gotham, where hordes of people were volunteering to help resolve the situation on the seventeenth floor.

Most of them claimed to possess special skills or "supernatural gifts." The lobby, as a result, was swarming with such a mass of humanity that the police were forced to set up a checkpoint at the entrance and take names with notes on what the individuals said they brought to the table.

Among other arrivals at the Gotham that day was Miss Evelyn MacDonell—the self-styled "Angel of the Bowery"—who had come up from the Beacon Relief Mission with her father. She had been the subject of a 1911 silent film and was an undisputed hero of the era. MacDonell maintained that she had rescued thousands of men who found themselves in desperate situations like Warde's by "reading them Scriptures and inspirational poems that uplift the soul and alter the perception of the man."

A fellow dressed in an all-white outfit explained that he was "an army man" who could "expertly use the ancient art of jujitsu" to capture John. Next to him, a female faith healer with "scientifically worked-out slogans and incantations" insisted on kneeling in the lobby and praying loudly and constantly.

Hundreds of suggestions were being called into the Gotham's switchboard operators with ideas for rescuing Warde. One man telephoned from Rochester, New York, to say that the police should put him on a regimen of chamomile and ginger tea because that "removes the poisons in the brain that are gathered from reading smut." A woman thought it might be wise to "drop a giant net over the entire hotel so Mr. Warde would have nowhere to fall."

Another caller offered to bring his carrier pigeons to the floor above Warde to defecate on him, saying, "There ain't nobody who'll take a shower of bird shit and keep standing there. It's a foolproof plan."

Dozens offered to just go up there and push him off, as if ending the standoff was the ultimate goal. Some had compassion. Others were as crazy as the man on the ledge, or perhaps more so.

A Sister Lumina claimed to have discovered, in the Bible no less, a way to magnetically extract poisonous metals from the body that caused mental illness. If she could get close enough to him, she suggested that she could pull out the offending elements and "the man will simply walk off the ledge unaware of anything that had besieged him. He will be as new."

Neither Sister Lumina, nor the army man, nor the pigeon breeder, nor the Angel of the Bowery was ever given the opportunity to test their powers.

Among those who were rebuffed more than once by the police was a twenty-two-year-old Greenwich Village blues singer and self-proclaimed fiancée of John Warde, who was adamant she could save him from a spectacular plunge.

The *Daily News* later reported that the girl, Camilla LaMont, had turned him away from suicide several times in the past, and that she felt frantic and helpless as she had viewed the scene play out from below. Explaining to reporters that she had met Warde at a cocktail party in Scarsdale, New York, the previous fall, she said that, after a series of dates, she considered herself engaged to him.

Miss LaMont said she was stopped on the hotel steps by an officer who scoffed at her story and told her, "I don't care whether you're his girlfriend, his sister, or his mother, there ain't no way you're getting in here tonight." And she didn't.

The street scene was pure pandemonium by now.

Bookies had set up shop on each street corner and were offering changing odds. At the moment, it was 8 to 5 against jumping. Each time John bent over the edge, however, the odds flipped toward taking the leap, and men lined up to lay down their hard-earned paychecks. Money was continuing to change hands rapidly.

A woman—who was clearly either just seeking attention or was part of a publicity stunt—walked in a provocative dress through the middle of the open circle that the police had cleared at the base of the hotel and wiggled her assets to the crowd's delight. When she reached the center, she turned to the crowd and began throwing kisses, spotlighted by the outer glow of one of the searchlights.

As she did, a man in the crowd yelled out, "Look out, lady! The fella just jumped, and he's gonna land square on top of you!" The woman screamed and ran for dear life in her high heels before tumbling into the arms of an onlooker, to the absolute delight of everyone. The laughter even made its way up to John, who was following the action from above.

The cops in the crowd also had their own opinions as they awaited the outcome, whatever it might be. "He sure picked himself a good spot," an officer by the name of Hannigan said.

"Yep," his partner replied. "He picked a spot on the building where there was no chance to get at him. No balconies on that part of the building. You can't drop a loop over him from the roof because of the overhang. He must be a pretty smart guy. I bet the brass are real frustrated."

Cabbies, whose taxis were now frozen in place, had reached their own breaking point and inexplicably began laying on their horns, causing a cacophony of confusion and firing up the crowd once again. The traffic cops were doing their best to quell this uprising, though there was little chance that could be done.

Sergeant Murphy, along with Hannigan, were pounding on the hoods of the taxis with their nightsticks and yelling, "Hey, this is already enough of a nightmare. We don't need you making it worse! Stop honking yer goddamn horns. You're driving me crazy. Save it for New Year's, will ya?"

One of the cabbies—standing next to his taxi with arms crossed—yelled back, "Hey, officer, how are we going to be able to get through? I got a big fare waiting for me. . . . I ain't gonna lose it over some jerk walkin' on a ledge. Let us through, for God's sake!"

Hannigan snapped back, "You better take it easy, fella. That's a real person up there. Have a heart, buddy."

"You know him?"

"Not really, but kind of. I mean, one of my buddies is up there with the guy right now and trying to talk him down. The word comin' down is he's real crazy, you know. Bats in the belfry kinda thing." Hannigan twirled his finger alongside his head to illustrate his point.

"Sure, copper, but what do you want us to do about all this, though? My cab's overheating, and I'm burnin' up gas! This is costing me money. . . . Go do your job, will ya?"

"Just hold your horses. . . . There's something bigger than you going on here. Have a little sympathy, will ya? My buddy's working on it, I told you."

"Well then, tell your buddy to just ask the kid to jump and get it over with, will ya?" That brought peals of laughter from the crowd and even a smile to Hannigan's face. Everyone was growing tired of the drama.

"Okay, okay, all you's guys get back in your cabs and shut your traps for a change!"

"Yeah, sure. Easy for you to say. You're drawing a paycheck whether he jumps or not. It ain't no skin off'a your nose."

"Excuse me, officer, I have an important appointment for a job." A pretty young woman interrupted the conversation between the cop and the cabbie from the back of an adjacent taxi. "I'm late already, and I really need this job. Can you move these cars, please?"

"Well, if they are expectin' you today—"the policeman responded. "I'd say get out and walk." Perturbed, the woman rolled up her window, but not before muttering, "How inconsiderate!"

A group of street toughs were sitting on the edge of a flower box planter and were surveying the scene with some interest. "Look at 'im . . . like a bug taking a walk. Just a tiny little thing up there causin' all this commotion. I still have my service M2. I could knock him off from here. One clean shot, and it'd be all over with."

Then, with horns blaring, sirens screaming, and a roar from the crowd that resembled the start of the Kentucky Derby, Sergeant Sean Murphy looked up and saw John Warde hundreds of feet up, teetering precariously, with his toes over the ledge and his eyes squeezed shut. His hands were high overhead with his fingers interlocked.

He looked like the perfect image of an Olympic diver.

11 Hour Nine

Charley Glasco looked down at his new Bulova wristwatch—the one his wife Margaret had given him on his thirty-fifth birthday—and noted that the hour was pushing 8:40 p.m., but there was no darkness on the upper facade of the Gotham because searchlights set up by the police were crisscrossing the exterior of it. They gave the scene the look of a Hollywood premiere, and the photographers were continually shooting their flashbulbs despite pleas from the police to stop.

Glasco wanted with all of his heart to rescue this poor kid, but both his patience and his energy were wearing thin. The sun had set twenty minutes earlier, and it felt to the patrolman like an ominous sign.

If that was the case for the nearly exhausted traffic cop, it must have been multiplied many times over for John Warde, who was now standing alone on a ledge two hundred feet in the air in pitch blackness, except for the occasional sweep of a searchlight that was instantly blinding and disorienting.

Barely wedged into the slight outcropping of the architectural floral decorating, it was clear that his legs were beginning to shake, and his feet seemed to be going numb. He would occasionally kick them against the limestone wall as if to wake them up.

Wrapping his arms around his body to provide some emotional comfort, John seemed to be growing more sullen and moody. Glasco sensed a disconcerting despondency sweeping over him.

His mother had given up on him, as had his father many years earlier. He could hear the chants of "Jump, jump, jump, you coward bastard! Be a man!"

"My sister doesn't think I'm much of a man, you know," John said. "She sometimes calls me a pixie. She thinks I'm weak. A failure. She says I have no character . . . wants to commit me to the loony bin. I don't think I'm crazy, you know, Charley. . . . I'm just different. Different from other people. Different from other . . . men. I just can't get past it. I just can't."

Glasco's back was aching unbelievably, and it was almost hard for him to concentrate on John's words, which were softer now, more breathy and erratic.

The cop found his mind wandering a bit. He was starving at this point, and he had a headache that wouldn't stop even after incessantly popping Bayer aspirins throughout the ordeal.

The multiple doses of Benzedrine were also affecting him. It was becoming harder to focus, and nothing sounded better at the moment than lying down for a few minutes on the bed in the room. He knew he couldn't, but the bed in the room sounded like heaven.

There was something about John's tone that now had his attention. It had shifted noticeably. After talking about how the Yankees had a good shot at winning one hundred games that season, and with Gehrig, Dickey, and DiMaggio, the World Series was nearly a lock, they moved on to the movies.

John had just seen *The Adventures of Robin Hood*, starring Errol Flynn and Olivia De Havilland, at the Roxy. Charley and Maggie hadn't really had the extra money for dates lately, so he was drawing on memories of *King Kong* and *The Wizard of Oz*.

They had both run out of things to discuss and found themselves enduring long stretches of awkward silence between conversations.

In the end, the two were reduced to talking about the weather. New York was in the midst of a daunting heat wave, breaking a record on this day when the mercury surpassed ninety-four degrees in Manhattan. Though the sun had set earlier, the heat had not diminished, and even high in the sky, both John and Charley were feeling it now.

Dr. Presner eventually stepped in to share the load, though he, too, was wearing down. Accompanied at the time by Dr. Shilder and joined by another psychiatrist who happened to be a guest at the hotel on vacation from Chicago that day, the trio were putting their heads together to see if they could come up with any fresh perspectives.

As soon as the three were in the window, John caught them completely off-guard with a challenge. Looking at them intently, he stated, "If any of you can give me any reason to live, then I give you my word I will come in. Any reason for living, and I'll put an end to all of this."

It was silent for nearly two minutes before Dr. Shilder made the first attempt at an answer.

"Well, Mr. Warde, I would say it is different things for different people. For some, it is friends, activities, careers, new adventures, and the pleasantries of life. For others, religion, learning, creativity, and the interchange of thought."

The Chicago psychiatrist followed Shilder with an additional perspective. "And to that, I would include family, John. The warmth that comes from belonging to a family. The interpersonal relationships that give meaning to every day."

Warde, the bright young man that he was, paused momentarily. "I'd venture to say that the two of you don't really believe a word of what you are saying. You've been trained for years to repeat those very words, but you know—and I certainly know—they are empty and specious. They come off your lips, and they fall to the ground. You embarrass yourselves by offering such trivialities."

The two clinical psychiatrists—who had studied Sigmund Freud, Carl Jung, and Emil Kraepelin for years—had no response.

Finally, Dr. Presner, who knew John Warde better than anyone among the doctors, said, "John, we don't have an answer. It has to come from within you. Only you truly know the answer to that."

"Then there is no answer," he replied solemnly. "I didn't think there was. I didn't think you could come up with anything, but I wanted to give you a shot at it. I have no friends, my parents have abandoned me, no career, no hobbies, no affection for any woman, and no interest other than finding fine clothes and going for drives in the countryside.

"How sad, really. Great minds like yours and no one can effectively give me a reason to live. One acceptable answer and, I assure you, I would have come in." With that, he turned away and looked in the opposite direction. Lighting yet another cigarette, he closed his eyes and drew smoke deep into his lungs in the abject loneliness of the night.

The doctors walked away, feeling that they had failed.

John's life would now be in the hands of an untrained, uneducated, unsophisticated traffic cop who wrote parking tickets for a living—yet one who overflowed with compassion.

There seemed to be something deep and problematic on John's mind, Charley Glasco would report later, but he didn't know how to find out what it was. The kid appeared to be stuck on something that he couldn't get out.

Charley was trying to be patient, but he was growing tired of the lighthearted and shallow chatter they had been reduced to. Since the beginning, he had been pondering over and ruminating on what might have caused all this, what was going on in John's brain that was telling him death was a better option than life.

"There has to be something, some little spur in his mind that was poking and poisoning everything else. But what was that thing?" The officer didn't dare say it out loud, but he knew he had to find out what it was. It was his only hope to save this sad soul.

"Different from other men? Is that what you said?" The statement John had just said, though weakly, was suddenly resonating with Charley. "You said that you just can't get past it. What do you mean by that, Johnny? What can't you get past?"

"That I'm not like other men. I'm different. I already told you. I don't really want to talk about it."

In Officer Glasco's many years on the force, he had learned that whenever someone brings up some topic and says they don't want to talk about it, they probably do. John wanted someone to draw it out so that he could answer cryptically, allowing him to find relief from a painfully kept secret.

"Why don't you whisper to me what you mean? Sometimes I find that for people who need to share something, this is the best way to do it. You know, just a little whisper right in my ear." He wasn't sure if John would go for it.

"No . . . no, no, no. It's just a gimmick to grab me when I lean over to whisper to you. I'm not an idiot. I'm not falling for that."

In reality, Glasco hadn't thought for a moment about making a play for John. His concern was sincere, and he was committed to the belief that if he could find out the source of John's inner pain, he could convince him to come in. It seemed like a very important moment.

Perhaps the most important of the last ten hours.

"How are you different? You seem like a regular Joe to me. Just a normal guy going about his business until, well, until, you know, all this happened. What makes you so different from me except for the fact that I write parking tickets?"

At this very moment, John Warde took in a big breath, leaned down about halfway, and motioned for Glasco to approach him. The officer held up both hands to indicate that he had no intention of pulling off any monkey business.

Then, in one of the most significant moments in the entire situation, John bent down and began to speak into Glasco's ear. He talked for over a minute, while the officer nodded and patted the young man lightly on his left shoulder. Charley appeared to be comforting, sensitive, and empathetic. John seemed to be talking freely and easily. The conversation felt important and continued.

After two full minutes, Glasco pulled back and said, "Thanks. Thanks, John, for talking to me. I appreciate it. I really do. It means a lot."

John wiped his eyes with the sleeve of his shirt several times and then turned his head toward the architectural element that had provided him with the only support he had enjoyed over the past many hours.

"Have you always felt that way? You've always had these feelings, I guess you'd say?" Glasco continued sincerely. "And you feel that you just can't get past it? Am I right? Can't get past being different from other boys?"

John nodded. He couldn't speak at first, and then he did, still facing the granite ornament. "My father has never really been around, you know. He has always been a highly regarded man, no doubt, but I'd say drunk most of the time. My mother is very stern and religious but not very stable. She had certain expectations for a boy. I don't think I lived up to those. She made me hate my father. My sister always said there was something wrong with me. I have no real love for my family, other than Katherine, of course."

Charley was starting to get an idea of where he was going with this.

"But in high school, I mean, you felt 'normal' then. And they told me you had a fiancée. Is that true?"

"Well, I mean, she's a swell gal, but . . . but I can't be with her. It's hard to explain. I can't talk about it, but I can't be with her, that's all."

John was looking down at his feet, shuffling them nervously. Still, it seemed he appreciated having Charley there to listen like a priest in the confessional booth, albeit nearly two hundred feet in the air.

The cop, for his part, was not convinced there even was a fiancée. There was something about the man that just didn't fit with that picture.

"John, I been married for some time now, and it isn't all peaches and cream, you know. Not for anyone. She gave me a great kid, and she's great in the kitchen, but it ain't as bad as you're thinking. Not at all. I'm sure once the two of you's married, everything'll work out fine. I'm sure of it. And if you're saying that you're scared about your wedding night, well, lots of boys are. We just don't talk about it . . . being men and all.

"You just need to decide to come on in, and we can talk about this some more. Sit down and have a beer or two and just talk like men. There are also people, you know, that can help who do this for a living. Real smart professionals, you know. Fine people, I hear. Why, I know this guy at the station that went to a shrink and . . ."

John interrupted. "It's not gonna work, though, Charley. You're not listening to me. I'm different. I can't change. I've tried, and I can't change. I've prayed and prayed, and I can't change. The Bible says, 'A leopard can't change its spots,' and I can't either. It's no good, I'm telling you. I just can't get past it . . . just can't. Just can't get past these feelings I have."

Charley noticed that John had moved closer to the edge as he spoke. He was now, once again, lifting himself on the balls of his feet like a diver on the high dive, readying himself to take the plunge. It appeared to be a moment of decision, and Charley's heart was racing.

"Hey, son, you don't wanna do that. C'mon now, don't do anything foolish just because you feel different from other fellas. Hey, if I asked a hundred guys at the precinct if they feel there's something about them that's 'different,' a hundred of them would say, 'Hell yeah.' Everyone feels the same, John. We all got issues."

John responded softly. "You know, I just came up here in the first place to get some attention. You know, to come up with a story for Mr. Manelli. He told me that if you can't find a story, then make one. So I did. But now it feels all different. There are real things to deal with. It would be too embarrassing to come in. Besides, all the people want me to jump. I don't want to disappoint them."

With this, John was done talking. He seemed to have moved into a more morose, more reflective stage.

"Oh no, please don't say that, John. No one wants you to jump. No one. Not your mom and dad, not your sister or fiancée, not any of the cops in here. Not Mrs. Valentine. And if you hear anyone saying something like that from down below, well, they're the crazy one. They're the ones I wanna lock up if I can get my hands on 'em.

"But listen to me, John. We're all pulling for you, kid. 'Specially me. I'm pulling for you. I really like you, kid. I really, honestly do. If you come in, you know we could do something together. Go fishing, maybe. You like to fish?"

"Yeah, I like fishing. My dad and I used to fish when I was little. We'd go over to Hempstead Lake, sometimes to the Jones Beach Fishing Pier. I liked it. It was fun."

"Well, then, we gotta do it! I got some days off owed to me, so maybe we could go this weekend? Sound good? Come on in, and we'll sit down and make some plans. Let's catch us some mackerel . . . some whoppers!"

John did not respond for a few minutes.

Instead, he was fixated on the mob below. Looking in all directions, he could see that both Fifth Avenue and Fifty-Fifth Street were filled from sidewalk to sidewalk, and then from there for as far as he could see. The searchlights were sweeping back and forth across the hotel facade while, by this point, a single spotlight was fixed on him. He felt like a fly under a microscope.

"I can't get past it, Charley. I just can't. I've tried everything. I've begged God to change me, but he doesn't do anything. I can't get past it. It's no good . . . I'm just no good."

Glasco had no words.

Days later, when he was interviewed by the investigating team at the NYPD and then after that by reporters, Glasco refused to say what John Warde had whispered to him in confidence, saying, "He told me a secret but only if I promised never to tell anyone else. I told him at the time that I was a man of my word, and I don't intend to change that now. His secret will die with me."

John lived in an era that offered no grace for anyone who strayed from the lines of moral, social, and religious tolerance of the early twentieth century in America. As a result, for anyone who fell into that category, life was a prison with little or no hope of escape. This undoubtedly was John's reality, especially with the fear of an impending wedding day and a honeymoon night looming.

Many years later, while he was working on a screenplay for a movie based on this dramatic true story, writer John Paxton accessed eyewitnesses, police reporters, reporters' notes, and memories from bystanders who were present on that day. To depict this aspect of the subplot, which was never addressed openly, he has John's fiancée coming to speak to him on the ledge.

Although that did not happen in real life, this portion of the script—based on the writer's interviews—provides insight into the mind and soul of the man who was making the most important decision of his life.

In the movie, the fiancée asks John if he truly loves her. Tortured from within, he cannot answer her. She asks a second time, telling him that she loves him dearly.

John is silent, sweating profusely. She then tells him that she has memorized a portion of a letter he once wrote to her that has left her puzzled. She recites his own words back to him.

In a moving scene, his girlfriend reminds him that he once wrote that when he was away from her, saying that he would stare at the empty doorway and whisper silent words of love to her. At the same time, she noted that he described that he felt unable to touch her. That he could not bring himself to press his body next to hers. That his soul could not embrace her, ending with a stark and painful statement that he had no power to give her what she needed.

Officer Glasco could feel all of this in the moment, and he later shared how badly it hurt him to be unable to help. Although he could feel that John was beginning to unravel further with time, he felt powerless to convey to him that he truly cared and sincerely wished to help. He felt that there were inner demons in the boy that were beyond his ability to control.

The cop would empathetically tell Warde that, to him, he looked like just a regular ol' Joe, the kind of fellow that he'd like to have for a friend. Going even further, he thought that—under different circumstances—they would probably be friends.

"'Of course we could,' he said back to me. So, I leaned far out the window—as far as I could—and stretched my right arm forward to shake his hand. The expression on his face seemed to me to be a mixture—he wanted to trust me, but he didn't know if he could. So with my open hand to him, he did the strangest thing.

"With just the tip of his index finger, he touched the palm of my hand for a fraction of a second. Then, one by one, he let each of his fingers rest on my hand and moved them around real slowly. After a few seconds, he pulled back his hand. He was real melancholy when he did this. Thoughtful, you know, kinda affectionate.

"I'm not sure what he meant by it, but I can tell you it meant something to me. Like he wanted some human touch or something. Like he wanted to trust. I'm tellin' you it meant a whole lot to me and even makes me sad to think about it now.

"I remember I said, 'Maybe, son, you don't trust me much, but listen, John, I trust you. I believe in you. You're someone special, and I surely don't want anything bad to happen to you.' I was . . . well, I was getting emotional at the time.

"There was nothing but silence after I spoke. The roar of the crowd had diminished a bit, as they were also growing weary of the wait. After a minute or two, John responded.

"'I just can't get over that fence,' he kinda muttered to both me and himself. 'I've got a momentous decision to make. This thing has got to be thought out. I have to make a decision. It's a big one, you know, Charley. A really big one, 'cause I'm not sure how I can go on feeling the way I do inside.'

"'Sure, I appreciate that, John, I do,' I said. 'So maybe I can help you.'"

Charley Glasco continued relating the story to his friends, and when he reached this part, he said, "Poor John just looked at me and told me, 'Thanks, but I have to work it out alone. Between me and my God, I guess. I have to. I'll be working it out, I promise you.' So then I told him, 'Well, whatever you work out, John, I want you to guarantee me not to let anything bad happen to you. Can you do that, John? Don't forget that we're all in here rooting for you.'

"He never answered me, you know, and that has always haunted me. He never even said one word.

"He was sitting out there alone except for a mourning dove that had landed next to him and was cooing, you know, with that sad, sad sound."

And with that, John William Warde felt even more alone.

12 Hour Ten

Things seemed to be building to a climax—although no one dared mention such a thought, in case they might jinx the outcome. Still, there was a feeling in Rooms 1714 and 1716 that this could not go on much longer. Reporters were approaching final copy deadlines for the next morning's paper, and there was a sense of unease and frustration mounting—as if Warde had personally decided to make their lives more difficult.

There was a similar vibe on the streets, where tens of thousands of onlookers were now growing weary of standing in the dark waiting for something to happen. It was becoming increasingly apparent that there was mounting exhaustion from all of the tension caused by intently staring at one man high on a ledge for so many hours with no end in sight. On the other hand, Warde was appearing less tense as time went on and, if anything, he seemed to be refreshed by tall the attention.

Large phosphorescent flares were now burning along the streets, illuminating the crowds who were growing increasingly listless and anxious, waiting for a *resolution*—a word that meant, in this case, for the jumper to finally take the leap that he had been teasing them with for the better part of an entire day.

It was as if he owed it to them.

The reality was that law enforcement and the rescue team had run out of ideas. Many of them, in fact, were secretly hoping for him to jump, and it seemed as if the only person standing between those eager to see him slip off the edge and John Warde himself was the ever-patient and infinitely compassionate Charley Glasco. At this point, he had invested a great deal in the young man and refused to abandon hope.

John continued to survey the scene below—crowds that stretched out endlessly in every direction—while every window across the street and within the Gotham was thrown, wide open with people hanging out of them as if they were watching a ballgame. With most of the spectators tuned in to radio station WOR, Dave Driscoll's voice could be heard echoing through the steel and glass canyons of Manhattan and reverberating into the streets.

John Warde was also hearing the broadcast—with repeated reports that it appeared he might jump at any moment—and it was unsettling to him. Glasco kept motioning to the officers in the room to get people to turn down their radios, and before long they were going door to door in the hotel, asking guests to lower the volume. On the ground, through bullhorns, the police were doing the same for the people in the adjacent apartments and rooms across the street.

Still, the circus seemed to be reaching a fever peak.

Shortly, the radio broadcasts filled the air with play-by-play announcers talking over each other.

Charley felt, for the first time in a while, that John was struggling with exhaustion. He would repeatedly shake his legs and feet, which appeared to be falling asleep, and wave his hands back and forth to keep himself alert. At times, his eyes appeared to be at half lids, and at others they were almost unnaturally wide open.

Gulping in big breaths of the evening air, he seemed to find a renewed fascination in the taunting crowds below. While steadying himself against the large floral element at his side, he would begin to rock rhythmically on the balls of his feet, lifting himself up or leaning dangerously forward to get a slightly better view of the street activities.

Glasco was concerned, worried.

"Hey, Johnny, gotta take a quick bathroom break, and then I'll be right back. Don't do anything foolish while I'm gone, 'cause I wanna tell you about what's happened in the Yankees game. They went up by six runs in the sixth over the St. Louis Browns in the second game of the doubleheader. DiMaggio's on a tear. . . . I'll tell you more in a bit."

* * * * *

Mort Lawrence, a respected journalist from the *Capital Times* in Madison, Wisconsin, had managed to talk his way up to the roof of the Fifth Avenue Presbyterian Church directly across from the Gotham. From there, he had both a ringside seat with his army-issued field glasses and a bird's-eye view of the activity on the seventeenth-floor ledge. The following day he would file his eyewitness account.

> I studied the kid carefully through the powerful binoculars I used in the service. From my position, I could see him clearly.
>
> He no longer was the carefree youth he had been reported to be earlier in the day. He had all the appearance of an animal at bay. His eyes were intent and piercing. I felt like I could almost see his heart pounding in his chest.
>
> Warde's gaze darted about from side to side and above and below him as if he were looking for an enemy. Everything seemed erratic. He no longer

was under control. His face was red with a flush that showed through a coating of soot from the smoke in the city.

(Lawrence, 1938)

Lawrence went on to describe in feverish detail the events as they unfolded through his binoculars in play-by-play style—Warde's hands nervously grasping at the corners of the columns behind him "as black as though he had on gloves." Periodically, his hands would slip and slide down the stone wall as his fingernails scraped the limestone. "It made me cringe. His face was sweaty, grimy, almost muddy."

The reporter would later record that Warde would reach cautiously with his left hand for a cigarette extended to him by Patrolman Glasco, after which Warde cupped his hands to light it and then would smoke it frantically in short, rapid, and nervous puffs as they conversed—at least Glasco was. "Warde's feet were pawing at the ledge," he would write. "A panting, animalistic trait could be seen over and over again."

About then, a reporter friend asked him what the time was—it was a little before 9:55 p.m.—and as Lawrence glanced back into his binoculars again, he watched "breathlessly," the rescue net being raised higher and higher from below the ledge. Simultaneously, two men were inching along the same shelf on either side of Warde, though out of Warde's view, and were getting closer and closer to reaching the young man.

> It felt like it was a race with time. Any moment, it seemed, one end of the net would be flipped up, and Warde would be trapped—and saved—perhaps against his will.
>
> I saw there was a strange activity going on, however. Glasco disappeared from view, and then the kid followed him to the window. At the same time, one window above Warde, on the 18th floor of the hotel, a policeman and a fireman were being lowered in life belts, I assume to grab him.
>
> All this activity, you must understand, took place within a few seconds. About the time it would take for a few feet of film to be run off. It was happening very quickly, which seemed quite odd at the time because the day had just crawled along with virtually no action whatsoever. My reporter friend turned and said to me, "I got a bad feeling . . ."

Glasco had, in fact, disappeared back into the room to talk to the men now heading up the rescue effort.

"I don't think we got much time left, Captain. He might not wanna jump, but I think his legs are gonna give out at any minute. He's gettin' weak, and at some point, he'll just fall. I'm pretty sure. So, I came up with a plan. . . . Hear me out.

"He ain't eaten a thing that counts in over ten hours, and he ain't taken a bathroom break or had a bath in all that time. He's livin' on Lucky Strikes and water for the most part. I'm thinkin' that if we promise him that we'll clear out the room and lock the doors, then he can just come in and rest a bit. But we gotta be true to our word. Can't be a trick, or he'll see right through it and do somethin' bad.

"If he comes in, I'll bet'cha dollars to donuts that he'll lie right down there on the bed and just rest his legs a bit. He'd have to. No man wouldn't after being on his feet and not movin' all day. When he lays down, I'll ask if I can come in and talk with him. By that time, he'll just give up, I'm sure of it.

"And if he don't, then I'll just bear hug him until you guys can come in. I don't wanna hurt him, though, and I need a promise from you on that. He's nothin' more than a scared kid that's all mixed up about some feelings he has inside. Some things he needs to work out with his Maker. And there can't be no monkey business in the room neither. If I give him my word, then it's gotta mean something. So, do we got a deal?"

It was a bold request for a traffic cop to make to men who were his superiors at the highest level, but Charley Glasco passionately felt that John's life was in his hands. He would be willing to risk his own career to save the boy.

With no other options, Anderson and the rest of the team said they would consider the plan. Most of his other ideas had failed, though progress was being made through several strategic moves—it was just that they were taking infinitely longer than anyone expected. Aside from Glasco's shot-in-the-dark plan to clear the room and give Warde time to rest and take a shower, there were three fronts upon which Anderson was gambling.

From both sides outside the rooms that had been the center of the day's activities, officers were slowly and stealthy inching their way along the ledge toward John without his knowledge. Blocked by ornamental outcroppings, they were out of view.

The second prong in Anderson's attack involved two expert rescuers being lowered in bosun's chairs by ropes attached to the roof. Again, because of a large overhang, this action was outside of John's line of sight.

Rigging up rescue harnesses, Alpine fashion, the men seated themselves in canvas chairs and were being lowered from windows above. They hoped that the others below could hold Warde's attention while they dropped to his level and snatched him.

Finally, the most extensive effort—which had been in progress for some hours—involved pulling up a massive cargo net, borrowed from a steamship, from one floor below. Now, on the sixteenth floor, one side of the net had already been securely attached to the side of the building. On the opposite edge, ropes were fastened at the corners lowered from the eighteenth floor, one floor above Warde.

The plan—regarded by police as foolproof—was to pull up the net quickly and trap Warde between it and the building before he could react.

Failing this, the net would be pulled out under John's ledge without him being aware of it, so if he leaped, he would be instantly trapped like a butterfly in a net. All of this, however, had been fraught with problems from the beginning.

The net—which was actually two nets stitched together—had gotten tangled in the process of putting it out of the relatively small windows, forcing several men to climb inside the thing and try to straighten it out while dangling more than 180 feet in the air. For most of the last few hours, it was nothing but a giant knot with three men trapped inside.

Still, all three approaches were underway, and Anderson held out hope that one or all of them would do the trick. All he needed was a little more time.

To buy that time and get everything in place, however, the head cop told both Dr. Presner and Charley Glasco to keep Warde entertained for what he thought might be another hour.

Glasco took on the chore and—tearing open a new pack of Phillip Morris cigarettes—started all over right from the beginning. He talked about his wife and kid. They talked about going on vacation, Cubs baseball, and their favorite recreational activities. John shared more about swimming, lying on the beach in the sun, and building up his physique with dumbbell exercises.

Glasco would later comment, "Clearly, John's body was important to him. He went on for some time about how he enjoyed getting the perfect tan and often mentioned the satisfaction he felt from achieving a smooth build with fine muscles. It was the look he was after, not the strength."

The two men continued, with Charley often checking his watch to see how much of the hour he had managed to chew up. It was not going as quickly as he had hoped.

So, they reviewed the batting averages of the Yankees, discussed their mutual dislike for the Dodgers, compared their favorite songs and dramatic shows on the radio, and discussed their favorite meals—and every movie that Charley could think of that he had seen in the last five years.

He passed John cigarettes now and then—always with his left hand. John smoked and listened, but he didn't answer the questions Glasco kept shooting at him. Whenever he finished a cigarette, he dropped the butt on the ledge, carefully extinguished it with his heel, and placed it neatly in the pile of butts he had been gathering.

After Glasco had gone over everything he could think of, he paused. There was nothing else to say after nearly eleven hours of talking.

Then John said, "I really wish someone could have come up with some answers for me . . . for my problem, you know. I really do, Charley. I wish someone had answers for me."

Inside Room 1716, a young man—Andrew Courtney—was talking to the chief inspector. "He's been a friend of John's since they were kids together," Anderson explained to Glasco. "I'm thinking maybe we let his buddy take a crack at him. You take a breather, Charley, and let's see what happens."

With that, Anderson motioned for the friend to head over to the window. "Go ahead, Courtney. See if you can get anywhere with him." The young man went to the window and leaned out. John took a minute or two to recognize him and then said, "So, Andy, what do you want?"

Andrew paused, hunched his shoulders, and said, "I dunno. My parents just sent me up here to talk with you. I don't really got anything to say. So, me and the boys is wondering . . . are you gonna jump or what?"

Warde threw a lit cigarette at his face, and Andrew responded with a crude gesture, which effectively ended that experiment.

Glasco was sitting on the bed and rubbing his left leg, which had gone to sleep. He hoped this last effort would work and, if not, at least he'd get a bit of a break to nurse his tired body.

"How's it with that net?" he asked one of the cops.

"Should be all set in a few minutes, Charley. You think he can see it?"

"No, but I think he'll see those bosun's chairs when they come down from above."

"Well, they'll have that net ready in a few shakes, and then there'll be nothing to worry about."

"Gosh, I sure hope so. It's been quite a day, and still I got all those stubs on my parking tickets to process before I can go home."

With all of Anderson's efforts moving much too slowly or fouled up in some way, Glasco was increasingly feeling at a loss as to how this could end up anything but badly for the NYPD. The commissioner was no doubt watching all of this closely, and the chief inspector knew that he had some skin in the game as well.

However, Anderson had something up his sleeve—a last-ditch effort.

Returning to Glasco's plan of luring Warde into the room with food, soda pop, a hot shower, and a soft bed, he turned to the patrolman and said, "Okay, Charley, let's do your thing. I'll try anything now. You go talk to the kid, and I'll clear the room. And you got my solemn word that there won't be no monkey business, neither."

As the patrolman returned to the window to explain the offer to John, Anderson was busily shooing everyone out of Room 1714 and then shouted back that the room was clear.

But it wasn't.

Chief Inspector Anderson had directed two of his best men—one who had recently won the department's "Fastest Handcuffs Award"—to surreptitiously hide themselves in the suite where they couldn't be detected. One was in the bathroom, where they thought John might head first, and one behind a large sofa divan at the far end of the room, nearly against the wall. Whether he was coming or going, they were certain they could grab him one way or the other.

Glasco, in the meantime, was having a hard time convincing the young man that he could be trusted.

"Johnny, you been out there a pretty long time now, kid. Ten, eleven hours, somethin' like that. I dunno for sure. You must feel awful. You're covered in soot, and your white suit is almost black. Your face looks like mud, son. Look at your nails. . . . You've bitten them down to the elbow almost.

"I'm tired, so you gotta be exhausted. Gotta be starvin' too. You ain't eaten in a long time, and I'm sure you gotta take a piss, so listen up now. I'll make a deal with you.

"Here's what I'm suggestin'. I'll clear out the room in here so it's totally empty. Not a soul. You come in, and I'll have some food here waiting for you. A sandwich or a burger or something. Whatever you like.

"If you want to, you can come in and have a good wash and get that dirt off. You'll be feelin' better in no time. Get freshened up a bit, and then lie down and take a load off.

"Those dogs of yours gotta be barkin' by now. I'll have a couple of cold beers here waitin' for you too. Then, whenever you feel rested up, you can, if you want, just come on back out here on the ledge, or you can call it a night, and I'll drive you home. Okay? That'll be your own decision, though. You decide what you want to do, and I'll be right by your side."

"But how do I know that you'll do it?" John asked. "How do I know this isn't some trick just to get me inside and then jump me?"

"Really, Johnny? Ain't I been straight with you from the get-go? Have I ever lied to you 'bout anything?"

"Well, you did say you were a bellhop, and that wasn't true."

"Okay, you got me there," Officer Charley chuckled at John's quick retort, and that made the kid smile too. "Yeah, all right, I did do that . . . but that was only on account I didn't wanna spook you or nothin' if you didn't like cops for some reason. I was just trying to help, that's all."

"Yeah, yeah, I know. You been straight with me. I'll admit that. You're a good guy, Charley. We've had our moments, for sure, but you're a good guy all the same. But still, how do I know this isn't some setup?"

"Well, John, because I say so. You got my word on it. Anyone who knows me will tell you straight out that my word is my bond. I'll shake on it if that makes a difference to you. Whatever it takes, son. I just know you need some rest.

"And tell you what. You lock the door behind me when I go out. I'll leave the key to the door right here on the window sill so no one can get in or out. You an' me'll have the only keys, and on top of that, I'll guard the door from the outside myself. I won't let nothin' happen to you, John. You got my word on that.

"So look, I'll give you a half hour, and then we'll come back in. This room will be empty for a full thirty minutes. I'll time it. You can look in at any time and see that the room is empty."

To prove his point, Glasco shoved back both sides of the heavy white drapes in the window so that John could see the room was empty. The officer kept pushing hard, believing this was their best chance to resolve the situation.

"Another thing, Johnny, if anyone tries to get in, they'll have to go through me, and there ain't no one that's gonna do that. I was a boxing champ in the infantry, you know. So listen, kid, you gotta be tired. I surely am."

"Yeah, gotta admit I am. I'm pretty tired," Warde responded. "I'm afraid my legs are starting to cramp, and that won't be good for anyone. I'll think it over." His voice and manner were not very friendly, but perhaps it was just utter exhaustion. He looked at his wristwatch and then glanced back at Glasco.

"All right, John, you think it over. If you get cleaned up, I believe you'll find you can think clearer. Here's the key on the sill where only you can get to it. I've pulled back the curtains so you can see for yourself that the room's empty. Be back in thirty minutes. You have my word on it."

"Hey, I'd like a sandwich if that isn't much of a problem. And some cigarettes. Phillip Morris, if it isn't a bother. No beers, though. A soda pop sounds mighty fine, though. But I don't really wanna trouble anyone."

"No bother, son, no bother at all. Just give me a couple of minutes after that to make sure the room is completely clear, the food is delivered, and then I'll give you the high sign, and I'll go out the door. You come lock it right away, and the whole room will be yours for as long as you want. No one else has a key to this room but me."

John nodded and looked at his wristwatch again. Glasco withdrew, walking backward, and then opened the hall door. As he did, the food and drinks were brought in on a silver tray and placed next to the bed on a nightstand.

Minutes later, Glasco shouted, "Okay, Johnny, take it away!" He went out and slammed the door loudly so that there was no mistaking his exit.

Charley Glasco allowed himself a big sigh of relief. The ordeal was finally coming to an end. He was confident he'd be home in time to hold his daughter and enjoy that liver and bacon dinner, certain that the second John stretched out on the bed he'd fall asleep, and in no time the whole thing would all be over. He could tell the kid had given up the fight. He could hear it in his voice.

Outside the door, with his ear pressed up to it, Glasco called back to the men who had been holding the rope that secured him.

"Thirty-minute break, fellas. Grab a smoke or a drink or go to the john. Hopefully this is the end of it, but we'll see." The men scattered, but Glasco kept his hand on the doorknob just in case. He was committed to making sure no one entered, and he was willing to put his own life on the line.

"I want to talk to the boy. I can save him. I have a message from God for him."

Charley Glasco whirled around to see a gaunt man with blazing eyes, wearing a high, stiff collar and the cut of a long coat that had gone out of style years before.

"I can save that boy," the preacher announced. "He doesn't understand the fear of God, that's all. I will explain it to him, and that will save him. I can assure you of that." The man stepped forward forcefully and lurched for the doorknob. Glasco shoved him back violently.

"Sorry about that, Reverend. Nobody but nobody is getting in that room right now. Maybe if you'd call back in an hour or so and ask to talk to the chief inspector personally." The cop was trying to be polite, but he could feel the anger welling up within him. Glasco was intent on protecting Warde at all costs.

The clergyman turned away impatiently, pushing his way through the crowd, and moved down the hall toward the Fifth Avenue end of the building—his Bible waving wildly in the air and Scripture verses spouting from his lips.

Glasco glanced at his watch. Only five of the thirty minutes had passed. Room 1714 was painfully silent.

* * * * *

On the other side of the door, gingerly inching his way toward the window from his perch on the ledge, John crouched down low and peeked into the room, his hands clutching the frame tightly. The room was empty, as promised. Staring for a minute to make sure there was no movement, he dropped one leg over the window sill and steadied himself.

His leg was shaking, quivering, and he wasn't sure at first if he could support himself. He paused to catch his breath.

Next, John pivoted around and sat on the edge of the sill with both legs in the room, his hands on his knees, and his head slightly bowed. He could feel the relief, the calm, the sense of peace washing over him. He lit a cigarette and took in a long and satisfying pull of smoke into his lungs. It was over. He knew it. Charley knew it. The cops outside knew it.

Everyone was ready for this excruciating ordeal to be concluded.

In the safety and security of the empty room, John—his eyes darting in every direction—moved cautiously toward a plate that held a cheese and mayonnaise sandwich. Next to it were some potato chips and a dill pickle slice, along with two orange Nehi sodas.

Outside, there was a roar as the man in the white shirt and pressed slacks suddenly disappeared from view. It was a source of great joy and answered prayers for some and the basis for immense disappointment for others. All those hours, all that time spent, an entire wasted evening—and no one had jumped.

John Warde took a couple of minutes to gather himself and then grabbed one of the chilled orange sodas on the side table next to the bed. He popped off the cap, the cigarette still dangling from his lips.

And then it happened in a split second.

The handcuff expert, peeking from behind the sofa, was stunned to see a gaunt man wearing an old-fashioned clerical collar enter the room through the side door that was connected to Room 1716.

Inexplicably, no one had remembered to lock that door.

Instantly, the crazed man was in the face of an equally shocked John Warde and began shouting in the sing-songy voice of a Pentecostal evangelist.

"The fear of the Lord is the beginning of knowledge, but fools despise wisdom and instruction. The fear of the Lord prolongs life, but the years of the wicked will be shortened. The fear of the Lord is to hate evil and pride and arrogance and the perverted mouth! Son, the fear of the Lord . . ."

For a second, everyone froze.

Then, immediately leaping from behind the sofa, the first of the hidden officers bolted toward the preacher in a full sprint. At the same time, the bathroom door flew open and the second cop came flying out squarely in Warde's direction with handcuffs in hand.

Startled, John dropped the soda to the floor and knocked over the plate of food in the process as his arms extended with open palms to signal the man to stop. At the same time, he took a few backward steps in the direction of the open window without ever taking his eyes off the policemen.

Outside the door to Room 1714, someone yelled over to Charley that something was happening in the room and he'd better get over there quickly. At the time, Glasco was on the hotel phone telling his wife to heat up his liver and bacon dinner. She was just starting to ask what had happened to end it all when he heard the commotion.

Dropping the receiver, he took off in a dead sprint toward the door and broke through it. As he did, he saw that the people in the room were in a standoff: four people in a triangle staring each other down in complete silence.

Forgetting the preacher, who was now being dragged out of the room by a couple of officers from Room 1716, the cop with the handcuffs took a step toward a visibly frightened John and scowled.

"Look, buddy boy, the gig's up. Ain't nowhere else to turn now, fella, because as soon as you make a move, we'll be all over you. It's all over now—hear me?—and that's good for you, see. You'll be in the nuthouse, but at least you won't be a flapjack on the sidewalk."

Cringing at those words, Charley Glasco, however, put an end to that.

"What the hell's going on? Where did you guys come from!" Glasco was furious. John Warde was shaken and trembling. "You guys get outta here, leave me and John alone! I made a promise to the boy and intend to keep it."

Then, turning to Warde, he began to plead.

"I'm awful sorry, John. That idiot got in by mistake. He sneaked into the next room on me and came in here through the side door. I thought it was locked. There's just so many people in that next room, they didn't even notice him. I swear it won't happen again. C'mon now. Won't you give it another try, please?"

As he said it, Glasco knew there would be no other chances.

He had taken his shot, and fate had cruelly intervened in the form of a fire-breathing evangelist and betrayal by his brothers in blue. John's eyes were transfixed on Glasco. He appeared heartbroken. The one thing he could not handle was betrayal.

"Charley, you promised me," he nearly sobbed. "But you promised me it wasn't a setup! Who are these guys? What are you doing to me? Why would you do this?"

"Listen up, kid," the officer with the handcuffs said sternly. "It's all over now. Just kneel down right there, and let's take you somewhere where you can get some help." John would have none of it. He had backed up toward the large open window again, both of his arms outstretched, though they barely reached the side frames.

"Charley, Charley, you promised me. You gave me your word. I trusted you. Oh my God, it was all a trap, and I fell for it. Charley, you betrayed me!" John had his head in his hands. He was crushed.

"But I didn't, Johnny. I didn't! I swear to you. I didn't know nothin' about these men. I had no idea. The captain lied to me. He promised me there would be no tricks, no monkey business. They lied to me, too, John. . . . I'm as upset as you are."

There was desperation in the officer's voice. He could feel things slipping away. "You can trust me, Johnny. I promise. I had no idea about any of this. I'll never let it happen again if you just trust me. Please, Johnny!"

Glasco could see the kid's eyes darting around as if nothing was certain to him any longer. The ground beneath him had turned to sand. The fragile hold that he had on sanity seemed to be crumbling. As Glasco was begging him not to do anything rash, John put one foot behind him up on the bottom of the window sill, then lifted himself into it.

Now crouched in the rectangular space, he was perfectly framed by the white starched curtains and illuminated from behind by a giant spotlight.

For a split second, he was nothing more than a perfectly outlined silhouette, poised and still, as if he was posing for an avant-garde portrait.

Down on the street, the crowds had earlier begun to dissipate. The show was over. The kid didn't have the guts to take the plunge—at least, that was what they were saying. Nearly two hundred police officers were still milling around doing traffic control and smoking on the sidewalk in front of the entrance to the Gotham.

Hot dog and roasted nuts vendors and the pretzel pushcart had given up some time ago, and there was no more business for the opera glasses salesman. The night air was still, cold, and indifferent.

The spotlight continued to be trained on the blank spot on the ledge that John Warde had manned for nearly eleven hours without flinching.

Inside the window frame, however, John Warde held his position, his eyes boring in hard on Glasco—the man he had called his friend. Charley's hands were outstretched toward him. The two officers in the room had pushed themselves against the back wall.

"I couldn't have stopped them if I wanted to," Glasco continued to plead. "You gotta believe me, Johnny. I had nothing to do with this trap. Nothing! But now this is just between us . . . you and me, Johnny. No one else."

Glasco turned to the two officers at the back of the room. "Hey, you two jokers, get outta here! You hear me? Get the hell outta here now. This is just between me and the kid from now on. No detectives. No brass. No trick plays anymore. Just me and John here and not another soul from here on. So clear the room! Go on, get outta here, pronto!"

Like whipped and cowering puppies, the two men who had failed at their job left the room without saying a word. In seconds, it was once again only the two lead characters in what was increasingly feeling like the final act in a prolonged drama. In a few seconds, Dr. Presner entered the doorway of Room 1716. He didn't say a word, and the room was filled with tension.

Charley took one small step toward the window, his arms still reaching out like a compassionate father calling his frightened child.

John's frame visibly tightened.

Charley took a second step and said, "C'mon, buddy. You can trust me. None of this was my doing. I won't let anyone hurt you. I'll take you home to meet the missus if you want. You can stay with me for a while. Just relax and get better, you know. You can have a picnic with us. You know, just like we talked about. My little girl would love to meet you."

"Really?" John answered. "You think she'd like me?" There was a softness about him now. Perhaps a sense of surrender that ushered in some relief. "Maybe I could be her Uncle John or something like that. Think maybe I could?"

"Yeah, sure, Johnny. She'd love you, I'm tellin' you. You could give her piggyback rides. . . . She'd love that. And you know what I was thinkin'?"

Before Glasco finished his thought, John stood up full frame in the window and offered a wry but problematic smile. Taking the cigarette in his right hand, he looked at it briefly, rolling it in his fingers—and then, looking directly into the eyes of his friend, he said, "I know what to do now. I know what I'm supposed to do."

For a brief second—with feet together, arms outstretched on both sides, and head down—he looked like a crucifix frozen in time.

Then, gazing at Dr. Presner, he said, "I wish you could have convinced me that life is worth living. It was all you ever had to do."

13 Hour Eleven

It was exactly 10:35 p.m. when a photographer decided to take a running start halfway down the corridor that led to Room 1714 and managed to slice around Chief Inspector Alexander Anderson, Captain William O'Brien, and Captain Pat McDonald. Without stopping, he rushed past Charley Glasco and dropped to one knee with his camera pointed squarely at the man frozen in the window frame.

He knew it would be the shot of a lifetime.

His flashbulb went off with a loud pop, momentarily blinding everyone in the room.

With that, John stepped backward out of the window and held on to the bottom of the frame for a few seconds. Smiling at Charley Glasco in a kindly, grateful way that would remain with the seasoned cop forever, he said, "I've made up my mind."

Tragically, while fireman George McKenna and Patrolman Albert Miller were being lowered slowly from above, one of their feet scraped on the upper cornice. Warde heard the sound. His eyes darted up, and he saw McKenna's foot. He then glanced up to his right and saw the form of Miller being lowered toward him. The feet of the two men were almost level with his shoulders.

Next, he pivoted and took one half step toward the edge of the ledge, where the searchlight illuminated him once again in a giant circle as he flipped his cigarette out into the night air.

As the street exploded with cheers, the crowds instantly rushed back to their original positions and held their collective breaths. Looking down at them, he glanced back over his shoulder at Officer Glasco and spoke one last time. "The show must go on."

Facing the abyss, John William Warde stood on his tiptoes with his hands high overhead, his hands touching at their tips like a world-class diver.

Then he simply stepped out in perfect form into the night sky of Manhattan to the pops of a thousand flashbulbs.

Dropping feet first and straight down, his hands now at his sides, he appeared like a stone statue as he plummeted silently and solemnly downward.

Someone in the crowd screamed, "There he goes!"

Two floors under the ledge, the men who had been feverishly trying to fix the net underneath the seventeenth floor watched him sail by—just a foot from landing in the rope net—as one of the workers made a valiant lunge for him. The man just missed by a fraction of an inch.

If Warde had waited even a minute longer, he couldn't have escaped the net. It was just about in a position to close in around him when he fell. But to John Warde, it was the difference between now and forever.

Charles Leischner, an investment broker living just blocks away at the Essex House, would give a graphic eyewitness account of the leap in the *New York Daily News* on the same day. In an article titled "11-Hour Vigil on Ledge."

> I could see the policemen climbing out from the windows on the seventeenth floor. They were walking sideways with their arms stretched out against the back wall to maintain their balance. With every step, they were getting closer and closer. They were almost ready to reach him.

> With the men being lowered from above by ropes connected to a bosun's chair, and the giant net coming up from below, it looked like he was being hemmed in on all sides—except straight ahead. I'd have said they'd have him in a few minutes—maybe less—and then the show would be over.

Leischner's comments would reflect that of others from that day. Although many were crying out cruelly for the man to take the plunge, most felt that in the end he would not do it, that either from fear or boredom he would simply give up the ordeal and eventually climb back inside with the aid of his policeman friend. It was at that point, however, that the mood on the ground began to change.

> Suddenly—and as calmly as if he was enjoying a pleasant summer evening on the veranda—he stepped to the edge, stood there for a brief instant and looked out over the city skyline. Next, his eyes went down to the crowd that was chanting at him . . . and he just took off with the red ember of his cigarette preceding him.

> He plunged out and down, a tremendous leap, it seemed—barely missing the net stretched out below him by inches as a policeman lurched in his direction. It appeared to me to take a very long time before he reached the bottom, though I'm not sure in reality how long it actually took. It seemed like fully two or three minutes to me, though, I would say.

A magnesium flare was set off by one of the newsreel cameramen to catch the falling body on film. As he descended in full view of thousands of mesmerized onlookers, his body was outlined by hundreds of flashbulbs that were popping simultaneously and creating an eerie nighttime visual for the eager spectators that stretched out in every direction. Leischner's eyewitness account continued:

> The explosive flashes of the cameramen's bulbs outlined the slender, falling figure in mid-flight—not really in a dive but plunging straight down, hands at his sides, like a dead, inanimate weight. Shrieks and screams and moans came from all around me and filled the air like the sound of a locomotive.
>
> Several women by my side fainted and collapsed and subsequently were badly trampled as there was an immediate rush to get a better vantage point of the body coming down. In the background, I could hear the sirens of ambulances coming for the ladies.

The scene quickly changed to what was happening on the ground. After a collective gasp and a brief pause, the spectators rushed forward and into the path of the falling body as if it were a prize or a celebrity stepping into their midst.

> At least a hundred policemen—all with arms linked—as well as mounted police were trying desperately to hold back the crowd for fear the madman should kill even more in his leap by landing on those of us who were watching from below in addition to himself.
>
> The officers were crushed by the surging and unstoppable mob who swept them aside like little more than straw.
>
> It felt to me as if it took a full three minutes for the body to fall and that it appeared to almost be moving in slow motion, so captivating was the scene. I tried but simply could not manage to pull my eyes away.

Shortly after this, Warde grazed a stone shelf outcropping that jutted out from the sixth floor and flipped him forward, end over end, until he was once again descending feet first as before.

Continuing to fall at a high rate of speed, he hit the hotel marquee—a large steel and glass overhang with ornate ironwork that covered the sidewalk entrance to the Gotham.

Landing first on his stomach, his knees broke the glass top and crashed into the front edge with such thunderous force that it shattered and bent a large section of the ornamental steel scrollwork and showered the nearest bystanders with glass shards. The body, reportedly, struck the solid marquee with such force that it swayed back and forth momentarily—appearing to be on the verge of total collapse—and was left dripping with blood.

Both of Warde's shoes flew off high in the air—the shoelaces ripped apart—and landed in the crowd, which leaped for them as if for a bride-tossed garter at a wedding reception. They became two of the most treasured souvenirs of the day.

For a grotesque instant, the body hung half over the outer ledge of the damaged marquee under the harsh light of streetlamps and the eerie flicker of the flares of newsreel men. Then it agonizingly and slowly toppled to the street, where Warde landed face first on the curb of the sidewalk pavement, his head and arms ingloriously falling into the gutter as thousands gasped in horror.

One bystander had just arrived at the scene after an evening Broadway show and had been casually walking through the crowd when Warde jumped. He would later describe that the man fell like a ton of bricks—so swiftly that he could hardly follow the body until it struck the marquee. But after that, it seemed to him that the body moved in slow motion, noting that it felt as if it took five minutes for it to fall the mere twenty feet from the marquee to the street.

A second explosion of flashbulbs immediately went off, illuminating the entire scene and showing horrified police officers' and bystanders' expressions at the moment they realized what they had just witnessed.

The police officers, who had been enjoying a cigarette while they were shooting the bull and waiting for their shift to be over, were suddenly sprayed with blood when the marquee exploded over them, and they were dripping with it. Warde missed hitting, by a few feet, Homicide Squad Lieutenant John Moffett, who was just walking out from under the overhang.

The massive spotlight, which had formerly been trained on John's perch on the ledge, quickly reignited and turned to put a tight circle of brilliant incandescent light on the badly battered corpse. Blood began to gush out in every direction.

A priest sprang forward to administer the last rites, but John was well beyond hope. The priest knelt at his side for a moment, crossed himself, and then walked away, wiping his eyes.

The crowd began to scream and howl in unison. Glasco later told reporters that it sounded like the roar at the beginning of a horse race as soon as the announcer yells, "And they're off!"

Spectators who had pushed and shoved their way to hold spots along the front line next to the police barriers were sprayed with blood. Those closest to the body began to vomit. Several more women fainted. Others backed away with their handkerchiefs over their faces.

And then everything was silent, as if all of the air on earth had been sucked in and no one had exhaled yet.

When they came to their senses, the insatiable mob broke through the police lines and rushed toward the body, surrounding it in a giant circle that was reportedly thousands deep. Then, in a vain attempt to control the melee that was developing as the crowd rushed forward, the police also went into action.

Officers mounted on horseback galloped into the crowd and drove them back momentarily. Thousands still managed to duck inside the ropes. "The show's all over," the police said sarcastically as the mob swelled forward, not realizing they were echoing Warde's final words. "You can go home now. There's nothing to see here."

Leischner's article continued with a report from a bystander:

> The newsreel cameramen set off a second set of flares just as he crashed, which created a large volume of sparks and smoke that went high into the air and cast a red, hellish glow on the proceedings. The smell of sulfur was gagging. People were vomiting and then slipping on it.
>
> But people were crazed, desperate to see the body of the man they had been watching for so long. It was almost as if the crowd had been thrilling to a highwire trapeze performer at a circus who was working without a net . . . and then fell.

A second group was now rushing toward the hotel's entrance—pushing Sergeant Sean Murphy and other officers; Walter Vickers, the doorman; and valets out of the way—to hurriedly gather pieces of shattered glass.

In an eerie twist, shortly after John's leap, the new moon suddenly appeared in the night sky over the top of the Gotham, and in its bright light, souvenir hunters madly scrambled for bits of the broken marquee. One bystander remembered being approached by an obviously enthusiastic young man who held up a piece of glass with a wet, reddish tinge, exclaiming proudly: "Looky . . . I got me one!"

Giving the dozens of photographers, who had maintained a long vigil, enough time to grab their shots—a moment they had patiently waited for—they were soon joined by motion-picture men who began to grind away with their cameras as flares brightened the area. A man rushed in momentarily, turned the body over to snap a photo, and then returned it to its original position.

The police covered the body with the perforated red rubber mats from the hotel's entrance. Within seconds, a man rushed to the body, pulled away the mats, slipped Warde's wallet from the rear pocket of his trousers, and took off at a dead run.

The photos from this time provide a graphic representation of the sad and tragic end of John William Warde. Face down on the pavement, his starched white shirt and perfectly coiffed hair stand in sharp contrast to the true horror of the scene—his legs splayed out awkwardly at right angles from each other, and one arm curled toward his head as if he was viewing his flight to death.

Looking at it all from above, Charley Glasco was peering down at the tragic scene from the window in Room 1714. He burst into tears and collapsed on the floor in front of the window.

Dr. Presner went over to the officer and put both of his hands on the devastated man's shoulders without saying a word. There was nothing to say. Sitting there with his head in his hands, Glasco became aware that the chief inspector was now standing in front of him. Looking down at his officer, he said, "You did a good job, Charley. You acquitted the department well."

After a minute, Glasco pulled himself together. Then he turned without saying a word, put on his uniform cap, and attached his shield, pistol holster, and cartridge belt. Everyone in the room was staring at him. Not a word was spoken.

As he passed the photographer in the room, Glasco grabbed his camera and threw it against the wall, where it shattered, and the film uncurled into the light of the room. The photograph that cost a man his life was, fittingly, lost forever.

Making his way down to the ornate lobby of the Hotel Gotham, Glasco placed the bellboy uniform on the front desk and left the building without saying a word. Trying to forge a path through the now dense crowds, he cast a quick glance in the direction of John's body but couldn't bear to linger on it. "The pain, the loss was too great, I guess," he later reported.

Eventually, he checked back in at the station, where he put his gun, holster, and cap in his locker and then settled in behind one of the generic desks reserved for members of the traffic squad. There, he pulled out his leather book that contained the summons stubs from the tickets he had written.

After calling his wife, Maggie, and telling her to give up on the liver and bacon, Patrolman Charles Glasco spent the next three and a half hours doing clerical work on his summonses.

It was 4:15 a.m. when he finally walked through the front door of his Queens home.

Back at the scene, the New York Fire Department was bringing in large fire hoses to clean the pavement as the police forced everybody away from the area. After less than an hour, the crowd began to disperse—other than those who wandered by to point at a crimson-hued spot on the pavement—and soon New York began to forget John Warde.

14 After Hours

Shortly after midnight, John Warde's body was moved to an ambulance that had been parked ten feet away in front of the hotel since early in the afternoon and taken directly to the West Forty-Seventh Street Police Station. The officers in charge chose not to wait for the medical examiner to come to the scene, fearing that the mob would try to extract souvenirs from the corpse.

At the precinct station, the mangled body was placed in the back storage room on a makeshift table made of a sheet of plywood resting on two sawhorses. Throughout the middle of the night and into the early morning hours, a steady stream of cops, reporters, and their family members came through to view the flattened figure.

Those who came described it later as "little more than pulp, his face was completely flattened, his body looking more like a large sack filled with . . . mash. Every bone in his body was obviously broken. It was hard to think of him as ever having been human."

The next morning the corpse was transferred to the county morgue and then was sent to the New York and Brooklyn Funeral Home at 187 South Oxford Street in Brooklyn, where it was held awaiting direction from the family.

It would be two full days before the mortuary was notified and given direction on the disposition of the remains—a fact with which the newspapers had a field day. Repeatedly reporting that "the body has been left unclaimed," readers were left with the impression that the young man was such an embarrassment to the socially prominent Wardes that they could not bear to acknowledge him or deal with the horribly unpleasant situation.

Eventually, John's sister dealt with the uncomfortable responsibility.

During this time, the mortician said he received hundreds, if not thousands, of calls requesting to see Warde's body, which was displayed unclothed on a metal table. All were refused, but not all were turned away.

At the same time, New York City Deputy Mayor Henry Curran presided over a press conference where he shook Charley Glasco's hand and praised him—

with tears in his own eyes—for "one of the finest pieces of police work I've ever witnessed." Photos were taken, congratulations were shared, and a citation of commendation was awarded.

The morning front pages of nearly six hundred newspapers nationwide were emblazoned with three-inch-tall letters featuring sensational headlines along the lines of:

Man Thrills Thousands with Leap to Death
Bored New Yorkers Thrill to Plunge
New York Boredom Shattered by Suicide
After 11 Hours of Tedium, Onlookers Gasp at Leap
Man Thrills Crowd on Hotel Ledge before Tumble
Manhattan Watches Man Take Life in 200-Foot Leap
Thousands Gape at Spectacular Leap from Hotel Ledge
Gibes-Wisecracks Reach Jumper on Ledge
Thousands See Maniac Leap from Hotel Ledge
Morbid Man Ends 11 Hours of Indecision
Crowd's Gibes Turn to Gasps as Man Reaches Fatal Decision
Psychopath Provides Perverted Entertainment for New Yorkers
Maniac Stares Down at Death Ravine
100,000 in Horror Watch Man Die in Leap off Ledge
Psychopath Killed after Standing on Narrow Ledge
Joking Crowd's Laughs Turn to Screams

Both the Associated Press and William Randolph Hearst's International News Service—which would later become United Press International—immediately picked up the story. By the following day, it headlined every major newspaper in America and many worldwide. The articles were accompanied by garish and unfiltered photos—often taking up half of a full-sized newspaper page—which ran for several pages.

John William Warde, unknown throughout his lifetime, suddenly became a name and a figure recognized throughout the world in death.

Within minutes after his tragic seventeen-story suicide plunge, news services had carried the story around the world via telegraph and cable. In far-off Tokyo and Manila, in Berlin, Vienna, Rome, and London, down in South America and Australia, they read of John Warde, playboy son of a well-connected, wealthy family.

An almost magazine-length article went over Canadian Press wires to every province in Canada. Still, the readers asked for more.

The Reuters news agency cabled several lengthy stories to Great Britain. At least two London dailies received exclusive cables with accounts written by their New York correspondents.

Deutsches Nachrichtenbüro, the German news agency, reported that every major city in the country carried the story, and it was broadcast by both radio and television. The Havas news agency sent a detailed article to every French newspaper. The Japanese news agency Domel flashed news of the leap to Tokyo.

The Associated Press, besides the comprehensive coverage delivered to its domestic outlets, relayed the news to its South American members, including Mexico City and Havana, where newsreel footage was being airlifted to those markets overnight.

Discovering that their readers couldn't get enough of the sordid story, the publishers accommodated them by running multiple articles for days on end—usually several at a time—which included firsthand accounts and recorded conversations by reporters who had been embedded in Room 1716 nearly from the first minutes of the ordeal.

Over time, these grew in sensational content and included "never before revealed" information that titillated subscribers, while newsboys hawked the headlines from street corners.

As one might expect, there were also a series of moral judgments and editorials that decried both the sadness of mental illness—while conjecturing wildly on its causes—and the shocking reaction of a morbid crowd that was desperate to be satiated by a man's jump to his death. To some, John was a sympathetic hero. To others, he was a selfish villain.

Writer Joel Sayre, who reintroduced the story to a new generation on the tenth anniversary of Warde's tragic fall, wrote about the event on April 16, 1949, in his "That Was New York" column in the *New Yorker*.

> The next day, the nation's newspapers broke out with a rash of some of the worst editorials in the history of American journalism.
>
> The most offensive of these seemed to fall into three categories: those which compared John to the European dictators teetering on the brink of war; those which compared Patrolman Glasco to Neville Chamberlain trying to make Adolf Hitler see reason; and those which deplored mob hysteria.
>
> With a certain hypocritical irony, virtually all the newspapers which sermonized over sensationalism and mob hysteria with great alarm, simultaneously ran the ghastly pictures of John's broken body lying on the sidewalk.

These editorials, however, provide a priceless snapshot of the thinking of the time. In 1938, Hitler was beginning his rise to power in Europe while most Americans were supporting the nation's isolationist policies. President Franklin Roosevelt—his hands full trying to pull America out of the Great Depression—was caught in the crossfire.

Thus—for no logical reason—John Warde's act was imbued with political overtones and grandiose messaging that would never have crossed the mind of the poor, troubled young man smoking cigarettes in the evening air. Others, taking a more moralistic and sociological perspective, decried the darkness of humanity on display by the voracious mob that hungrily feasted on John's misery and mental illness.

Three days after the fatal event, an editor for the *Zanesville (OH) Signal* posted his thoughts on the matter under the headline "Audience to Violence."

> You may have already forgotten by now who John Warde was. There are several thousand who haven't, and who won't for the rest of their days. These are the people whom nearly 1,000 policemen tried to send away.
>
> They rented binoculars, they bought ice cream and peanuts, they laid wagers on what John Warde would do. These are the people who, for hour after hour, jammed the streets around the Hotel Gotham in New York, hung out of windows, and gathered on neighboring roofs. They shouted and cheered, and laughed, and yelled wisecracks—while some of them fainted. And yet they all kept staring and held their ground.
>
> John Warde, of course, was the young man who threw himself off of a stone ledge after an 11-hour standoff from a 17th-floor window.
>
> The young man, since his adolescence, apparently had an overwhelming conviction of personal inferiority which gave him the viewpoint that no effort was worthwhile, that life was not worth living. Though he was intelligent, well-mannered, and came from a socially prominent and quite wealthy family, his depressive mania made him seem "strange and queer" to others.
>
> Friends said today that all the efforts and pleadings, all the prayers of the approximately 100,000 persons who had looked up from the street at the dizzy height where he was perched, all the ingenuity of the technicians who devised a half dozen schemes to save him, had been doomed from the beginning to failure because the young man was deeply troubled within.
>
> For most of a very long day, John Warde could not make up his mind whether to leap to death or climb back safely inside. Firemen and police beseeched him to come on in, but there he clung on for hours.
>
> Thousands in the street below blocked traffic.
>
> The cameras clicked, and the television transmitter picked up his figure.
>
> It was very exciting.
>
> It was great publicity—whether the man died or lived.
>
> Living might have meant a ride up Fifth Avenue as a hero. Maybe offers by the radio, movies, and newspapers. Certain celebrity.
>
> Instead, Warde jumped to death. He settled his problems permanently.

Just as interesting was the reaction of New Yorkers—and presumably the tourists in town as well. New York folks seldom seem bothered by pressing business. They always have time for parades and spectacles.

The thousands who watched Warde for hours expected, of course, to be rewarded for their patience and thrilled by his jump. Otherwise, there would be no reason to hang around merely to see a person on a skyscraper ledge.

That, apparently, must be rather common.

But here . . . here was curiosity, anticipation, and the irresistible lure of death.

Such is the way with crowds—the "mob mentality," as it has been called. A most pleasant dread. Delightfully hypnotized by terror. A rather welcome change from the boring routine of daily life.

This, no doubt, is the explanation for the glorious greetings given to heroes of war and those that entertain us through daring circus acts as well as motion pictures that trade in exaggerated melodrama.

It should be no surprise then that mankind would thrill to the bizarre, to the dangerous, to the mystery and dreadful uncertainty of a young man teetering between life and death.

"I know I look like a fool," Warde remarked, a little while before he jumped. "Life does not hold anything for me now."

If John Warde looked like a fool, he had company. And you can be sure that life holds just a little less for those oglers and bug-eyed spectators now than it did.

Shame on you.

But not all journalists saw the events of that day through the same lens. While some were overcome with compassion, and others disgusted by the circus-like atmosphere of gawking New Yorkers, a few editors introduced other, somewhat perplexing perspectives.

In the throes of the Great Depression, and with a new Democratic president, Franklin Delano Roosevelt, elected to his second term of office, the nation was frightened and angry, and Republican leaders were quick to lay the blame on FDR's economic policies. Warde was almost always described as unemployed, although that had nothing at all to do with his choices on that day. Instead, it was a political indictment.

Most of the publishers of the day were proud members of the GOP. Thus, it was not surprising—though it was fascinating—that immediately after John Warde's fall to his death, the newspapers began publishing outraged editorials pointing the blame at Roosevelt's administration.

In such a highly charged political arena, the writers of these columns—and there were many—overlooked the role of mental illness to take an easy shot at the economic situation of the time as the cause for Warde's despondency and eventual death.

In St. Joseph, Missouri, the readers of the city newspaper were treated to the following editorial—a thinly veiled attack on the "minimum wage," which had only become law months earlier, as the ultimate cause for John Warde's desire to end his life.

John Warde as a Symbol
St. Joseph (MO) News-Press
Wednesday, July 27, 1938

> New York's precipitous skyscrapers, roaring subway trains and lofty bridges invite suicides, but rarely one so spectacular as John Warde's crowd-thrilling plunge last night.
>
> He selfishly chose an impeccably fashionable hotel alongside Manhattan's broadest, proudest thoroughfare—a spot in full view of all who would see—for his life's last drama. For 11 hours, he tied up traffic, paralyzed the business of the ritzy shops at his feet, engaged the attention of hundreds of policemen, and disrupted the routing of the ultraconservative Hotel Gotham.
>
> The scene that was witnessed by thousands, perhaps tens of thousands, of gawking spectators who followed with morbid interest the death watch that played out at an agonizingly slow pace along the edge of a New York hotel this week was horrific by any standard in civilized society.
>
> The more disturbing thought is that there may be, in this country, vast numbers of other John Wardes who, in moments of despondency, are entertaining plans of self-destruction. To this particular John Warde, just twenty-six years of age, the future looked dark. Too dark to live . . . but there was an even darker hand behind that decision, which may be invisible for most to see.
>
> It was a cowardly escape, moralists will tell us, but John Warde, emotionally disturbed and despondent, had coldly reasoned it out, had counted the cost, and to him, there seemed less horror in a plunge from the 17th floor of the Hotel Gotham than in prolonging the series of disappointments that had marked his life.
>
> Unquestionably there are, in every populous community, young men and women who will have no difficulty in adopting John Warde's point of view. Sentiments he expressed while clinging to that dizzy ledge have found their way into graduation essays and baccalaureate sermons. These are, without any doubt, singularly difficult times for American youth.
>
> Fortunately, few of them will be cowards like John William Warde.

Instead, the vast majority will have the moral stamina to face the music and fight it out. But, no doubt, scores of thousands of them are in a position to empathize with the young man who leaped to his death.

They know what it means to hunt for jobs and hunt them in vain. Everybody is deeply concerned over the plight of these young people, most of whom are idealistic, energetic and eager to take their place in the world of affairs but are unable to find that place of fulfillment.

The cause of their condition, of course, is economic.

The cure, when found, will be economic.

It is the tragedy of the United States that in its moment of greatest need, there should befall us a Democratic Administration that is utterly unable to perceive that the old remedies for depression, tried and proved, are the best after all, however barren they may be of dramatic appeal.

And this Administration has at its head a chief magistrate in Roosevelt who rejects wise counsel as uninspiring. "Panaceas" he calls the proposals of his political opponents. He demands novelties and experiments at a fabulous cost. To mention just one of them—the so-called "minimum wage"—is designed to "stabilize employment" but, in practice, puts employment at any wage beyond the reach of millions.

John William Warde was no doubt a casualty of such irresponsible and misguided economic thinking. How many lives of young, talented and hard-working men like Warde will be lost before the Democrats realize the costly error of their ways.

But a government doing these things, says the man in the White House, is a "government with a soul." It is a government working actively, he tells the young people, "to find an answer to your problem."

Relay that sentiment to Mr. Warde, I say.

John Warde is, in fact, typical of a large group of American youth. Few will follow his example—hopefully—but there are moments when they will have his outlook and when they will long for the old-fashioned Republican virtues in statecraft that encouraged—did not fight and destroy—the only agencies and institutions we have that are able to provide real jobs and keep the wheels of industry turning.

Mr. President, the body of John Warde lies at your feet.

This cynical interpretation of an unquestionably tragic event was echoed throughout many articles and editorials of the time from coast to coast. The disturbed nature of this handsome, wealthy, and entitled young man was evidently an affront to the "normal" white, Protestant, heterosexual, religious citizens of the day.

The idea that someone could "have everything" and yet be profoundly unhappy shook their underpinnings and, for some reason, left them angry—as if John had personally attacked their worlds. As if his "selfish and self-centered motives" were designed to be a slap in their faces.

John Warde's One Big Moment
Muncie (IN) Evening Press
Monday, August 1, 1938

> All of John Warde's life had been one of frustration. Or if not, he thought so. Even two previous attempts at suicide had left him as a failure. Living had become meaningless largely because his mind had become warped, and his self-blinded vision could see no future.
>
> Sensitive, shy, depressed—a victim of an inferiority complex—he never had been in a position to attract the attention of anybody of importance. Certainly, not many young ladies of his age.
>
> Few, except his relatives, knew he was even alive. But he decided that, whatever the cost, he would have his "one big moment"—a harrowing moment that dragged out into 11 hours, to be sure, but big.
>
> So he crawled out upon the balcony at the seventeenth story of a New York hotel in the downtown sector, perched himself perilously, and pretended to jump so that all the attention of Manhattan would be upon him.
>
> Sure enough, somebody saw him, and soon, thousands gathered in front of his perch to see whether he would indeed make the jump. Bookmakers bet two to one he wouldn't. Then, they switched: two to one, he would. Back and forth they went throughout the day.
>
> Soon ambulances and fire engines rolled to the scene, policemen appeared by the hundreds, nets were spread to catch him if he jumped. Many got near to him and pleaded with him to live.
>
> Thousands milled about the streets below, hawkers sold their wares, storekeepers shut up shop to join the throngs. To all pleas to step inside the hotel room, he turned a deaf ear.
>
> It was his one great moment, and he purposed not to be cheated out of it. He must have enjoyed his grim triumph, the great suspense, the knowledge that, for the time being, he was the focus of thousands of eyes, the center of the day's news of an entire nation.
>
> Finally, when it appeared he was about to be netted as a bird is trapped, John Warde cowardly acted. He jumped, and in a minute or two, his bruised, battered, lifeless body lay upon the sidewalk.

But, assuredly, he had his one day of stark, dramatic living, even if the price was tragedy. Not everybody has that moment. John Warde sure did.

The Curious Case of John Warde
Coos Bay (OR) World
Thursday, July 28, 1938

It was only in death that John Warde, 26, could find any triumph in life. Defeated in his ambitions, morose and moody, he stood for 11 hours on a hotel ledge while threatening to jump. Crowds gathered. Onlookers urged him to go back to his room. Others called for him to take the leap.

Finally, he obliged the latter.

Today, no person called to claim his body. He is now as alone in death as he was in life.

It is a weird case, to say the least, but psychologists have an explanation for it. Resentful of life's treatment of him, Warde resolved to gain attention—even acclaim—in death. In the end, he was nothing more than a selfish, self-centered fellow and all the ills of life were mirrored in his own mind.

But there is a bit of Warde in us all if we could give it play. Life can be, and often is, cruel for most people. Walk down Broadway or Market Street and note the faces—the scars of life on tired faces, the fear, the pain.

It is not strange that New York City reports more than one thousand suicides annually. These are men and women who could not stand the buffeting of life. These are the weak and frail. The feeble-minded and the spineless. Those that fear their own shadows. Who jump at the sound of a mouse's squeak.

However, the men and women who survive the battle of life—and who win regardless of circumstances—are not the self-pitiers, the envious or the jealous. Life jostles them about, but their hearts are strong. The mind refuses, on their part, to believe that their ills are more than the common ups and downs of this mortal existence.

For John Warde, there should be pity. Pity because he might have found in his span of life enough joy and beauty to drown out his own moodiness. Only to such people can the world give acclaim.

But, oh no, that is not John Warde.

His notoriety is only of today. Tomorrow, it will be forgotten. A big city is cruel. Life bustles on. It never pauses for the weak and whining among us. For while Warde was debating his own cowardly extermination, hundreds of new lives were being ushered in for their golden chance at eternal sunshine.

In another piece distributed nationwide, a popular columnist saw John William Warde as little more than an egotistical, self-involved spoiled child from the Hamptons who had never learned the value of hard work and self-discipline.

Instead, from this writer's perspective, he was selfish enough to play out his inner turmoil on Manhattan's grand stage because it was guaranteed to place the maximum number of eyes on him for the greatest number of hours.

Worse yet, he was costing businessmen thousands of dollars in revenue while mocking them.

One Man Halts Thousands
The Missoulian (MT)
Thursday, July 28, 1938

> It was very evident that John Warde wanted to die. He was unemployed and his reasoning powers had become sufficiently tangled so that he saw no hope in the future. Also, John Warde wanted to die in the most spectacular manner possible. It apparently was his desire that as many persons as possible should witness his death.
>
> Warde went to the seventeenth floor of a New York hotel and crawled out on the ledge between two windows. There, feverishly smoking cigarette after cigarette, the young man matched wits with those who would have saved him from himself. He was there for more than ten hours.
>
> Now see what can happen, even in a city as blase as New York.
>
> Nearly a thousand policemen were summoned to the immediate district surrounding the hotel in the effort to keep traffic moving. Rescue squads were called from both police and fire departments. But none could offer a feasible scheme to get to the young man who was standing on the very end of the ledge.
>
> In the meantime, office windows commanding a view of the scene were filled by excited clerks and stenographers. All work was suspended; even lunch was forgotten as these waited for the expected leap. Movie cameras were kept trained on the scene. Not one of the morbid wanted to miss the jump.
>
> Finally police hit upon what seemed to be a possible chance. They secured a huge net from the Coast Guard. Fastened at one end two stories below, the officers were bringing it up to the story above which John Warde stood, hoping thus to draw him in the huge net.
>
> The young man discerned their purpose. Before the net could be hauled up, he stepped off into space, his body whirling in midair, while watching women screamed as it struck the hotel marquee to roll off into the street, a broken, shapeless mass.

An Editorial: Glass Slippers and a Silver Spoon

Spokane Press

Friday, August 5, 1938

So, who was this young man who stole the attention of all of Manhattan?

John Warde was a self-centered, self-consumed society playboy who felt the world was his oyster. Despite privilege and wealth at his fingertips, he blamed his unhappy life on others, and when obstacles could not be surmounted by his weak moral courage, he chose to jump to his death.

These days, young people seem to possess all the confidence in the world. But confidence without differentiation between good and evil is a dangerous thing. A bandit may have as much confidence in himself as has an engineering student that he can accomplish his goals. The confidence of the first is destructive. The confidence of the latter is for the good of all.

Mr. Warde, sadly, falls into the former.

These days young people seem to possess a great deal of intelligence, but this also is a dangerous thing if not put to the right use.

Too many young people, like young Mr. Warde, seem to have been reared on the understanding that if they push hard enough, they can go out and demand what they want. Someone will just give it to them.

But they have not been taught that anything worthwhile requires hard work. They seem to believe that if they cannot get it on demand, then the use of coercion or manipulation is justified.

And for eleven hours, young John Warde did exactly that. He manipulated everyone around him. Manipulated his sister and good friends who had been caring for him. Manipulated the police and, in particular, a kindly cop by the name of Charley Glasco. Manipulated the cameramen, the reporters, the news stations.

And especially manipulated the thousands who gathered at his feet as if they were worshiping an idol.

But he was nothing to be worshiped.

The nature of man is such that he is of no substance or worth and never satisfied with what he obtains unless he has really worked hard for it.

The more that is handed to people, free for the asking, the more dissatisfied they become and the more they demand.

Mr. Warde knew wealth. Was catered to all of his life. Was nothing more than a dandy who tried to prance through life as if he had glass slippers and a silver spoon.

Unfortunately, he fell off his high ledge and crashed down hard to earth.

Perhaps most tragically, it is estimated that Warde's selfish act cost the city and merchants more than one hundred thousand dollars. Most terribly

> affected were the exclusive shops along Fifth Avenue—one of the busiest and wealthiest mercantile streets in the world—which lost virtually an entire day's worth of business.
>
> For 11 hours, this psychopath tied up traffic, paralyzing the business of the fashionable stores along the side streets for many, many blocks from the hotel, which also reported that they did little or no business during this period of time. Police lines barred customers and shop clerks who—almost to a man—were watching the drama that Warde was directing.
>
> The maniac also disrupted the routines of the elite and ultra-conservative Hotel Gotham.
>
> At least 1,000 police and firemen, two ambulances, an emergency truck, and many police cars were called to the scene. The actual cost to this city for these services alone has been estimated to be in excess of $30,000, which must be added to the total racked up by one man's foolish and self-consumed actions on one single day.
>
> What a waste!

It was not a waste for newsmen, however. By the end of the year, the story of John William Warde's death even overshadowed Hitler's invasion of Austria—which would eventually launch the Second World War—and was equaled only by Orson Welles's broadcast of H. G. Wells's *War of the Worlds*, which created a nationwide panic when listeners were convinced that aliens had landed in New Jersey.

15 The Aftermath

The key players in the standoff on that seventeenth-floor ledge at the Gotham all went on to lead somewhat normal lives, though they would be forever touched by the tragic events of that day.

John Warde's father, with whom his son was reportedly estranged until the end, was on a "motoring vacation" to Bennington, Vermont, for a hunting trip on the day that his son lost his life. Strangely enough, John Sr., a powerful railway and shipping executive in Southampton, had visited New York City that morning for a doctor's appointment but left by mid-morning for his New England vacation.

Ironically, he was only blocks away from Hotel Gotham where his son would ultimately meet his end. He had, in fact, left midtown just minutes before John Jr. stepped out on the ledge.

When the news was released regarding the tragic outcome, an appeal was sent out to the state police in New York to try and track down the father. His brand-new Austin cabrio roadster was eventually flagged down by the highway patrol in Vermont, where, in the company of a younger woman, the tragic news was delivered to him.

The patrolman who notified John Warde Sr. that his son had fallen to his death indicated that the father's only comment was that he had been a troubled young man for some time, and perhaps it was for the best for all in the long run.

Mrs. Katherine Warde, John's socialite mother with whom he refused to speak in his final hours, heard the news over the radio in her Southampton estate home where she was recovering from an illness. Several friends were with her at the time. Within moments, neighbors reported, the house blinds and drapes were drawn to a close, and the sound of sobs and wailing could be heard outside.

A family spokesman later emerged to deliver a statement for Mrs. Warde while wiping his own eyes. "There's nothing we can say at this time," he said in a sober and halting speech. "We learned about this only five minutes ago. We have no words at this moment. Mrs. Warde is not sure what she could have done to prevent this. At the moment, she is near collapse."

John's sister, Mrs. Katherine Bull, twenty-two at the time, was almost inconsolable and curled up on the bed in Room 1716 in the minutes after John's leap and wailed loudly for some time after he was gone. "Oh, Johnny, Johnny!" she sobbed. "I didn't mean it! I didn't mean it! I'd never send you back to the asylum. We would have taken care of you. Oh, Johnny, forgive me!"

Strangely enough—after so many hours of participating in the efforts to persuade her brother to come in off the ledge and enduring the long ordeal—his sister did not see him jump. Katherine had worked herself into such a frenzy that it was necessary to give her a sedative, and she was in bed, subdued and unaware, when he leaped.

After about a half hour under nurses' care, she suddenly jumped up and rushed to the open window in the room and tried to leap out to join her brother in death on the sidewalk below before three policemen restrained her. "Let me go to him!" she screamed hysterically at the officers. "I want to be with my brother! I want to die with him."

Those present reported that Katherine Bull reasoned and pleaded with officers past midnight, begging, "Please let me go, too. I want to follow John." Eventually a police matron escorted her away.

Later, she told reporters,

> He seemed to have a feeling that I was going to put him into a sanitarium again. Send him back to the asylum. So he just crawled out on the ledge shouting, "You'll never put me away!" Nothing could have been further from the truth, but I still blame myself. I don't know why he did it, but I feel I should have prevented it somehow. I thought until the very end that we'd save him. I really didn't think he'd do it.
>
> (Sayre, 1949)

Miss Camilla LaMont—John Warde's self-styled fiancée—also missed the death plunge in the end. After hours on the street and unable to make her way up to see her betrothed, the cocktail blues singer had gone to a nearby drug store for a cup of coffee and was sitting at the counter when she heard the roar of the crowd and a scream of "There he goes!" She later confided, "I was heartbroken, of course, but what are you gonna do?"

Dr. J. C. Presner, the hotel physician who had worked closely with the police to provide insight into John's mental state, declared that Warde's hours of vacillation ended when he ultimately concluded that there was nothing to live for.

"The young man's mental state turned dramatically in the last hour," the physician explained. "And I believe he had made a definite decision to die. He no longer wanted to live. He jumped, not because he feared the police, but because, finally, he had made up his mind that there was no purpose in living. There appeared to be some deep, dark secret within him that was worth dying over."

In fact, the psychiatric community continued to discuss his case—along with the philosophical and sociological implications—for many years to come. At the core of it all, however, was the question that they all knew John himself had so mightily struggled with: "Should he proceed to the 'grand finale' that the audience of up to one hundred thousand had for hours been awaiting, or return shamefully in humiliation to the ignominy of safety?"

In an August 8, 1938, article titled "Medicine: Manhattan Suicide," a team of psychiatrists contacted by *Time* magazine offered some clinical insights into Warde's situation. They diagnosed him as having *a manic-depressive psychosis with alternating fits of madness and despair, during which—in a moment of extreme depression—he took his life.*

In addition to his depression, they felt he was suffering from schizophrenia—a relatively newly diagnosed mental disorder. Interestingly, they added, individuals who suffer from this condition often have an uncanny ability to forget their bodies and remain for hours in one position, no matter how painful or precarious their plight. They concluded that Warde was able to maintain his eleven-hour vigil largely because of his condition ("Medicine: Manhattan Suicide," 1938).

Going even deeper, the psychiatrists suggested that perversity, immorality, and deviant behavior also accompanied this condition, and Warde perhaps became sexually aroused by the persistent efforts to rescue him. In the end, however, his intense desire to fight society and reject moral guidelines overcame his urge for life.

Further seeking to understand the psychological underpinnings of Warde's unexplainable decision on that fateful day, in another article published in the *Birmingham (AL) Age-Herald* a day after the event ("Body Unclaimed after Fatal Leap," 1938), two notable psychiatrists provided their insight. The article begins with a bracing description:

> John Warde—the nerve-sick "man on the ledge" who was the central figure in Manhattan's most spectacular delayed suicide—lay Wednesday night in the solitude of an east side funeral parlor. The 11-hour carnival of death that gripped thousands of New Yorkers in agonizing suspense climaxed Tuesday night with his plunge from the seventeenth floor of the Gotham Hotel.
>
> In the aftermath of the strange case, enacted amid a stage-setting of skyscrapers, neck-craning thousands, clicking newsreel cameras, magnesium flares, fainting women and even a television broadcast, medical experts joined the man in the street trying to answer the question: "Why did he do it—and why the way he did it?"

Dr. A. Arden Brill, noted psychiatrist and Columbia University lecturer on psychosexual science, interpreted Warde's prolonged debate with death as the manifestation of a schizoid-manic. The day after the jump, the doctor was quoted in the *Birmingham (AL) Age-Herald* article:

> He lived in his own dream world, out there on the ledge before he jumped. At one point, Mr. Warde ate a piece of cake delivered by the hotel's room service and said he'd accept a cup of coffee. He specified it was to have cream in it, and when he had tasted it, he handed the cup back. Not enough cream. Receiving it again, he returned the cup once more . . . not enough sugar. It was as if he was annoyed by not receiving the service to which he was accustomed.

The writer of the article, in attempting to answer the "why?" question by speaking with doctors who specialized in mental aberrations, noted that, ironically, John Warde was known to only a few people in his daily life, but his sensational act on the ledge of a New York skyscraper hotel made him known to millions—something he might have been seeking in death that he could not achieve in life.

He proposed that there were countless people like John suffering from the idea that they were superior to all others. He noted that this human quirk, however, is what psychiatrists and other experts in mental mechanics were now calling an "inferiority complex"—the exact opposite of what the person was expressing. These tortured individuals were convinced that their friends and acquaintances looked down on them, that they were rank failures in life, and that nothing could be done about their situation. Most of these people suffered in private.

Continuing on in the same article, he procured the expert opinion of Dr. Joseph Jastrow, New York psychologist, who pictured Warde—the self-embittered failure, the youth who "felt different" than other boys, whose every venture in life seemed doomed—as enjoying a final hour of triumph: "He stood up there alone, looking down on the great crowds, dominating a scene at last," he said. "He enjoyed every minute of it. This was the greatest moment of his entire life."

> So, Warde lingered for hours, towering over the weird life-and-death spectacle of his own creation, until dusk became darkness, and a plan to catch him in a giant net and pin him against the side of the building like a butterfly caused the situation to escalate.
>
> Then, John Warde decided to take the public way out—the grandest moment of his lifetime on the nation's largest stage. The publicity he obtained instantly made him a national figure—no doubt made him feel important and cured his complex. But, of course, it's too late now.

Without any hint of compassion, the writer continued with his analysis.

> In the long prelude to his death, he dangled his legs nonchalantly over the side of his 18-inch perch from time to time and seemed to enjoy teasing the crowds below. He swayed and poised his hands as though about to dive, drawing gasps from the crowds. Then, he would pull them back and laugh uproariously at times.
>
> Puffing dramatically on cigarettes with a certain mannered flair—flipping the butts out into the open air and consistently generating a roar from the anticipatory crowds below—the young man sipped glasses of water as if he was bored at a cocktail party. It all seemed a lark to him, a drama on which he was performing on center stage.
>
> Skipping, prancing and taunting the hungry onlookers below, he would occasionally bow as if it was his curtain call and he was entertaining cheers of "Encore! Encore!" ("Body Unclaimed after Fatal Leap," 1938)

However, according to more than one newspaper, perhaps the question that most confounded every Manhattanite following the tragedy was how could a man stand on a window ledge for eleven hours and ignore the inevitable calls of nature while pondering death?

Isabella Katherine Valentine—John's "Bella"—never gave a single interview on the subject after those comments and spent the rest of her wealthy and privileged life trying to put together the pieces of this impossible puzzle. She was sincerely weakened and refused to discuss the events of that day with anyone, as well as her unique relationship with Warde. Those who were close to her noted that "she was never the same again. Forever changed, altered, by John's death."

Patrolman Charles Glasco was the subject of countless articles over the days that followed, and he became a short-lived celebrity in his neighborhood and on the force.

The general consensus at the time was the John Warde had simply decided to jump during that last hour—he was tired and ready to die. Although he may have been indecisive during the afternoon hours, at the finish, he was at peace with his decision. You could see it in his eyes.

"If he hadn't died when he did, he would have in a day or two," Glasco said. "I'm sure of it. His mental state at the end had definitely turned to death.

"But all along, I tried everything I knew to do. I tried as hard as I could but just couldn't get anywhere with him. All afternoon, I thought we were becoming pals, and I was sure I'd get him back to his sister and family. But as darkness came on, he seemed to have changed. He got more like a frightened animal.

“In the end, though, I think it can mostly be blamed on the crowd. They had a bloodthirst about them. In those last moments, he told me, ‘Look at all those people down there. I can’t disappoint them. The show must go on.’ Nothing mattered after that.”

Officer Charles Glasco—though he was lauded for his valiant attempt to save the life of a troubled young man—would go on to live and work in virtual obscurity for the rest of his days. He eventually would be promoted to sergeant. His wife said that after the initial days following the event, he chose not to speak much to his family about the incident.

Specifically, he refused to tell his wife the secret that John had whispered in his ear on that fateful day on the ledge. “He was a man of his word,” his wife said, “and he never offered to tell me what it was that had driven the young man on that day in 1938 to take his life as he did. And, of course, I never asked. He had too much integrity to talk about it. Plus, I know he genuinely liked the lad. He had respect for him in the end.”

Living in the same house on Eighty-Seventh Street in Woodhaven, just down the block from his beloved St. Thomas the Apostle Church, Charles Glasco passed away peacefully on February 3, 1976.

John Warde’s former employer and others wanted to spin the story in another direction, promoting the story that he did not jump from the ledge, but rather his knees buckled from the weakness of standing so long without any sustenance, and he simply lost his balance and fell.

John Warde’s broken and bruised body was eventually claimed by his sister and subsequently turned over to be buried in Brooklyn after private funeral services were held at the New York and Brooklyn Funeral Home on December 29.

The mortuary director reported at the time: “John William Warde, who came from an esteemed and wealthy family in Southampton, had 26 cents in his pocket upon his 200-foot leap—the most spectacular suicide Manhattan has witnessed in years.”

Members of his family had requested and received police protection for the funeral service after they disclosed that they had received hundreds of letters from people asking permission to attend the rites and view the body. The time of the funeral had been moved up four hours, unbeknownst to anyone, to avoid the anticipated crowds.

John William Warde is now interred in the Nazareth Section of Evergreens Cemetery in Brooklyn.

He is simply recorded as grave 6994.

Obscure in life, infamous in death.

16 Fourteen Hours

As if the events of that day in 1938 were not memorable enough, the story continued on in several ways. Eventually working its way into pop culture—even while the original characters in the drama were largely forgotten—the story would become the focus of a major motion picture.

Twelve years after John William Warde plunged to his death on the corner of Fifth Avenue and Fifty-Fifth Street in New York City, filming began on the story of this tragic incident for a feature film titled *The Man on the Ledge*. Loosely based on the true events, it followed an NYPD officer's attempt to try and stop a despondent man from jumping to his death from the fifteenth floor of the fictional "Rodney Hotel," and many of the facts are fictionalized.

The film would win critical acclaim for Richard Basehart—later famous for his role in the television science-fiction drama *Voyage to the Bottom of the Sea*—who portrayed the young man on the building's ledge.

Paul Douglas—who would go on to star in nearly forty films—played the kindly police officer, Charley Dunnigan, and the movie would feature a large supporting cast of future stars, including Barbara Bel Geddes, Ossie Davis, Agnes Moorehead, Robert Keith, Debra Paget, and Howard Da Silva. It also notably represented the screen debut of Grace Kelly, who appeared in a small role along with Jeffrey Hunter—who would later find fame playing Jesus in *King of Kings*.

With a screenplay written by John Paxton, based on a 1949 article in the *New Yorker* by Joel Sayre, on-screen credits for the Warde biopic contain a statement saying that the film and characters depicted were "entirely fictional."

They were not, of course.

In fact, just shortly before its theatrical release, Twentieth Century Fox studio chief Darryl F. Zanuck changed the title from *The Man on the Ledge* to *Fourteen Hours*—also inexplicably changing the actual number of hours from the real-life event. It came after a personal plea by John Warde's mother—who a dozen years later was either still grieving the tragic loss of her son or embarrassed by it—so that the picture would not be as closely identified with him or their family.

Zanuck also considered changing the setting of the movie to Philadelphia or Chicago for the same reason. In the end, it was ultimately filmed at 23 Wall Street in New York and identified as such.

Sayre's article was published in the April 16, 1949, edition of the *New Yorker*, titled "The Man on the Ledge." Just days after the article was out, the rights to the story were purchased by Twentieth Century Fox, and the studio assigned Sol C. Siegel to produce it.

Famed and celebrated Hollywood director Howard Hawks was brought in on the project. Still, after reviewing the script, he adamantly refused to direct the movie because of its somber subject matter and depressing ending. Instead, he proposed making it a comedy starring Cary Grant—an option that Fox executives declined.

Henry Hathaway, a director noted for his realistic depictions in previous films, was next assigned to the project in April 1950. The screenplay was originally designed as a vehicle for Richard Widmark, who was to play the man on the ledge, with Robert Wagner scheduled to portray half of a romantic story that was set to play out on Fifth Avenue at the same time. The role of the cop-negotiator eventually went to Paul Douglas.

As mentioned, Grace Kelly made her movie debut in the film, beating out Anne Bancroft for the role. Her casting was announced at the last moment, creating a bit of a surprise because, to this point, she was only a stage and television actress of little renown.

It was on the set of this movie that the future Princess of Monaco would be noticed by Gary Cooper, who cast her as his bride in the western he was just getting ready to shoot, the now-classic *High Noon*. The movie—which has often been considered a metaphor for Hollywood's cowardice during the McCarthy red scare era—would thrust the ingenue into the spotlight and make her one of the world's most famous women.

Barbara Bel Geddes, who played Basehart's (Warde's) emotional fiancée—and later starred as Miss Ellie Ewing on *Dallas*—did not appear in another film until *Vertigo*, seven years later.

Hathaway ended up hiring more than three hundred actors to play bit parts and extras in the film, much of which was filmed on lower Broadway in Manhattan. Among actors performing in uncredited roles were Agnes Morehead (Endora from *Bewitched*), Ossie Davis (*Roots*), and Harvey Lembeck (later Eric Von Zipper in the *Beach Blanket* movies) as taxi drivers, as well as Joyce Van Patten, John Cassavetes, and Richard Beymer—who played the lead in *West Side Story* a few years later—and character actors Leif Erickson and John Randolph.

Filming began in June 1950 and wrapped in just six weeks with a modest budget. Interiors were primarily shot in Studio 8 at the Fox Studios in Century City. At the same time, some exteriors with the crowds were filmed at the American Exchange

National Bank building, located at 128 Broadway in Lower Manhattan. This structure has since been demolished.

In what is largely considered to be his finest film, Hathaway tried to avoid the monotony of filming a man standing against a wall for hours by cutting between the film ledge and the reaction of the crowd below through the clever and innovative use of distinctive camera angles. At the time, the filming was recognized for its innovative camerawork.

The movie represented no small challenge for actor Richard Basehart, who was forced to spend most of the filming pressed against a wall hundreds of feet in the air and barely moving a muscle. He eventually got so accustomed to this that he didn't feel the need for any bodily movement, rather learning to express himself by the slightest turn of his head, the puff of a cigarette, or the subtle gesture of a hand. He chose—most successfully—to allow his eyes and facial expressions to do the acting. It was considered a dramatic breakthrough at the time.

His stand-in on the ledge for most of the film was Richard Lacovara, a veteran Fox stuntman. There was a padded platform below him—in case he fainted or slipped. However, this was often removed for wide shots, making it a harrowing experience for anyone.

Even with the stunt double, Basehart still had to endure more than three hundred hours of standing on an actual high-rise ledge with virtually no movement and without being tethered, for fifty days of shooting during an unusually hot summer in New York.

Unfortunately, just prior to the start of filming, Basehart had badly sprained his ankle—the doctor said it would have been better if he had broken it—and his legs were ravaged by a serious rash from poison oak contracted on the grounds of his Coldwater Canyon home while cutting down a tree. He suffered terribly throughout the filming, with piercing pain from the sprain and itching and oozing legs that had to be tightly bandaged.

As if anything could be worse, Basehart's wife, costume designer Stephanie Klein, was diagnosed with a brain tumor during the opening days of shooting and died following brain surgery on July 28, 1950, during the final few days of production. The tragedy rocked the entire production and put Hathaway in the horribly awkward situation of deciding if they could wrap the production before Basehart needed to leave and make arrangements for his deceased wife.

As mentioned, the film's content also came with a significant amount of controversy, and it was a fight even to get it made. The movie originally ended with the young man falling to his death, as was the case with John Warde. A second—more acceptable—ending was also shot at the same time, with Hathaway, the director, clearly preferring—and lobbying hard for—the realistic ending and instructing the editors to cut it accordingly.

However, on July 17, 1950—amid the filming—Dionysia "Chickie" Skouras, the twenty-three-year-old daughter of Twentieth Century Fox president Spyros Skouras, jumped to her death from the roof of a Fox building. Still alive after the fall, she was nevertheless pronounced dead later at the hospital. The tragedy rattled the entire studio—combined with the eerily similar story being shot at the same time—and appeared to provide a death knell to the production before it was even completed.

Previews for the film had already been produced and were being played in theaters in anticipation of an August release. It immediately threw the project into chaos, and the trailers were halted.

On the day of her death, the *Clinton (OK) Daily News* published an article that told of the tragedy, stating, "Dionysia Skouras, whose father, Spyros Skouras, is president of the 20th Century-Fox Film Corp. and one of America's highest-paid film executives, died today a few hours after she leaped from a building. Her father's annual salary is about $500,000 [$10 million in today's money]. The Pretty Red-haired girl had been in a 'highly nervous condition'" ("Rich Playgirl Dies from Plunge from Penthouse," 1950).

It went on to explain that Miss Skouras had jumped from the roof garden of the Fox West Coast Theater Exchange Building of her uncle, Charles Skouras, who was also a motion-picture theater executive. "Chickie" Skouras—as she was known—had been visiting her uncle from her home in Greenwich Village, New York, and staying in the luxurious penthouse apartment atop the theater building.

Chickie had been known to struggle with mental issues for some time and was in town hopefully for some rehabilitation. An earlier report had revealed that on December 13 of the previous year, Miss Skouras—starting near her home—had led Connecticut state police on a wild hour-and-a-half, eighty-mile-an-hour auto chase, which resulted in her being shot in order to stop the car.

At the time, authorities said Skouras shook off several police pursuers in the wild ride along a stretch of highway and then through four communities before an officer stopped her with three bullets on Boston Post Road. Injured during the gun battle, she was treated by Dr. Allen Rother, who then took her to Hall-Brooke Sanatorium, a private hospital in Westport, Connecticut.

> Skouras was subsequently booked by Greenwich police on a charge of reckless driving and failure to possess a driver's license. Highway Patrolman Chauncey Dance, the last of the police pursuers who chased her, said he didn't fire until it was apparent only bullets could halt the maniacal driver.

Just seven months later, Chickie Skouras—the pretty, twenty-three-year-old daughter of a multimillionaire film executive—would lie mortally injured at the base of the Fox West Coast Theater Exchange Building—an eerily similar situation to Warde's drama on the eve of the film about his life.

The news, of course, was shocking—and chilling in its parallels—and Skouras immediately demanded that the film be permanently shelved and he, understandably, wanted nothing more to do with it.

Little is known about the behind-the-scenes negotiations that took place during this time. Still, six months later, *Fourteen Hours* was released with the ending that showed Basehart surviving his fall by grabbing the net intended to save him.

When the film was released in twenty-one countries, it met with critical praise, although it was far from a hit with the moviegoing audience of the time, which considered it a bit dark and unsettling for their tastes.

> Almost all the reviews concentrated on the "why"—why did this man go out on the ledge in the first place—something the script only hints at but refuses to answer. Maybe it was because, in 1951, they didn't want to address the real issues at hand.

Movie critics of the day went out of their way to compare the menacing landscape of concrete buildings to the restless crowds gathering below the ledge to see if the man lived or died. They noted that in the film, New York City was as much of a character as the man, his family, or the cop who found himself trying to talk Warde into reentering his hotel room, expressing that when night falls, the city may light up, but it does nothing to alleviate the shadows that seem to be wrapping themselves around the would-be jumper.

Indeed, the visuals in the film seem to reinforce that. For the many hours that John Warde was on that tiny ledge, he may have felt like he was the center of the world, but the film left little doubt that New York City would continue to exist in all of its glory and its horror regardless of how this personal drama ultimately played out. In the end, whether he lived or died, the man on the ledge appeared to be destined to be forgotten.

Fourteen Hours was ultimately nominated for an Academy Award for Best Art Direction and was listed as among the top ten films of 1951 by the National Board of Review of Motion Pictures ("1951 Award Winners"). For his performance in the movie, Basehart won the Award for Best Actor.

Despite several good reviews by prominent critics and a strong push by the studio to publicize the movie—with Paul Douglas even appearing on the March 12, 1951, cover of *Life* magazine as the film hit the theaters—*Fourteen Hours* was never able to gain much traction with the public and was not a moneymaker.

Bosley Crowther, however—the premier film critic of the era—covered the film, giving it a glowing review in the *New York Times*.

In his column on March 7, 1951, Crowther spoke specifically to the many New Yorkers who undoubtedly still vividly remembered the real-life case of the man on the ledge as a poor, unbalanced chap who lodged himself on the ledge of a local hotel one summer day and stood there teetering while the city held its breath.

Saying that they would no doubt be forced to relive those harrowing moments through this film, he nevertheless added that those who have no memory of the event would find gripping suspense, absorbing drama, and stinging social comment in this film.

In a series of glowing comments, he said the production was a hotly throbbing and brutally candid slice of metropolitan life. Further, he praised director Henry Hathaway's crisp, journalistic style, noting that the precarious situation of a person perched upon a narrow ledge, high above the streets of a city, was a natural for dramatic suspense. He especially felt the director used the universal phobias of falling and of dizzying heights to maximum effect in the movie.

Crowther went on to say that although the focus of the film was the man on the ledge, the accumulating drama—a traffic cop and the frantic, fumbling rescue efforts combined with the morbid, cruel crowds in the street—made for the "real emotional upsweep and the hard, staggering shocks in this film."

Crowther was especially taken by the scene the movie presented so starkly—a person teetering between life and death in view of thousands, exhibiting his free will to destroy himself.

Alongside that travesty are the reporters and heartless radio men and the curious crowds looking on in breathless horror or with lust for a death spectacle—hypnotized observers who emerge as the most pathetic of all in the film.

Crowther ends with a rare note of praise, calling the movie "a superior American film."

After its original release, the film seemed to have faded into obscurity, other than in occasional showings on TCM. When the movie was shown at a film revival in 2003, it was stunningly the last remaining print to have survived.

Ironically, however, *Fourteen Hours* was not the first time the story of John William Warde would be found in theaters across America. More than a decade earlier, the young man had been a headliner that drew packed movie houses from coast to coast.

During that time, he regularly outperformed such leading men as Jimmy Stewart, Spencer Tracy, Humphrey Bogart, Clark Gable, and Cary Grant.

That was because the film footage shot by newsreel cameramen representing Pathé News, Fox Movietone News, and Hearst Metrotone News on that fateful day had been edited—along with still photos shot by George Reinhart, Bob Costa, Walter Engels, and Harold Harris—into a "movie short" and distributed to theaters where it was heavily promoted.

The nearly four-minute film—over twice the length of the normal newsreel—featured melodramatic narration by such familiar announcers as Pathé's Bob

Danvers-Walker and Universal's Ed Herlihy and chronicled every hour of the Warde saga leading up to and through his dramatic leap.

At the penultimate moment, the movie proceeded in tantalizingly slow motion so that every second—literally—of the death dive could be enjoyed on a 25 × 45 foot screen in the horror of a darkened theater.

Newspaper advertising from the era for the newsreel—which preceded A-list double features—touted the film with banners and headlines such as:

> SPECIAL ENGAGEMENT! Complete Pictorial of Warde's Death Leap!
> HELD OVER! Sensational Film of Deranged Boy's Plunge to Death
> SCOOP! John Warde's 17-Story Death Leap
> EXTRA! John Warde's Leap to Death While 1000s Watch!

Proprietors of the movie houses reported in trade magazines that the Warde newsreel was a bigger draw than top moneymakers like *Snow White and the Seven Dwarfs*, *A Star Is Born*, *Captains Courageous*, and the *Adventures of Robin Hood*. It was regularly held over even as the double features changed.

In the end, the industry's trade magazines reported, "New York theater operators alone calculated that the newsreel footage brought in more than one million dollars in additional grosses"—an equivalent today of $19.8 million (Sayre, 1949).

Interestingly, a single fifty-four-second clip from the original Pathé newsreel still exists, as well as a second twenty-seven-second clip from the Universal newsreel that shows, in real time, the events of the day.

Although neither of the extant prints shows the falling body—a decision undoubtedly made out of fear of fainting women and audience panic—they perfectly capture the pandemonium of the day, along with the nonchalance of Warde as he both stands on the ledge and later sits with his feet dangling over the edge while watching the curious onlookers below.

On display are the crowds shoving for a position—lit by magnesium flares—backed-up taxis, the film crews and photographers, Hotel Gotham, and the Fifth Avenue Presbyterian Church, among policemen at work, trying hopelessly to control the crowds.

Also shown are firemen with the "rescue net" featuring a bull's-eye painted in the middle, a double-decker tour bus with riders staring up and pointing at Warde, and the final street scene as he falls with flashbulbs popping before a single, one-second shot of his body on the ground. Macabre as these are, they are a historical record of this tragic moment.

17 The Hotel Gotham

Yesterday and Today

No less of a player in the grand drama that took place on July 26, 1938, was the elite hotel that provided the backdrop for all of the activities of that day and—though it would experience many changes over the following seventy-five years—it continues to be a major Manhattan landmark.

The Hotel Gotham of that day would in fact fall into bankruptcy, partly because it could not acquire a liquor license as it was too close to the Fifth Avenue Presbyterian Church, which refused to allow it.

Some years after John Warde's fall to his death—and the wave of negative publicity that followed—the Metropolitan Life Insurance Company acquired the hotel. Desiring the maximum leasable retail floor space, the company gutted many of the hotel's public rooms and transformed guest rooms into offices. With that, the extraordinary lapsed into the ordinary, and the glamour of one of the world's great hotels was no more.

Although it would change hands as office space over the years—and cease to be remembered for the tragic events of 1938 by most New Yorkers of subsequent eras—it never went away. Today, the 1905 Beaux Arts building stands proudly as before, and looking much the same from the sidewalk as it did on that day, but with a new clientele and ambiance.

Today, the hotel is an elite destination called, simply enough, The Peninsula, self-described as "Fifth Avenue's Most Glamorous Address." A stay currently costs guests up to $2,750 per night.

It now boasts twenty-three floors, fifty luxury suites, and four restaurants. The historic property was purchased for $127 million in 1988 and, after a massive renovation effort, now has received the AAA Five Diamond Award for thirteen consecutive years, as well as being named one of the greatest hotels in the world by *Travel + Leisure* magazine.

Prior to its current state, the hotel went through several acquisitions but—seemingly with a curse attached to it—ended up repeatedly in bankruptcy after more than $300 million in renovations. When it was finally obtained by its current owner, the new group promptly put another $45 million into the property.

These days, the luxury hotel is best known for its fitness center, which is located on the top floor. With a glass-enclosed pool and sundeck, the hotel's spa is one of the largest and grandest in New York City, with a floor area of thirty-five thousand square feet spanning three floors.

Ironically, the location of the five-star spa is where much of the action took place—including Bill Klotzbach's failed lasso attempt—as part of the strategy to prevent John Warde from tumbling to his death. It was also where the commander of the city's chief rescue team had assembled with the idea of dropping a net over "the target"—their generic name for the man on the ledge—and trapping him there in place.

Today, as wealthy guests frolic and relax in the hotel's solarium, few of them will be aware of the dramatic events that took place in the same location where they are enjoying a seaweed wrap with sliced cucumber–covered eyes.

Hotel Gotham—as much of a character in this spellbinding drama as were John Warde, Charley Glasco, the Valentines, and Katherine Bull—would more than once find itself in the public arena again with shocking news.

In fact, just four years after Warde's stand—almost to the date—the New York Police were once again dealing with a man on a ledge at the Gotham, and Manhattanites were struggling with *déjà vu* as a similar storyline looked to play itself out.

On June 24, 1942, George Bryant, sixty-three, of Queens, romped for some time on a ledge of the Hotel Gotham's twentieth floor beginning at 7:30 a.m. Dressed in blue-and-white pajamas, Bryant entertained the mesmerized crowd—more than 240 feet below—from the ledge for a while. He then went back into a room for a few minutes before reappearing on the ledge, still wearing his pajamas.

A reporter for the *Brooklyn Citizen* covered the event on that day, writing in an article that

> an elderly man had strolled along a ledge of the Hotel Gotham twenty floors above Fifth Avenue, Manhattan, "in search of some air." After waving cheerily to passersby he sat down on the narrow ledge and kicked his feet into space but he came obediently to his room when police arrived.
>
> ("Man on Ledge Tells Police 'Out to Get Air,'" 1942)

Ironically, the police were called to the hotel by Walter Vickers—the same doorman on duty when John Warde jumped—and Patrolman Hanford Bova responded. Entering his room with a passkey from the desk manager, he peered out of the large inset window at "Bryant prancing and dancing, apparently to music in his head alone."

As late as 2018, the name would surface again. The Gotham Hotel—now in a new iteration with a different address—would be the scene for yet another high-rise suicide leap, this time in a horrifying mother-and-young-son leap that would shock the nation and revive memories of John William Warde.

On May 18 of that year, Stephanie Adams, forty-seven, *Playboy*'s Miss November 1992, jumped with her seven-year-old son Vincent to their deaths amid a bitter custody battle with her chiropractor ex, Charles Nicolai. They leaped from the twenty-fifth-floor penthouse suite of The Gotham Hotel around 8:15 a.m. Reportedly, Adams was distraught when she was told she couldn't take her son on a European vacation because of a court dispute.

The deaths came as Adams waged a fierce court battle with her estranged husband. Apparently their relationship was so toxic that Adams would only meet Nicolai—who had visitation rights for Vincent—at the First Precinct in Tribeca for handovers. "It ensured that no violence took place," a friend reported.

Adams came out as *Playboy* magazine's first lesbian centerfold in 2003. The former Wilhelmina and Elite model-turned-author had written twenty-five self-help books and was quoted as saying, "Just because I look a certain way and have expensive tastes, it doesn't mean I'm shallow. Style and looks don't mean lack of brains, sweetheart!"

But if the old haunt known as the Gotham—now The Peninsula—hoped to escape its tragic past, that was not to be, as in 2010 a new story emerged in virtually the same spot where John Warde made it one of the most famous buildings in the world.

Perhaps the most dramatic of all the events connected to the Warde leap—and the subject of a sensational trial—centered on a would-be suicide/murder that occurred just one floor down from the exact ledge where John once stood in 1938.

The beyond bizarre events in February 2010—ones that in so many ways mirror the madness and the tragedy of that day more than seventy years earlier—supply an equal amount of psychological drama and puzzling outcomes as John Warde once delivered, if not more.

In the same location—virtually in the same spot—where Warde would take his leap to his death, a stunning mother-and-son tale unfolded that is worthy of a full-length treatment of its own.

It was there—this time just one floor down in Room 1603—that a frightened, desperate, and unhinged mother in her thirties by the name of Gigi Jordan would take the life of her eight-year-old autistic son. She believed he had told her that he wanted to die because he had been sexually molested, tortured, and tormented at the hands of his father. In the end, apparently she didn't feel there was any way she could protect her child from the dark forces she believed had surrounded him, and in her mind, his death was the only merciful option.

Locking herself and her son in the $2,300-per-night luxury suite, she navigated a strange and inexplicable series of events that eventually had her writing a rambling twenty-six-page "suicide note" before giving her son a lethal dose of powerful medications and taking some herself.

When police broke into the room after a tip, they found the boy on the bed and the mother sitting on the floor up against it, surrounded by nearly *six thousand* pills scattered on the floor and babbling incoherently.

She was also worth more than $40 million.

As tragic as that would prove to be, the story is far, far from that simple. It involves allegations of hit men from the Chicago mob, heart-pounding races around the country, lawsuits and countersuits, a stunning trial testimony, and a deep dive into the heartbreak and exasperation of autism. Jordan was ultimately convicted in 2014 of killing her son, Jude Mirra.

It was a story that continued to make headlines for years as Gigi's legal team kept her complex appeals case alive while she lived in a penthouse apartment in Trump Tower with an electronic tracking bracelet on her ankle. After moving to Brooklyn, she was found dead on December 30, 2022. The city medical examiner's office ruled that the death was a suicide by asphyxia.

The Gotham, it would appear—in its every iteration—is no stranger to bizarre deaths and sensational lives.

In fact, the hotel's storied past would seem to surface every few years even as the world around it changed. The Gotham took on a new face and image, and life rolled along to modern rhythms. For a while it seemed to never recover from the darkness that hung over it from John Warde's fateful decision to slip out a window on July 26, 1938, but today it stands as a grand testament to its drive to survive.

OVERTIME
AN APPENDIX

The days that followed John Warde's leap were dominated in the press by countless articles on the dramatic events of July 26, 1938. It reached virtually every state and most continents, and the facts, emotions, and perspectives varied widely by source.

Most were heavily editorialized—intending to send a moralist, political, or philosophical message to their readers. As a result, they today give modern readers a fascinating glimpse into the mindset of the 1930s in America.

Excerpts from several articles are reproduced here for those who enjoy a deeper dive into a historical event.

These have been carefully selected from hundreds that were published because, beyond a retelling of the events, they reflect the editorialization and commentary that followed—some of which might prove uncomfortable to more modern and empathetic ears.

Death: The Publicity Hound
By Dale Harrison,
Duluth (MN) News
Monday, August 15, 1938

It happened weeks ago, yet still in my mind's eye I see him standing there—the Man on the Ledge. Why is it that horror etches its memory more deeply than happiness?

He was a madman, surely—and what a show he gave! What a mad, gruesome, sickening show! And how avidly, even sadistically, we New Yorkers scrambled for front-row seats!

You read it on the front pages. Perhaps you saw it in the newsreels. The radio outdid itself with its round-by-round accounts. The new television industry used the event to reveal why it might be the medium of the future.

Death was certainly a publicity hound that day!

The man, you remember, was John Warde. The name is not important. Even the fact that he died is of no concern at the moment. The importance rests in the fact that a madman was able—for more than eleven hours—to make all the forces of sanity and civility in America's greatest city look stupid and helpless.

I was no better than the rest of the morbid tens of thousands who fought and connived for a chance to stare at human tragedy. It was only easier for me than the rest because my press pass, which provides open access to newspapermen, got me a front-line vantage point.

The crowd—including me—that watched John Warde taunt death from the ledge of the Hotel Gotham, 17 dizzy stories above 55th street, was as enthused as though it were viewing an aerial artist at a circus. But as emotionless and disconnected as if it were watching cows graze in a field.

No one in the crowd really gave a damn whether John Warde jumped or not. They were more than content simply to be entertained on an otherwise boring, hot summer Tuesday.

They even joked. A cab driver, brought to a halt by a red light, leaned from his cab window, looked up at the imperturbable John Warde standing on the ledge, and shouted: "Go ahead and jump! If you don't, you're yellow!"

They poked fun. They taunted the poor kid. Calling him by name, he became their little puppet. A plaything.

Gamblers moved about in the crowd. They made bets on John Warde. They wagered he would jump, but then later, the odds switched, and the betting was on the side that he wouldn't. I heard it was 8 to 5 at some point, though I'm not sure which way the odds were leaning at that point. Money was changing hands quicker than I could follow it. Bookies were having their biggest day of the year.

Men and women came with field glasses, the better to see the face of this man who—mad as a hatter—still was outsmarting the best minds of the city who were trying to prevent his suicide. They commented on his clothes, his choice of haircut, the fact that he fashionably tucked his tie into his starched shirt, the shine on his shoes, and his personal smoking habits.

More than one person wondered what brand he smoked. More than one person asked how he could refrain from using a restroom for so long. More than two dozen formally filed their suggestions with the police on how to resolve the situation.

Newsreel cameramen pointed their lenses at the man and moved their cameras up and down, practicing so that when he jumped, they would get every inch of the plunge. It was the final dress rehearsal for what was certain to be the curtain call.

And why? So they could record on celluloid the self-destruction of a madman. So they could show it in theaters everywhere and satiate the American public's taste for morbidity. So they could make their career mark. So they could make some money off his misery. There might be a big payday ahead, and that made everything worth it.

I watched John Warde for perhaps an hour. It was certainly no longer. The manner in which he stood there, nonchalant, a bit bored and seemingly half-amused, reminded me of John Barrymore in one of those sophisticated, man-of-the-world roles he plays so effectively.

I grew tired of it after a while. Not that I was superior for turning away. I just grew tired of the ordeal. What a sad statement about my own character. I realize that now.

John Warde smoked cigarettes. Lots of them. Obviously a chain smoker, he lit one cigarette from the dying butt of the last. You could see the smoke roll from his mouth like little clouds of utter disdain for us jackals who gaped at him. He used it as his tool to toy with us.

I, for one, was struck with wonder at his air of complete indifference. Most people get dizzy looking down from such heights. John Warde looked down for the better part of eleven hours, sometimes with a half smile on his face, unconcerned, completely calm. At times, he seemed to enjoy all the activity below. At times, he was nervous as a cat.

And when he himself grew bored with the meaningless monotony of it all, he simply stepped off the ledge, pausing only long enough to put his hands overhead like an Olympic diver and sail into the darkness.

When he leaped, women screamed. Several swooned. Somehow, I didn't care about them. They had stood there for hours, secretly hoping to see death snatch John Warde from the ledge. When it happened, they couldn't stand it. It was the ultimate display of hypocrisy. Wanting so badly to see him jump and then turning in horror when he fulfilled their wishes.

This was no doubt the best day of the year for newsmen and newspapers. Publishers too. Circulation is certain to skyrocket. Newsboys will make more in a day than they do in a month.

But the "Man on the Ledge" was nothing but an annoyance to others. He interrupted traffic on Fifth Avenue for hours, delaying the important business of life while he parlayed with death. Hundreds of extra policemen were required. Business in the entire area was paralyzed. An otherwise respectable hotel became an innocent victim of a lunatic.

There is indeed a lesson here.

It takes a crazy man to show us that we're all crazy too.

"Death Carnival" Ends as Man Flies Past Net

Pittsburgh (PA) Press

Wednesday, July 27, 1938

John W. Warde, a 26-year-old neurotic playboy who played about the fringes of high society in privileged Southampton, today was New York's most spectacular suicide.

In full sight of the hypnotized gaze of thousands massed along Fifth Avenue, Warde plunged from the 17th-floor ledge of the sedate and luxe Hotel Gotham on which he had perched for nearly 11 hours. Once he hit the sidewalk, it was a horrific sight that caused many to cover their faces and others to gawk in delight. Women screamed and fainted.

And then, with that, the carnival of death was over.

Just as he was about to be trapped like a wild animal in a net—cunningly devised by police and firemen—Warde plummeted head-first onto the glass and steel marquee of the hotel and then dropped on the street after spraying shocked onlookers with blood.

Warde was described by his acquaintances as a young man who was accepted by the society set of Southampton yet was not part of it. He was an outsider, a frustrated playboy who never in his business or social life could ever feel he had succeeded in anything.

He was comfortable around girls, especially his sister, but never attached to any until recently—which appeared to come with great unease—according to friends.

To Southampton's social families, he was known as a "pleasant and nice" young man—well-dressed, fastidious, and nicely mannered—who was welcome in their homes when they were not entertaining formally. But not during more sophisticated or important occasions. They considered him erratic at times.

"He always felt himself an outcast. Different than the other boys," a fellow classmate remarked. "There was something quite odd about him at times that just made him not fit in well."

"If he could be convinced that anything in his life was worthwhile," Patrolman Charles V. Glasco reported. "Then, he said would come back into the room. If the doctors could convince him that his life was worth living, then he would've given the whole thing up. They tried but, I guess, couldn't come up with an answer."

And so this is the end. The broken corpse, as the midnight bell tolled, was lifted onto a canvas stretcher to be taken to the morgue, where stunned relatives never got around to claiming it as of late today.

Like Hamlet, John Warde couldn't make up his mind, and thus spent a long, excruciating afternoon debating whether "to jump or not to jump."

Like Hamlet, he spurned well-meant advice.

And like Hamlet, his end came in violent tragedy.

According to reports of his conversation, while perched on a building ledge in New York City on Tuesday before jumping to his death, John Warde said he felt he couldn't disappoint the thousands who had gathered to see what he was going to do.

But crowds have no will, nor have they heart.

John Warde's audience didn't necessarily want him to jump. It was merely sufficient that he intended to jump—an exciting enough premise for this mob.

Unfortunately, the young man had the bad luck of running afoul of one of the deepest pitfalls of reasoning when his mind was already in turmoil.

Indeed, the grief caused by attributing to crowds a will they cannot possess is beyond estimate. Athletes have risked permanent injury for fear of losing prestige in the eyes of a crowd by quitting the game when they were hurt. Politicians have been stimulated by crowds to say and do things that jeopardize their careers and injure public welfare.

What John Warde feared was his own disappointment if he failed to reach a dramatic climax before a screaming, demanding audience.

He wasn't the first to confuse what he wanted with what he thought a crowd wanted and then make the poorer of the two decisions.

Was It Suicide? Well, Not Really

Ventura County (CA) Star

Wednesday, July 27, 1938

New York's neurotic 11-hour, one-man hippodrome ended, as it inevitably had to end, in the victim's plunge to death on the sidewalk 17 stories below. The coroner will write it down in his book as suicide, but we cannot help wondering if the tragedy maybe was not more on the order of manslaughter, with many, many accessories to the crime.

The hysterical sister, the overwrought wealthy friends, the "water and cigarette handing friends," the encircling cameramen, the frenzied hotel employees, the policemen and firemen making well-intentioned efforts at rescue, the gaping, waiting crowds below—did not each of these play a distinct part in setting a scene from which there was no retreat?

Did they not dramatize and magnify a petty and foolish exhibition from which the exhibitionist could only escape by a leap of self-destruction?

What would have happened had the sister simply told the brother, when he climbed to the window ledge, that he was acting childishly and that she would be happy to discuss their differences, but only after he returned to the hotel room?

Or had the firemen, policemen and friends left him alone and unnoticed?

Or, perhaps, had the attention of the crowds never been attracted by the tiny dot of a sight overhead?

It is a safe guess that after a few minutes of fresh air and solitary thought, the excited individual would have come back into his room and, in time, gone about his normal business. There is nothing in the accounts to indicate that when the 26-year-old man stepped out of the window, he was contemplating suicide.

There are rumors he was doing it to impress someone or as a newspaper publicity stunt. Some report that he was merely throwing a tantrum to frighten his sister, with whom he had a minor quarrel.

It is scarcely conceivable he would have stayed there 11 hours had death been his real objective.

But when the attention of the whole city—and later the entire country—was centered on this rebellious figure—on the ever increasingly hysterical efforts to dissuade him from the leap that he had threatened—then the doom of John Warde was sealed. He found himself suddenly cast in the role of hero of what was being falsely exalted into a great tragic occasion. He reacted as an emotionally unstrung man had to react.

He leaped to his death—the result of his state of mind—which, in the circumstances, was the pitifully inevitable thing.

Yet it wasn't John Warde who gave, in his spectacular suicide, the poorest account of himself.

No, it was the crowd of spectators that gloated over the last minutes of his sorry life.

Those circus crowds in Rome, which watched with hope to see the lion crunch the Christian in his jaws and turn thumbs down on the whipped gladiator, were no different than this New York crowd of 200,000, some reports say.

One can only feel sorry for John and other people like him. There's nothing humorous about the mental malady from which they suffer. And yet, the episode reminds one of a story that insists upon being repeated over and over and over again.

A Mass Craving for Sensationalism

Rutland (VT) Daily Herald

Thursday, July 28, 1938

At first glance, it seems incredible that thousands of New Yorkers could mill about stiflingly hot streets or sit calmly in office windows eating their dinners while they waited for a man to kill himself.

There is, for the most sensitive, a terrible fascination about such a situation.

It is inconceivable that any in the crowd below wanted to see him leap to his death, but even while apprehending with dread the horror of the slightest misstep on his part, they are held, almost against their wills, to see what he will do.

The inevitable cameraman is there to record the tragic spectacle. Reporters are busy supplying details to an eager public. But, after all, these people who watched a man die must not be judged too harshly. His audience no doubt will maintain that they were victims as well—victims of a mass craving for sensationalism.

John Warde was mentally upset, if not insane.

Something in his heredity, in his 26 years of experience with life, in his inability to hold a job, had robbed life of its dearness to him.

The motive for Warde's act remains obscure.

He suffered from a manic depressive psychosis, which elevates its victims to extremes of exhilaration only to plunge them into depths of despair. He had attempted suicide twice before and feared he would be sent back to a hospital where he once received treatment.

His mother said he had been in love with a woman he did not feel he could marry for some reason. The youth himself threw little light on his mental problems during his many hours on the ledge. Once, he said: "I have a momentous decision to make. I have to think this thing out for myself."

He refused to say what "this thing" was.

A Deranged Leap to Death

Burlington (VT) Free Press

Thursday, July 28, 1938

It is difficult for a sane, well-balanced person to imagine the deranged state of mind that causes a man to stand for eleven hours on the ledge of a building 17 stories above the street and threaten to jump if he is approached.

Then finally jump just as desperate measures are being taken to save him.

It is a pity that such a state of mind cannot be discovered in advance of such an episode and the victim kept under supervision. For such a derangement of mind often results in the injuring of others also.

If society would give a fractional part of the attention to trying to help such people before they reach such a crisis than that which is given to them when they reach it—as evidenced by the multitude of people who stood for hours to see what John Warde would do—the story of the human race might be quite different.

But, the fact is, few people give much attention to the Biblical injunction to be their "brother's keeper" until it is too late to do any real good.

When a man or woman has reached that mental attitude, which leads to the act of suicide, it is often too late to do very much for them. Sometimes, they may be restrained for the moment, but they are likely to make another attempt later and keep trying until they succeed.

What we need is to study the forces in our civilization that are driving people into that state of mind, with the hope that we can get to the root of the trouble and do something about it.

Probably the trend toward false and shallow goals in living is the principal difficulty.

People strive for money, power, bodily comforts, selfish passion—which some people call love—success of a sort that fades almost as soon as it is achieved. If these are not achieved, or if they fail to satisfy when achieved (as they usually do), then there comes the feeling that life isn't worthwhile and that the thing to do is end it quickly.

Why did the crowds watch John Warde for hours? Because each watcher saw in himself something of their own discouragement perhaps.

If John Warde had been able to give a thought to others, he never would have taken that leap or remained on the ledge to cause so much trouble for so many people. His was an entirely selfish viewpoint. He refused to listen to the pleas of those who tried to save him.

He would not even listen to his mother's voice over the telephone when an extension phone was placed in his hands. It was apparent that his mind was so completely occupied with his own troubles that there was no room for the thoughts of others.

Such events make interesting reading for the curious and thrill-seekers, but they show a pitiable side of human nature which is becoming all too prevalent in these days of hectic and misguided living.

Mob Plays Its Usual Part in Suicide Leap

By Maxine Garrison,
Pittsburgh (PA) Press
Thursday, July 28, 1938

John Warde didn't want to disappoint the crowd—and that curious throng may be to blame for his tragic act.

100,000 people who collectively decided the fate of one.

Indeed, 100,000 people watched 26-year-old John Warde jump to his death from a window ledge 17 floors above New York's Fifth Avenue on Tuesday.

The pleas and ruses of his friends, his mother, his sister, a psychiatrist, a priest, an eloquent patrolman, physicians, dozens of policemen and firemen, and the whole of that crowd of 100,000 failed to divert the young man from his suicidal intentions. He stood there for 11 hours asserting his desire to die, and eventually, he jumped.

Picture him there, completely distraught and yet exhilarated, doubtlessly insane yet seemingly as lucid as the best of us. His white shirt and dark trousers silhouetted him against the walls of the hotel, a target for the attention of everyone who passed below. And for most of an entire day, he stood there with only an 18-inch footing between himself and death.

High above the street, Warde, toes on the edge of the ledge, looked down throughout the long ordeal. Women glanced up and away. Many hurried on, fearful of the end they thought would come at any moment. Office workers, businessmen, stenographers, female shoppers, men, and women going to lunch forgot their plans for the day and simply watched and waited.

Waiting . . . waiting . . . waiting to see a man die—for 11 suspense-packed hours, crowds of New Yorkers waited, eyes focused on the 17th-floor ledge of a hotel where John Warde was debating whether to live or die. Ice cream hucksters did a land office business. Police were fervently attempting to hold back a crowd by clearing space where his falling body could most likely strike them.

He had made up his mind to kill himself, of course, and seemed almost to relish the effect he caused by wavering. Often mirthfully stopping to dangle his legs and feet over the edge to get a guaranteed rise out of the crowd, he looked like a young man on the edge of a dock refreshing his feet in the Hudson River.

He even answered questions with the playfulness of a child, saying, "I'd rather jump than see the Dodgers."

He did jump, though. And before he jumped, he answered one of the pleas to stay by saying, "Look at all those people down there. I can't disappoint them."

So, yes, let's do look at all those people down there.

Perhaps they deserve as much attention as that lone figure standing seventeen stories above. They, his audience, played a leading role in the spectacle. Perhaps they decided the course of its denouement.

They had begun to gather soon after he appeared on the ledge. Ordinarily intent upon whatever pursuits they followed in their own little world. 100,000 people forgot those pursuits in the thrill of watching a man who might die before their eyes.

They choked up traffic on one of the busiest streets in the world.

They made business impossible in many shops.

The statistical experts who pop up so quickly with emergency figures tell us that the event cost the hotel several thousand dollars and the city and the merchants another $150,000.

There they were, 100,000 upturned faces agape at the gruesome excitement that might be in store. Some screaming up to the young man, "Don't jump!" Some crying, even. Among them passed ever-ready hawkers, this time calling, "Get'cher binoculars here!"

There they were, 100,000 individuals became a mass.

People who individually would have gone about their business, ignoring another's tragedy or trying not to interfere. People who, caught in the mass, lost themselves in gawking at something that did not concern them, something which might have been solved more happily had they not been there.

People no longer people, because they were a mass.

It happened only the day before yesterday, but it is the story of mobs since time began. Lynching mobs, wild with the thirst for blood. Terror-stricken mobs fleeing from burning theaters (said by firemen to be a far worse hazard than the fire itself). Revolutionary mobs, with always a Madame La Farge to sit placidly knitting while the guillotine chops off heads.

Few people would recognize their own faces—could they see the photographs captured on that day during the mob scene—for they would not like to admit to their abominable behaviors.

The Greater Tragedy: A Less Spectacular Loss
Montreal Gazette
Monday, August 1, 1938

It is difficult to describe the sickening feeling that weighted the hearts of New Yorkers last Tuesday as millions read and witnessed the tragedy of John Warde, the young man who climbed out on a 17-story ledge and held an eleven-hour conference with himself before he decided to leap to his death.

For out-of-towners, it was another fascinating attraction in a city filled with them. For some of us here who could almost touch him with our fingertips and yet were helpless to prevent him from carrying out his own horrible scheme, it was a nightmare come to life.

The best minds in New York cajoled, pleaded and argued with Warde. It is estimated that more than $100,000 was spent in the effort to save him from self-destruction. The police department, the health bureau, the army, the navy and the coast guard combined in a herculean attempt to preserve what was left of a broken mind.

It just so happened, however, that while Warde made his tantalizing defiance like a tightwire act in front of an adoring audience, 99 other persons also died in New York, according to the records.

Among these 99 was another suicide.

It wasn't spectacular. It didn't even rate a line of type in the newspapers. It was covered merely by a police report which stated that a Mrs. Mary Smith, 33, a recent widow, was found dead in her one-room apartment on the Upper West Side. The gas jets were found on. No note was left. There were no known relatives. No one called to claim the body.

Apparently, no one held out any hope that would cure her acute unhappiness. None of her neighbors had spoken to her lately. She was wretched and alone. A young woman who lived in lonely sadness and unrelenting misery for many years.

The tragedy of Mary Smith happens every day in New York and, I suppose, all over the world. Few read about those. Fewer care about them. But the exhibition of suicide by John Warde brings vividly to mind what happens in a less spectacular way every day.

I have no suggestions to make. No moral message to point out.

I merely thought it should be written that sadness and tragedy are hiding in plain sight in our city every day, and we, consumed by our own desires, blindly pass by without notice.

Thousands Watch Man Leap 17 Floors to Death
By William S. White,
Rutland (VT) Daily Herald
Wednesday, July 27, 1938

Talk, talk, talk. For 11 hours on end, it was nonstop talk that kept John Warde on the Hotel Gotham's 17th-floor window ledge while exasperated rescuers sought vainly to save him. Policemen, firemen, friends, relatives, priests, doctors—and a few oddballs—all talked to him, pleading, cajoling, and begging, but Warde shook his head to all inducements.

"Look," he said sheepishly, pointing at the crowd. "Everybody's looking at me. I know I look the fool," he muttered morosely. "Life would not hold anything for me now. There is no future for me."

Then, in a flare-lit scene of hysterical horror, John Warde, 26 and unemployed, leaped to death last night from the perch to which he had clung.

His body landed on 55th Street near Fifth Avenue amid scattered screams rising from among the many thousands who, for hours, had stood morbidly bemused. At first there was a long, corporate moan and then—bursting out of that monotonous tone—a series of sharp, individual screams emerged. Countless women fainted while ambulances screamed into the area to take them away.

The whole area was alight with photographic flares, and noise exploded from the crowd as shattered glass flew high into the air and glittered as a reflection of the flares.

Some of Warde's last words were heard by Dr. G. C. Presner, a city health department physician, who had talked with the young man frequently during the day.

"He implied that there was something in his soul that he could not seem to get past. I do not know what that was, unfortunately. I wish I did."

As darkness fell, spectators forming one of the greatest midtown traffic jams in the city's history—like New Year's Eve or Election Night—could make out only a white blur on the ledge: Warde's starched white shirt.

Pedestrians had been ordered out of a block-long area around the hotel on Fifth Avenue, but thousands jammed into neighboring side streets and eventually made their way back to the hotel's entrance. Hawkers selling ice cream, peanuts, and cheap binoculars strolled through the throng doing a bang-up business by all accounts. A street vendor sold buttons promoting the event.

Hundreds in offices near the hotel stayed on after work, sent out for supper, and held their grandstand seats on window ledges and balconies. Rooftops were thronged, some spectators sitting in deck chairs, others eating dinner.

It appeared to be an evening of fine entertainment for these folks and without the cost of one of the spectacular productions currently on Broadway.

Today, the throngs who saw John Warde jump wondered what queer obstinacy and indecision kept him waiting—poised there with his back against the side of the building, half-crouched, staring moodily down into the night-darkened chasm where the flashbulbs of cameramen flared like fireflies far below.

In all that time, he had kept thousands mesmerized in morbid suspense—an estimated 35,000 who watched him from the street, from bus tops, from windows and the roofs of nearby buildings. They appeared transfixed by the tiny figure of a man in a white shirt, who drank incredible quantities of water through the long afternoon while police cajoled him in vain attempts to dissuade him from thoughts of suicide.

With the coming of night, however, he had become a pale blur as darkness crept up the limestone walls of the Hotel Gotham on Fifth Avenue and 55th Street, a blur sometimes faintly picked out by the glowing spark of a freshly lighted cigarette.

In the beginning, fear had chilled the hearts of all who saw him. But fear had passed, and speculative talk was exchanged. Then there were sorry gibes, arguments, mockeries, wisecracks. He had become a spectacle for the bored and listless who demanded to be entertained as if a circus had come to town.

Obscure in life, Warde, a 26-year-old unemployed bank teller and hopeful newspaperman, became perhaps the biggest human focal point in the city for a day. He was the answer to the mob's desires, though he was probably the last to understand his role for them.

And so a kind of perverted holiday spirit grew upon the crowd that watched him on his dizzy perch. There were overtones of cynicism and mockery. He wouldn't jump, they said. Not by a long shot, they answered. Amateur psychologists debated the point.

All agreed he wouldn't jump. Not a chance.

The police tried new and innovative means of saving him—hoisting up a cargo net they had borrowed from a ship—before it all came to a sudden end. The pale blur detached itself from the gloom high above. In a quick moment, Warde was seen flying out into the night air. A horrified gasp from the first onlookers, then a roaring scream from the entire crowd as Warde plunged to his death.

All the devices the police and fire departments could think of had failed. The appeals of his mother and sister, the persuasive words of a pastor and priest and several psychiatrists had gone for nothing.

Hour by Hour until a Morbid Climax

By John Ferris,
Casper (WY) Star-Tribune
Wednesday, July 27, 1938

High above the street, Warde, toes on the edge of the ledge, locked down. Frightened women glanced up and away. A crowd quickly gathered. Sidewalks were jammed on both sides of the street. Crowds ceased swarming along Fifth Avenue and stood motionless, waiting in dreadful anticipation of what appeared certain to transpire in front of their eyes.

Warde lighted a cigarette—the first of several dozens he was to smoke before death—blew the smoke in a big, voluminous cloud, watched it for an instant and then looked down at the gathering spectators. He seemed intrigued by the attention and watched for some time.

The mental doctor tried to talk him back into the room. The sister began a long series of pleadings. A young woman from a sales-talk agency tried to convince Warde he ought to come in. A priest and a tent-revival evangelist. A "lady of the evening" tried to use her obvious charms to attract his attention. Phone calls from his mother didn't help. A cop with an aching back dedicated hours to the rescue effort.

To all the pleas, he simply shook his head or answered that he had nothing to live for.

Among the youth's final words to Dr. GC Presner were: "There's no way out of this. I have been up here so many hours trying to convince myself that things can change . . . but they can't, and they never will. I am who I am."

Earlier, however, his mind had appeared clearer as he gazed out, fascinated at the growing throngs beneath him. Here are one reporter's notes of this fateful day with an hour-by-hour accounting:

1 pm. By the afternoon, the crowds still were growing, but some of the tension and fear among the crowd had departed. Here and there, a man appeared with binoculars. People joked about the man on the ledge. They were calling him Jumpin' Johnny. An ice cream vendor sold his wares as quickly as he could hand them out. "Business ain't never boomed like this," he told a reporter. "Wish I could have this every day."

2 pm. Police began clearing the streets of all except newspapermen and photographers. People retreated to their offices after lunch, their apartments, or far down the street, where police held them in check with barriers. No one was leaving, however, as their greatest fear was to walk away before the leap happened and would be forced to miss it.

Police and firemen arrive and carry a net, a scaling ladder, and coils of rope into the hotel, along with bosun's chairs, tentatively prepared to swing down to Warde from above and snatch him unawares.

3 pm. Walter Vickers, the doorman of the Gotham Hotel, emerged with a broom, carefully swept the sidewalk and looked benignly around before going back into the hotel. It appeared to be just another day for the hotel employee who was either unaware of the action overhead or was paying no mind to it. One suspects the latter.

The crowd started wisecracking, making fun of the young man and calling him a coward—imploring him to show some courage and step off the ledge. Women giggled, men began chanting for Warde to jump. Warde—watching it all with amusement from above—took a drink of water, flexed his sore leg muscles, and once again teetered on the edge.

4 pm. Concrete workers at the construction site on the corner finally knocked off for the day and departed with hardly an upward look. They headed to the local watering hole, making crude gestures as they walked by without ever looking in his direction. The wisecracks continued, and the spirit among the crowd was more circus-like. Popcorn and peanuts were being sold by vendors who normally work at Ebbets Field.

5 pm. Manhattan traffic is in a snarl as homeward-bound shoppers and office workers jammed the streets beyond the police lines. Traffic slowed down and then came to a complete halt. Bus drivers slowed their double-decker buses to a crawl to allow passengers a chance to look up and catch the sight.

Word came from above that a medium had tried to persuade Warde not to die by explaining his destiny according to the stars.

The jokes only grew stronger, more cruel. Now and then, police handed the man on the ledge more water. He smoked more cigarettes and gazed down. He appeared to be growing tired, however. Sometimes leaning against the stone wall, sometimes sitting on the ledge and dangling one foot, much like a small boy on a fishing dock on a lazy afternoon.

6 pm. Police served Warde a cup of tea. He had requested Earl Grey. The pleadings went on while he sipped the beverage. The crowds made fresh jokes, repeated old ones. Now, they were growing weary. A group of teen-age boys were hollering for him to prove that he was a man and jump. A certain tedium set in. The crowds were growing restless but refused to leave for fear of missing the event.

7 pm. The after-dinner crowds began appearing. He spoke once or twice on a handset telephone given to him by the police. His mother called him from Southampton. He hung up. Everybody in the street was certain he wouldn't jump. He'd lost his nerve, they said. Cabbies were laying odds. The big money was on him being a chicken.

Dusk slowly enveloped Warde. He began pacing, one might say, nervously.

8 pm. The impending darkness brought fresh activity from police. Reports of many plans to save Warde made the rounds. Then the big cargo net arrived and, after a great deal of trouble, started its upward flight. The crowd sensed that a conclusion was in the offing. A new buzz rippled through the crowd as if they were getting a second wind.

9 pm. "It won't be long now," everybody said. "They'll land that baby in the crib." People are rubbing their hands with glee. There is an excitement in the air.

10:38 pm. They were anticipating watching the net trap Warde when he came tumbling off the ledge, but instead, he was hurtling directly toward the bug-eyed crowd. People seem literally transfixed by the falling body. Mesmerized.

In the end, they seemed well-rewarded for their long wait.

BIBLIOGRAPHY

"11-Hour Pleas Fail to Avert Death Plunge," *Buffalo (NY) Times*, July 27, 1938.
"17-Story Dangler Leaps to Death," *Harrisburg (PA) Telegraph*, July 27, 1938.
"17th Story Stepper Seen as Schizoid-Maniac Type," *News Press (FL)*, July 28, 1938.
"1,000 Police Work in Vain to Rescue Warde," *Owensboro (KY) Messenger*, July 27, 1938.
"1951 Award Winners," NationalBoardsofReview.org.
"100,000 Watch Mad Youth Pick His Fate," *Port Heron (MI) Times*, July 27, 1938.
"A Crazy Young Man Defies Pleas 17 Stories Up on a Hotel Ledge, Leaps to Death," *Standard-Star (NY)*, July 27, 1938.
"A Deranged Leap to Death," *Burlington (VT) Free Press*, July 28, 1938.
"After 11 Hours This Was His Decision," *Blackwell (OK) Daily Journal*, July 27, 1938.
"All Efforts to Rescue Youth Fail," *Press Democrat (CA)*, July 27, 1938.
Allen, Frederick Lewis. *Since Yesterday: The 1930s in America*. New York: Harper & Row, 1939.
"A Mass Craving for Sensationalism," *Rutland (VT) Daily Herald*, July 28, 1938.
"Arguments Fail to Halt Suicide," *Emporia (KS) Gazette*, July 27, 1938.
"A Roman Amphitheater," *Honolulu (HI) Star-Advertiser*, July 28, 1938.
"Audience to Violence," *Zanesville (OH) Signal*, July 30, 1938.
"Between Life and Death," *Birmingham (AL) Post-Herald*, July 28, 1938.
"Body Bounces Off Marquee," *Boston (MA) Globe*, July 27, 1938.
"Body Unclaimed after Fatal Leap," *Birmingham (AL) Age-Herald*, July 28, 1938.
"Box Office: The New Pictures," *Time*, March 12, 1951.
"Brief but Supreme," *The Commonweal*, August 12, 1938.
Brien, Donn. "Photographers Cover a Suicide," *Popular Photography*, October 1938.
"Broken Body of John Warde Lies Alone in Death," *Carthage (MO) Evening Press*, July 27, 1938.
Burton, Hal. "Maniac Threatens 17-Story Leap as Thousands Watch," *New York Daily News*, July 27, 1938.
"But Why," *The News and Advance (VA)*, July 29, 1938.
"Camera Shows Youth's Leap to Death from Hotel," *Journal Times (WI)*, July 27, 1938.
"Camera Snaps Death Dive," *Anderson (IN) Herald*, July 28, 1938.
Celona, Larry, Khristina Narizhnaya, and Tina Moore. "Playboy Playmate Took Young Son on Fatal Leap from Gotham Hotel," *New York Post*, May 18, 2018.
"'Come In, John, We Love You,'" *Hutchinson (KS) News-Herald*, July 27, 1938.
"Crowd Moans as Body Flips Over and Over," *Des Moines (IA) Register*, July 27, 1938.
"Crowd Sees His Bizarre Night Leap," *Hickory (NC) Daily Record*, July 27, 1938.

"Crowd's Gibes Turn to Gasps as Man Reaches Fatal Decision," *Lancaster (PA) New Era*, July 27, 1938.
"Crowds Ignore Suicide's Body in Morgue after Bizarre Death," *Tulsa (OK) Tribune*, July 27, 1938.
"Crowd's Jibes Hushed by 17-Story Plunge," *Fort Worth (TX) Star-Telegram*, July 27, 1938.
Crowther, Bosley, "Fourteen Hours: Fox Film about Man on Ledge Ready to Jump," *New York Times*, March 7, 1951.
"Curious Search for Souvenirs after Warde's Suicide Plunge," *Boston (MA) Globe*, July 27, 1938.
"'Death Carnival' Ends as Man Flies Past Net," *Pittsburgh (PA) Press*, July 27, 1938.
"Death from the Ledge," *New York Daily News*, July 27, 1938.
"Death Plunge Horrifies Crowd," *New York Daily News*, July 27, 1938.
"Death Spot Is Magnet for Crowds," *Palo Alto (CA) Times*, July 27, 1938.
"Death Wins in Grim Drama 17 Floors above Street," *Birmingham (AL) News*, July 27, 1938.
"Defying Rescuers on Seventeenth Floor Ledge," *Lincoln (NE) Journal Star*, July 27, 1938.
"Despondent Man Leaps to Death from 17th Story Ledge of New York Hotel after Deliberating Course for 11 Hours," *Portsmouth (VA) Star*, July 27, 1938.
"Dizzy Vigil Ends in Leap," *Durham (NC) Sun*, July 27, 1938.
"Down, Down, Down," *Dayton (OH) Daily News*, July 27, 1938.
"Eerie Scene at 55th Street and 5th Avenue Is Lighted by Movie Flares," *Kansas City Times*, July 27, 1938.
"Eleven Hours of Suspense Ended by Death Leap from Lofty Fifth Avenue Hotel," *Columbia (SC) Record*, July 27, 1938.
"Fatal Leap from Hotel Ledge," *Appleton (WI) Post-Crescent*, July 27, 1938.
"Father on Vacation; Doesn't Know of Leap," *New York Daily News*, July 27, 1938.
Ferris, John. "Hour by Hour until a Morbid Climax," *Casper (WY) Star-Tribune*, July 27, 1938.
"Fifth Avenue Throngs Watch Suicidal Plunge," *Daily Sentinel (NY)*, July 27, 1938.
"Former Bank Teller Kills Self in Jump," *The La Crosse (WI)*, July 27, 1938.
"Fourteen Hours: True Story of Boy Who Jumped from Hotel Window Is Basis of a Taut Drama," *Life*, March 12, 1951.
Frink, Carol. "Warde's 'Death Wish' Explained by Dr. Lind," *Washington (DC) Herald*, July 28, 1938.
"Funeral Rights Held for Your Suicide," *Cumberland (MD) Evening Times*, July 28, 1938.
"Futile Love for a Woman May Have Caused Spectacular 17-Story Leap," *Chattanooga (TN) News*, July 27, 1938.
"Gaping Throngs Hold Breath before Leap," *Harrisburg (PA) Telegraph*, July 27, 1938.
Garrison, Maxine. "Mob Plays Its Usual Part in Suicide Leap," *Pittsburgh (PA) Press*, July 28, 1938.
"Gibes-Wisecracks as He Pondered," *The Plain Speaker (PA)*, July 27, 1938.
"Gotham Crowds See Fatal Jump to Pavement," *Niles (MI) Daily Star*, July 27, 1938.
Harrison, Dale. "Death: The Publicity Hound," *Duluth (MN) News*, August 15, 1938.
"High on Ledge, He Ponders Plunge," *Des Moines (IA) Tribune*, July 26, 1938.
"Hopeless Love for Woman Probable Cause of Death Dive," *Rock Island (IA) Argus*, July 27, 1938.
"Hoping for the Best," *Rutland (VT) Daily Herald*, July 28, 1938.
"Is Life Worth Living?," *New York Times*, July 28, 1938.
"'I Want to Be Left Alone!,'" *Beatrice (NE) Daily Sun*, July 27, 1938.

"Jobless Man Holds Spotlight on Dizzy Perch," *Shawnee (OK) Evening Star*, July 27, 1938.
"John Warde as a Symbol," *St. Joseph (MO) News-Press*, July 27, 1938.
"John Warde Chooses Spectacular Way Out," *San Antonio (TX) Light*, July 27, 1938.
"John Warde Dies in Most Sensational Suicide New York Sees for Years," *Chippewa (WI) Herald-Telegram*, July 27, 1938.
"John Warde's One Big Moment," *Muncie (IN) Evening Press*, August 1, 1938.
"John Warde Suicide Leap 17 Stories," *Columbia (SC) Record*, August 3, 1938.
"Joking Crowd's Laughs Turn to Screams," *Springfield (MO) Leader and Press*, July 27, 1938.
"Large Net Hoisted," *Vincennes (IN) Sun-Commercial*, July 27, 1938.
Lawrence, Mort. "Appeared Like an Animal at Bay!," *Capital Times (WI)*, July 27, 1938.
"Leaper Fools a Crowd," *Kansas City Star*, July 27, 1938.
"Leap Follows Mother's Plea by Telephone," *New York Daily News*, July 27, 1938.
"Leaps 17 Stories to Death; Climaxes 11 Hrs. on Ledge," *Daily Record (NJ)*, July 27, 1938.
"Leaps to Death as Thousands Watch," *Miami (FL) Herald*, July 27, 1938.
"Ledge Percher Plunges to Death as Thousands Watch," *Modesto (CA) Bee*, July 27, 1938.
"Ledge Sitter Attracts Crowd; Plunges to Death," *Argus (SD) Leader*, July 27, 1938.
Leighton, Isabel. *The Aspirin Age*. New York: Simon and Schuster, 1949.
Leischner, Charles. "11-Hour Vigil on Ledge," *New York Daily News*, July 27, 1938.
"Madman Dives 17 Floors to Death," *Wisconsin State Journal*, July 27, 1938.
"Man, 26, Ignores Please of Relatives, Leaps to Death," *Taylorville (IL) Daily Breeze Courier*, July 27, 1938.
"Maniac Stares Down at Death Ravine," *Vicksburg (MS) Evening Post*, July 29, 1938.
"Man Leaps 17 Floors to Death after 11-Hour Vigil on Ledge," *Capital Times (WI)*, July 27, 1938.
"Man on Ledge Tells Police 'Out to Get Air,'" *Brooklyn (NY) Citizen*, June 24, 1942.
"Man Picks John Warde's Hotel to Stand on Ledge," *New York Daily News*, June 25, 1942.
"Man Plunges to Street after Waiting 11 Hours," *Riverside (CA) Daily*, July 27, 1938.
"Man, Poised on Ledge for 11 Hours, Leaps to Death in New York," *The Express (PA)*, July 27, 1938.
"Man Promises to Emulate Hotel Jump," *Atlanta (GA) Constitution*, August 22, 1938.
"Man Thrills Thousands, Leaps to Death," *Wisconsin Rapids Daily Tribune*, July 27, 1938.
"Man Who Thrilled Throng Now Lies Alone in Death," *Fort Pierce (FL) Tribune*, July 27, 1938.
"Medicine: Manhattan Suicide," *Time*, August 8, 1938.
"Men of Great Faith," *Radio Guide Week*, September 17, 1938.
"Miss Skouras Psycho Patient," *Times Herald (DC)*, January 11, 1950.
"Morbid Beg to Peek at Ward's Body in Casket," *Herald-News (NJ)*, July 28, 1938.
"Morbid Crowds Linger at Scene," *World-News (NY)*, July 27, 1938.
"Morbid Man Ends 11 Hours of Indecision," *Huntsville (AL) Times*, July 27, 1938.
"Morbid Throng Sees Youth Fall to Death," *Ironwood (MI) Daily Globe*, July 27, 1938.
"Mother's Plea to Son Fails," *Akron (OH) Beacon Journal*, July 27, 1938.
"New York Crowds Gape Up as Young Lunatic Leisurely Ponders His Dive to Death," *Life*, August 8, 1938.
"New York Man Plunges to Death While Crowds Watch from Street," *The Daily Progress (VA)*, July 27, 1938.
"New York's Curious Shun Bloody, Crushed Body," *Muskogee (OK) Times-Democrat*, July 27, 1938.
"New York Youth Leaps 17 Stories in Suicide Plunge," *Niles (MI) Daily Star*, July 27, 1938.

“No One Views Shattered Body of John Warde,” *Redwood City (CA) Tribune*, July 27, 1938.
“‘No Other Way Out’, Youth’s Final Words,” *Austin (MN) Daily Herald*, July 27, 1938.
“No Spectators Today after Leap,” *Parsons (KS) Sun*, July 27, 1938.
“NY Boredom Shattered by Suicide,” *San Antonio (TX) Light*, July 27, 1938.
“One Man Halts Thousands,” *The Missoulian (MT)*, July 28, 1938.
“One Man’s Selfishness Costs City a Fortune,” *The Missoulian (MT)*, July 28, 1938.
“On Ledge 11 Hrs, Dives to Death,” *New York Daily News*, July 27, 1938.
“Picks Warde’s Hotel to ‘Get Air’ on Ledge,” *New York Daily News*, June 25, 1942.
“Playboy Leaps 17 Floors after 10 Hours on Ledge,” *Kane (PA) Republican*, July 27, 1938.
“Plunge Is Fatal for Skouras Girl,” *Daily Times (NY)*, July 18, 1950.
“Plunges from 17th Floor to End His Life,” *Capital Times (WI)*, July 27, 1938.
“Police Say Tear Gas May Have Saved Jumper,” *Boston (MA) Globe*, July 27, 1938.
“Police Wound Miss Skouras with Shots in 80mph Chase,” *Mount Vernon (OH) Argus*, December 13, 1949.
Price, Jack. “Suicide Leap Harrowing Ordeal for Cameramen,” *Editor and Publisher*, July 30, 1938.
“Psychiatrists Seek Reason for Leap,” *San Francisco (CA) Examiner*, July 27, 1938.
“Psychopath Killed after Standing on Narrow Ledge,” *Daily Times (IA)*, July 27, 1938.
“Rich Playgirl Dies from Plunge from Penthouse,” *Clinton (OK) Daily News*, July 17, 1950.
Rogers, Agnes. *I Remember Distinctly: A Family Album of the American People*. New York: Harper, 1947.
Sayre, Joel. “The Man on the Ledge,” *New Yorker*, April 16, 1949.
“Seek to Answer Question Why Man Jumped to Death,” *Intelligencer Journal (PA)*, July 28 1938.
“Shattered Body of Man Who Staged Suicide Teaser Unclaimed,” *Birmingham (AL) Post-Herald*, July 28, 1938.
Shellenbarger, Marion. “Body Deleted,” *Life*, August 29, 1938.
“Sister Vainly Begged Warde to Quit Ledge,” *New York Daily News*, July 27, 1938.
“Skouras’ Daughter Killed in Leap,” *Los Angeles (CA) Times*, July 17, 1938.
“Souvenir Hunters Pick Up Glass from Marquee Hit in Fatal Jump,” *Evening State Journal (NE)*, July 28, 1938.
“Spectacular New York Suicide,” *Free Lance-Star (VA)*, July 27, 1938.
“Story of Warde Circled Globe,” *Standard Sentinel (PA)*, July 27, 1938.
“Suicide Plunge Ends 11 Hour Ledge Vigil,” *Argus-Leader (SD)*, July 27, 1938.
“Suicide’s Death Leap Thrills N.Y.,” *Windsor Daily News (Ontario, Canada)*, July 27, 1938.
“Suicide Televised,” *Radio Craft*, October 1938.
“Suicide? Well, Technically,” *Ventura (CA) County Star*, July 27, 1938.
“Takes Fatal Plunge after Long Debate,” *Hutchinson (KS) News*, July 27, 1938.
“The Case of John Warde,” *The World (OR)*, July 28, 1938.
“The Curious Case of John Warde,” *Coos Bay (OR) World*, July 28, 1938.
“The Greater Tragedy: A Less Spectacular,” *Montreal (Canada) Gazette*, August 1, 1938.
“The Old Gotham Hotel, Now the Peninsula New York,” *New York Times*, January 3, 1999.
“Thousands Are Thrilled for 11 Long Hours,” *Democrat Baker Herald (OR)*, July 27, 1938.
“Thousands Gape at Spectacular Suicide at New York Hotel,” *Capital Times (WI)*, July 27, 1938.
“Thousands Scream ‘Don’t Jump!,’” *Wilkes-Barre (PA) Times Leader*, July 27, 1938.
“Thousands See Maniac Leap from Hotel Ledge,” *Elmira (NY) Star-Gazette*, July 27, 1938.

"Thousands See New York Man Leap to Death," *Daily Democrat-News (MO)*, July 27, 1938.
"Threat Finds Realization in Morbid Climax," *Casper (WY) Tribune*, July 27, 1938.
"Thrilling Scenes of the John Warde 17 Story Leap to Death," *Johnson City (TN) Chronicle*, August 5, 1938.
"Throngs on 5th Avenue View Scene of Leap," *New York Times*, July 28, 1938.
"Thwarted Love Drove Warde to Spectacular Suicide," *Belvidere (IL) Daily Republican*, July 27, 1938.
"To Bury John Warde," *St. Joseph (MO) News-Press*, July 28, 1938.
"Traffic Jam Costs $130,000—Barkers Sell Binoculars," *Berwick (PA) Enterprise*, July 27, 1938.
Tucker, George. "Man about Manhattan," *Fargo Forum (ND) Herald*, August 18, 1938.
"Waiting Thousands in NY See Leap from 17th Floor," *Lincoln (NE) Star*, July 27, 1938.
"Waits 11 Hours, Then Leaps to Death," *Evening World-Herald (NE)*, July 27, 1938.
"Warde Alone in Death after Hotel Plunge," *Richmond (VA) News*, July 27, 1938.
"Warde Burial Advanced," *New York Times*, July 30, 1938.
"Warde Had Tried to End Life Before," *Great Falls (MT) Leader*, July 27, 1938.
"Warde Makes Plunge into Eternity," *Times-Tribune (PA)*, July 27, 1938.
"Warde Pictured as Bitter Failure Wanting to Dominate One Scene," *Atlanta (GA) Constitution*, July 28, 1938.
"Warde Plunges to Death," *Lincoln (NE) Star*, July 27, 1938.
"Warde Rites Friday," *Emporia (KS) Gazette*, July 28, 1938.
"Warde's Leap Cost City Near $100,000," *Star-Herald (NE)*, July 28, 1938.
"Warde Suicide Pictures," *Variety*, August 3, 1938.
"Was It Suicide? Well, Not Really," *Ventura (CA) Country Star*, July 27, 1938.
"When Why Is an X," *Wilkes-Barre (PA) Record*, July 27, 1938.
White, William S. "Thousands Watch Man Leap 17 Floors to Death," *Rutland (VA) Daily Herald*, July 27, 1938.
"Whole World Read of Warde," *Fargo (ND) Forum Herald*, July 29, 1938.
Winchell, Walter. "On Broadway," *St. Louis (MO) Post-Dispatch*, August 28, 1938.
"Window Ledge Sitter Leaps to Death," *New York Post*, January 1943.
"Woodhaven Cop in Daring High-Rise Drama," *Queens Courier*, February 5, 1976.
Wright, Sewell Peaslee. "Flash! Suicide!," *The Author and Journalist*, September 1938.
"Yorker Who Jumped from Hotel Forgotten," *Greenwood (MS) Commonwealth*, July 27, 1938.
"Young Unemployed Bank Teller Leaps from Hotel Building as Throngs of New Yorkers Watch," *Hinton (WV) Daily News*, July 27, 1938.
"Youth Leaps after Perching 11 Hours on 17-Story Hotel," *Reno Evening Gazette*, July 27, 1938.
"Youth Plunges to Death after 11 Hours on Ledge of New York Hotel," *Tampa (FL) Times*, July 27, 1938.

INDEX

ABOUT THE AUTHOR

For nearly forty years, **Jerry Jamison** has been an award-winning advertising copywriter with over sixty national writing commendations during his career. Following his years as a copywriter, Jamison turned to a career as a novelist, generating more than thirty books in a wide range of genres. He currently focuses on stories based on true events and crimes in history that are largely undiscovered. Jamison graduated from Westmont College with a degree in sociology and lives in Chula Vista, California. You can find him at https://jerryjamison.com.